SPORT ANALYTICS

The increasing availability of data has transformed the way sports are played, promoted and managed. This is the first textbook to explain how the big data revolution is having a profound influence across the sport industry, demonstrating how sport managers and business professionals can use analytical techniques to improve their professional practice.

While other sport analytics books have focused on player performance data, this book shows how analytics can be applied to every functional area of sport business, from marketing and event management to finance and legal services. Drawing on research that spans the entire sport industry, it explains how data is influencing the most important decisions, from ticket sales and human resources to risk management and facility operations. Each chapter contains real world examples, industry profiles and extended case studies which are complimented by a companion website full of useful learning resources.

Sport Analytics: A data-driven approach to sport business and management is an essential text for all sport management students and an invaluable reference for any sport management professional involved in operational research.

Gil Fried is Professor and Chair of the Sport Management Department in the College of Business at the University of New Haven, USA. He has been a sport management practitioner for over 30 years and a faculty member for over 20 years. He is the author of ten books, including some of the world's most widely used sport management textbooks, such as *Sport Finance* (with DeSchriver and Mondello) and *Managing Sport Facilities.*

Ceyda Mumcu is an Assistant Professor of sport management at the University of New Haven, USA. Her primary focus is on sport marketing and international sport management, and she has interests in quantitative research methods and the use of analytics. Before becoming an academic, she was a professional basketball player for eight years in the Turkish Women's Basketball League.

SPORT ANALYTICS

A data-driven approach to sport business and management

Edited by Gil Fried and Ceyda Mumcu

Routledge
Taylor & Francis Group

LONDON AND NEW YORK

First published 2017
by Routledge
2 Park Square, Milton Park, Abingdon, Oxon OX14 4RN

and by Routledge
711 Third Avenue, New York, NY 10017

Routledge is an imprint of the Taylor & Francis Group, an informa business

British Library Cataloguing-in-Publication Data
A catalogue record for this book is available from the British Library

Library of Congress Cataloging in Publication Data
Names: Fried, Gil, 1965– editor. | Mumcu, Ceyda, editor.
Title: Sport analytics : a data-driven approach to sport business and management /
edited by Gil Fried and Ceyda Mumcu.
Description: First edition. | New York : Routledge, 2017. | Includes
webography. | Includes bibliographical references and index.
Identifiers: LCCN 2016025146 | ISBN 9781138667129 (Hardback) |
ISBN 9781138667136 (Paperback) | ISBN 9781315619088 (eBook)
Subjects: LCSH: Sports administration—Statistical methods. | Sports
administration—Data processing. | Sports—Marketing.
Classification: LCC GV713. S67784 2017 | DDC 796.06/9—dc23
LC record available at https://lccn.loc.gov/2016025146

ISBN: 978-1-138-66712-9 (hbk)
ISBN: 978-1-138-66713-6 (pbk)
ISBN: 978-1-315-61908-8 (ebk)

Typeset in Bembo
by Keystroke, Neville Lodge, Tettenhall, Wolverhampton

Visit the companion website: www.routledge.com/cw/fried

DEDICATION

Gil Fried – I would like to dedicate this book to my wonderful children Gavriella, Arieh, and Rebecca. All the hard work I put in every day is to hopefully inspire you and show that we always need to work and play hard in order to live our lives to the fullest.

Ceyda Mumcu – I would like to dedicate this book to my mentors: Dr. John Barnes, Dr. Nancy Lough and Dr. Scott Marley. Your influence has been instrumental to my development as an individual, a scholar, and an educator. I am thankful for your endless support and guidance, and even more grateful for helping me find my passion.

Prof. Gil Fried and Ceyda Mumcu, PhD,
University of New Haven

CONTENTS

ILLUSTRATIONS

Figures

Photographs

Tables

CONTRIBUTORS

There are a number of professionals who contributed directly to this text and we list them alphabetically below.

Dr. Khadija Al Arkoubi, Associate Professor, University of New Haven.

Ben Alamar, Director of Production Analytics, ESPN.

Benoit Ammann, Deputy Director – High Performance Sports Analytics/Technology & Education, Singapore Sports Institute.

Brian Anderson, Chief Human Resources Officer at ECP-PF Holdings Group.

Mike Boissonneault, Production Operations, Human Resources and Business Leader professional and recently retired from ESPN.

Nicole Chua, Executive – High Performance Sports Analytics/Technology & Education, Singapore Sports Institute.

Evan Dabby, Executive Director, New Jersey Youth Soccer.

Dr. Peggy Keiper, Assistant Professor – Entertainment, Sport & Promotion Management, Northwood University.

Kimberly L. Mahoney, PhD, Assistant Professor, University of New Haven.

Jeff Meeson, Vice President, Octagon, Inc.

Dr. Lisa Miller, Professor, American Military University.

Juline E. Mills, PhD, Professor, University of New Haven.

John Morris, Executive Director of Business Intelligence and Analytics, New York Mets.

Russell Mucklow, Managing Director, AwareManager.

Maria Nibali, PhD, Director and Founder, Sport Scientist – MODUS PERFORMANCE SCIENCE (Australia).

Joash Ng, Executive – High Performance Sports Analytics/Technology & Education, Singapore Sports Institute.

Takao Ohashi, Attorney-at-law (Partner), Toranomon Kyodo Law Office.

Michael Rennie, Conditioning Coach and Sport Scientist, Sydney Swans Football Club, Australia.

Lindsay Salt, Account Manager, Octagon, Inc.

Brian Smith, Senior Vice President Human Resources, Octagon, Inc.

Krishna Vasist, Head – Business Development, moonwalkr, Bengaluru, Karnataka, India.

Dr. Dylan Williams, Assistant Professor, Sport Management, University of Alabama.

Kevin Wittner, Director, Insights & Strategy, Octagon, Inc.

The authors/editors of all chapters and case studies expressly disclaim that any information contained herein is derived directly from or with the consent of their respective employers and is for illustrative purposes. The opinions here represent solely the opinions of the authors and do not represent or reflect the opinions of their employers.

FOREWORD

Data and algorithms are driving cars, managing stock portfolios, and fundraising for political campaigns. The explosion of data has affected virtually every industry and every part of our lives. The impact of data has been driven by both new sources, increased availability of data, and new technologies that allow for faster and deeper analysis. The internet has allowed businesses to track consumer behavior in a much richer way, companies, such as Facebook and Twitter, are recognizing that the data that they collect is incredibly valuable and are monetizing that value by making the data available to marketing firms and other businesses, and advances in computing power and machine learning have allowed for deeper insights and in real-time.

The sport industry has certainly not been immune to these advances and, both on the field and on the business side, data analysis is becoming not only normal, but a vital part of any team's decision-making process. On the sport side, coaches and general managers are competing on a daily basis and have found ways to use data analysis to gain an edge on their on-field competition. That can be strategic decisions on the field, better player evaluation, more targeted player development, and even improved player training and health. Each team integrates data and analytics differently into their decision-making process and finds different types of competitive advantages. But it is generally accepted that more information can only help you gain an edge on your competition, so not using the information provided by data is simply making it harder to win games.

The same is true for the management of the business side of sport. Instead of competing against other teams on the field of play, teams are competing for fans' dollars and attention with an increasing number of options. Fans have a growing number of channels, streaming services, social networks, and other sources of content to grab their attention. As the competition increases, teams are finding new ways to use the information that good data analysis can provide to manage their finances, engage fans, and increase the efficiency of production.

One way teams are using analytics to advance their business interests is in the realm of fan engagement at the park. The Boston Red Sox have monitored the flow of fans into the stadium, in particular looking at which entrance a fan uses, relative to their seat location. Using this data, they modeled the location of their concession and memorabilia stands to improve the fan experience. They optimized the location of these stands to minimize lines and the distance fans would have to travel to find food and souvenirs. This improves both the fan experience and the team's bottom line as fans tend to spend more and return to the park more often when they have a good experience.

This is just one example of how fans can be directly impacted by good analytics. Given this importance, it is vital for professionals in the sport industry to understand the power of analytics and how to incorporate it into decision making. This is not to say that every professional is now required to be able to build data infrastructure that can handle big data or code machine learning algorithms to optimize social media content, but the more the professional understands the power and possibility of analytics, the more likely it is that they will be able to help their team truly gain a competitive advantage by using this new type of information.

That is why this text is a valuable tool for any aspiring sport professional. Taking the reader into a variety of areas of the business side of sport and explaining not only what could be done, but also what has been done and how it was done, gives the reader a set of concrete examples to draw on as they progress through their career. Perhaps they will join an organization that already has a highly developed set of analytic tools; the case studies here will allow them to be instantly more comfortable with the application of analytics in a variety of situations. For those that join organizations who perhaps lag behind the industry standard in analytics, this text will help them recognize the deficiency and diagnose it. With that type of knowledge, they will become incredibly valuable assets to their team.

The one word of caution I would offer the student being exposed to the power of analytics for the first time is to take the time to understand not only the power and potential of analytics, but also its limitations. Data can be incredibly valuable to a team, but if it is not handled properly, over emphasized, or misinterpreted, analytics, like all types of mishandled information, can lead to poor decision making. Use the case studies contained here to expand your idea of what is possible and understand what analytics can and cannot do.

The power of analytics is still in its early stages. As new data sources come online, and computing power continues to increase, the use cases for analytics and its impact on the sport industry will continue to expand. Engaging with analytics now allows you to be ahead of the game, knowing exactly where the game is headed.

Ben Alamar

Ben Alamar, Director of Production Analytics, ESPN

ACKNOWLEDGMENTS

We would like to thank all the folks at Routledge for their help through this entire process. They took a risk on a book in an area that was just starting to gain traction and we are very happy they trusted us with this opportunity.

We would like to thank all the members of the College of Business, the University of New Haven, and our wonderful colleagues in the Sport Management Department. We also would like to thank our students who have been in our various sport analytic classes over the years and have helped shape the material we have used in this book. They have served as our guinea pigs for material and the various assignments that are contained in the instructor's manual.

We also would like to thank all those folks in sport and related industries who have contributed to our knowledge and a good number have contributed in both small and large ways to this book. That is especially true for those who contributed by writing case studies and chapters for this book. The University of New Haven is especially blessed to have some great corporate citizens in our back yard such as WWE, ESPN, and Octagon and we appreciate all their help and assistance.

To all those who helped make this book possible – thank you.

INTRODUCTION

Gil Fried and Ceyda Mumcu

Data is everywhere in the sport field. The concept of using data to make sport decisions was popularized by the *Moneyball* book and movie. While player and sport-related data has garnered the greatest amount of publicity, fueled in part by the growth of fantasy sports, sport data has been around for hundreds of years. Gamblers regularly relied on data to know which horse or team to bet on. Coaches routinely utilized data to evaluate talent and potential for players. Likewise, on the business side of sport, executives regularly tracked attendance and broadcast revenue as just some data points to determine success. This text focuses on the business side, rather than the player side, of sport analytics to help executives more effectively manage their enterprises.

Data has significantly evolved over the years. That evolution has tracked how literacy has also evolved. It used to be that literacy meant knowing how to sign your name. Then it evolved into writing and reading Latin. Today, being literate means being able to read and understand a newspaper in your own language. But with so much data out there it can be argued that data literacy is the ability to wade through all the textual, audio, and video data that everyone consumes on a daily basis. For example, how much information can be gleaned from all the various search engines out there? If I were to enter my name (Gil Fried) into a Yahoo or Bing search it would produce 116,000 results. While all might not be about me, there would be a significant number of results associated with me, some accurate and maybe some that are not. If a Google search was undertaken it would produce 593,000 results. If someone was interested in really knowing about me, Gil Fried, how many sites would they have to visit? Just because there are so many results associated with my name does not make the available information the right material or the material I or you want to read. That is why being data literate is so important. Without knowing what data to look for, a person can spend years searching through data and not finding the right material.

Many people talk about "Big Data" which often refers to data volume or the task of processing large amounts of data that are often beyond the computing firepower of traditional work/home computers. Some people define "Big Data" as the collection and processing of their personal data as they search the internet or send emails. While these are correct interpretations of "Big Data," they represent a very narrow definition of "Big Data" as big data is so much more. "Big Data" is the ability to take significant amounts of data, analyze the data, and then develop approaches to solve numerous problems from where the flu is going to hit, to where crime will most likely occur, to how to effectively sell tickets to sport fans.

"Big Data" though can be called something more appropriate – decision analytics and intelligent action. Decision analytics focuses on taking all the data to help make better decisions and take intelligent actions in the real world. These terms focus on how you derive value from data to make evidence-based decisions. The action part of these terms is that the resulting conclusions need to be applied to important issues and problems. The process, as we will see throughout this book, is that we have to frame the problem, find the data (if possible) to answer the problem, analyze the data, and then take action to see if the right question was asked and answered. As an example, the long commute time and pollution caused by idling cars is a major issue affecting numerous people. Through using data, researchers were able to develop protocols and algorithms to appropriately time stop lights to reflect true traffic movement. In a recent application of the question and data to a solution, Pittsburgh, PA, ran a pilot program that reduced urban travel times by 25 percent and reduced emissions by 21 percent through reduced time waiting at intersections (Data Analytics, 2015). The problem was wasted energy and pollution from cars. The data included traffic usage, the number of cars, where people were driving, how long it took to commute and many other data points. This data was analyzed and a strategy was conceived of and then implemented that could be evaluated later on to determine if the strategy and execution worked. This is the approach used throughout this text. Identify a problem, explore the data, collect any necessary data, analyze all available data, develop a strategy using that data, and then execute a deliberate strategy based on the data.

We approach data in his text with the assumption that data can answer the question, what happened? This can be examined in terms of how many tickets were sold, how many members renewed their gym membership, how many employees received a favorable evaluation, or did we meet our budget as just some examples. While such information is very important, it does not necessarily answer the question, why? Why were we able to sell more tickets, why did some members not renew, why do our best employees leave, or why are we going bankrupt as examples. That is where our industry needs to develop a correlation between the questions asked (framing), the data collected, the data analyzed, the answered obtained, and decisions made in response to the data.

The use of data to help executives more appropriately manage their organizations can be seen in numerous examples across numerous divisions within any sport organization. The question often raised by those looking at data is: are we in fact examining the right issues with the correct data and making the correct correlation between the various data points? Numerous people like to espouse an example and extrapolate it to the general. For example, just because someone pitched a no hitter does not mean they or any other pitcher will always pitch a no hitter. As some scientists say, the plural of anecdote is not data (Levitt & Dubner, 2014). Several examples can help show the proper context data can have in the sport and fitness industry. These are only two of many examples, but will help show how pervasive data is and how it can either help identify a problem or generate more problems.

Are you obese? That is a rhetorical question, but it raises an important concept. Who determines what constitutes obesity? Is being 20 percent overweight the standard? Does it vary from country to country and even between states/provinces within a given country? Is obesity really that big of a problem and can there be arguments either for or against obesity being such a major concern? Are more kids sitting on couches playing video games rather than engaging in sports? These represent some of the questions that surround the issue of sport/fitness and a major health issue.

This leads to an intriguing question – what is fueling the growth of fitness in the United States and across the globe? Obesity is one element possibly affecting the fitness industry and obesity has been fueled by cheap and tasty food and tangent issues such as the reduction in cigarette consumption (which serves as a stimulant – burning more calories and an appetite suppressant) or the transformation of our society into an information economy rather than the prior farming or industrial economies where people burned more calories working (Levitt & Dubner, 2015).

A change in how we view being overweight can have surprising ramifications. For example, some prior standards for boat capacity pegged the average boat passenger at 140 pounds. It should be noted that in the 1960s the average American male weighed 166 pounds and the average woman weighed 140 pounds. By 2007 the average male weighed 191 pounds and the average woman weighed 164 pounds (Penn, 2007). Thus, if a boat carried 40 people, it would assumably be able to handle a total weight of 5,600 pounds. After a boat accident in 2014 where 20 passengers died after the boat capsized, New York Governor George Pataki changed the rule and set the average weight at 174 pounds. The boat did not have too many people (it carried 47 passengers), it was just the total weight envisioned when the 140 pound average was used had changed over the years and the boat was not able to handle the passengers' weight (Levitt & Dubner, 2015). Similarly, the Federal Aviation Administration also added ten pounds to the average passenger weight to help airlines calculate plane cargo loads (Penn, 2007).

The United States government is attempting to undertake numerous steps to address the obesity problem facing its citizens. These attempts have been undertaken for years, but a new push was made by the First Lady, Michelle Obama, in 2010 through launching a new initiative called Let's Move. Some of the initiatives undertaken under that effort include:

- providing healthier school meals;
- improving access to health;
- getting children more physically active;
- coordinated efforts across multiple federal government agencies such as:

  - Health and Human Services was to release new guidance for standards for physical activity and nutrition. This included a new push for better food labels.
  - The United States Department of Agriculture (USDA) was to update the Dietary Guidelines and Food Pyramid to provide parents with helpful information about nutrition and was to work with Congress to improve food in schools.
  - The Federal Trade Commission (FTC) was to monitor how food is marketed to children.
  - The Department of Transportation (DOT) and Environmental Protection Agency (EPA) were to promote walking and biking to school.

o   Federal agencies were also going to make funds available to local communities, including $35 million in physical education program grants to schools from the Department of Education (The White House, 2010).

The White House was trying to leverage government resources to help solve the obesity problem. The complexity associated with obesity and solving its carnage shows how complex solutions can be to what otherwise might be considered a simple issue and solutions. Data can help show the extent of the problem. For example obesity is responsible for more than 160,000 "excess" deaths a year. The average obese person costs society more than $7,000 a year in lost productivity and added medical treatment. Lifetime added medical costs alone for a person 70 pounds or more overweight amount to as much as $30,000, depending on race and gender (Freedman, 2011). Even with such data, obesity is a growing concern and has not declined since the launch of Let's Move. For kids aged 2–19 years, the prevalence of obesity has remained fairly stable over the past decade at about 17 percent and affects about 12.7 million kids (Center for Disease Control, 2012). The Unites States is not alone, even though it leads the world in obesity. According to a 2013 Global Burden of Disease study, there has been a 28 percent increase in obesity globally and from 1980 to 2013 the number increased from around 800 million to over 2.1 billion obese people. The majority of these obese individuals came from ten countries in order of occurrence – the United States, China, India, Russia, Brazil, Mexico, Egypt, Germany, Pakistan, and then Indonesia (Matilda, 2014). In China the percentage of over-weight men has grown from 4 percent in the 1990s to over 15 percent by 2007. Chinese women increased in obesity from 10 to 20 percent during the same time period (Penn, 2007). Similarly, more than one-third of African women and one-quarter of African men are obese and those numbers are expected to increase another 10 percent through 2016 (Penn, 2007).

To help combat obesity several European and Scandinavian countries have implemented taxes on sugar, soda and junk food. Similarly, Mexico has started taxing junk food and sodas, requiring clearer labels on food, ending junk food marketing targeting children, and only providing healthy foods in schools. In 2000, Australia implemented a 10 percent tax on soda, candy and white flour bakery products. Lastly, several countries in Europe (including France, Spain, and Greece) have implemented community based intervention programs to help combat obesity (Hyman, 2014).

Even with all the knowledge and strategies, it would be assumed that sport participation numbers would increase as individuals want to pursue a healthier lifestyle. However, the numbers show that sport participation among America's youth has experienced a steady decline from 2008 to 2012. For example, soccer participation dropped by 7.1 percent, baseball participation dropped by 7.2 percent, and basketball participation declined by 8.3 percent (Reed, 2014). It likewise would also be assumed that more children would be participating in physical education classes. The Center for Disease Control recommends 60 minutes of vigorous physical activity on a daily basis. In 2009, less than 20 percent of kids participated in at least 60 minutes of physical activity on a daily basis (Center for Disease Control, 2010). These numbers are actually better than the non-government research. Independent research showed that less than 6 percent of high schools offer daily physical education to their students. Even when physical education programs are in place, most students are not engaged in vigorous physical activity for the majority of their class time. It is estimated that boys only spend about 18 minutes engaged in moderate and vigorous activity and girls spend about 16 minutes (Fairclough & Stratton, 2005).

The lack of physical education programming also has reverberated to the youth sport market and general sport participation numbers. Participation numbers are down for almost all major sports over the past ten years. Are people being turned off from some of the major sports? Can that trend be changed? It should be noted that while participation numbers for many team sports have declined, many individual sports, such as skateboarding, kayaking, snowboarding, and archery, have shown increased participation (Penn, 2007). This might be a sign that big sports have gotten too big and people want to engage in smaller sports and carve their own path. As one author wrote, this does not mean that sports are dying in America, rather they are shifting from a communal rite to a personal one (Penn, 2007). This can be a very interesting trend to track, and the data can help us know the numbers, but we always have to revert back to the question – why? Theories abound concerning why, but what does the data say? For example, archery numbers spiked supposedly due to the release of the *Hunger Games* movies. In another example, football numbers have shown a dramatic decline after the release of research on sport concussions. People often make knee-jerk reactions, but are the number of concussions higher in football or soccer? This example highlights that data and analytics might fall to the wayside to hysteria, panic, and other fears.

It is not just the government that is making strides to address the issue. Insurance companies also have been working with larger employers to provide their employees with discounts to join health clubs. UnitedHealthcare offers a Fitness Reimbursement Program that provides smaller employers with money back for members who go to the gym on a regular basis. Employees need to show their membership ID when going to over ten larger chains and some independent gyms. Employees get reimbursed $20 per month (to an annual maximum of $240) for every month they visit the fitness center at least 12 times (UnitedHealthcare, 2015). The problem is that many employees who take advantage of the discount have great intentions, but stop going to health clubs in large numbers.

One way to address whether someone is actually "cheating" and not going to health clubs is to use fitness trackers that have gained popularity over the past several years, whether Fitbit, Garmin, Jawbone, Apple watch or a host of other manufacturers. New York-based Oscar, a relatively new health insurance company focused on using technology to communicate with customers, announced in February, 2015, that it would be giving all of its customers Misfit fitness trackers. These customers will receive $1 each time they hit their daily goal for steps taken – up to an annual total of $240 – distributed each month in an Amazon gift card. Other insurers, such as UnitedHealthcare, offer a health management app that connects to tracker devices. Insurers Aetna and Cigna report that many employers they work with are providing discounts or rewards to employees who use a fitness tracker (Shemkus, 2015). The success of fitness trackers led Fitbit to launch a public offering of its stock in 2015. As part of its regulatory filings for selling its shares, the company indicated that only half of their 20 million registered users were still active as of the first quarter of 2015 (Jesdanun, 2015). Industry research highlighted in the same article showed that about a third of the trackers bought get abandoned after six months.

Abandoning fitness trackers is only one of the areas being abandoned by those interested in fitness. Those who join and then abandon gyms are a major concern for the fitness industry. Here are some critical gym membership numbers:

- The average number of days a gym member actually goes to their gym each week – 2 times.
- Average monthly cost of a gym membership – $58.00.
- Amount of gym membership money that goes to waste because of underutilization – $39.00.
- Percentage of lost membership value – 33 percent.
- Percentage of people with gym memberships that never use them – 67 percent.
- Annual gym and health club industry revenue – $21.8 billion.
- Annual number of people that use a gym or health club – 58 million.
- Average age of gym member – 40 years old.
- Number of US gyms and health clubs – 30,500.
- Number of gyms and health clubs worldwide – 153,000.
- Approximate number of health club members worldwide – 131.7 million.
- Total global health club industry revenues – $75.7 billion.

More than half of members join a gym or health club to:

- feel better about themselves;
- look better;
- lose weight.

The most common reasons people give for not going to the gym are:

- they're too tired;
- because of work obligations;
- due to family obligations;
- no training partner;
- it's too expensive;
- they don't have time;
- the gym isn't convenient.

(Gym membership statistics, 2015; Averkamp, 2015).

From all this information we might try to draw the conclusion that obesity is a major issue in the United States and other parts of the world. The increased availability of cheap (and unhealthy) food, the downward trend in smoking, the more sedentary lifestyle people are pursuing, and the perceived lack of time/money to engage in fitness might all contribute to the rise of obesity. We also might draw the conclusion that fitness technology and fitness facilities are a possible solution. Likewise the numbers could show that some people are avoiding exercise, have multiple excuses for not working out, or that exercise is not taken as seriously as it should be. Numerous statistics can be viewed in so many ways and data can often be manipulated to serve the user's goals. This leads to significant confusion and individuals often twisting data to serve various needs. This also helped spur the need for a book that helps examine some of the data available in the sport industry to try to explain what the data means and how it can help us deliver sport and fitness in a more economical and successful manner.

The rush to use numbers to help prove or disprove some type of correlation has led to a flood of books and trivia-related publications. One of the popular series is the Freakonomics series of books. The authors (Levitt & Dubner, 2014) relied on several simple ideas:

- Incentives are the cornerstone of modern life – people do things for rewards.
- Knowing what to measure, and how to measure it, can make a complicated world less so.
- Conventional wisdom is often wrong.
- Correlation does not equal causality – just because two things are similar does not mean that one caused the other.

These basic ideas can be applied to the obesity and fitness example above. People undertake fitness often for a reward. They might be interested in obtaining a rock-hard body, becoming a competitive athlete to win an award, they could change their lifestyle due to medical issues, they might have a goal to lose a certain amount of weight, or they might want to obtain a discount on insurance premium. The more rewards someone has and the greater their desire to obtain those rewards, the more dedicated they will be.

There are so many possible variables to measure to address the problem of obesity, that those trying to solve the problem need to really understand the root of the problem and then what to measure to be effective. Is obesity linked to fast food restaurants, less kids engaging in exercise, or numerous other possible theories – all of which can be measured, but which also can raise serious concerns and might expose sacred cows that politicians might not want to address? For example, if the obesity issue is linked to family dynamics and the decline in two parent households, there might be significant correlation, but if no one wants to address the issue for political correctness than maybe the problem will never be solved because everyone will try to avoid the real issue.

Similar to old wives tales/remedies, conventional wisdom and how we examined issues in the past are often wrong. How doctors treated diseases, for example, can show the harm in conventional wisdom. Most people would think hospitals are the safest area and the least likely area for someone to catch a bug. However, that is exactly what happened to many people who got staph infections and other diseases. It wasn't until some researchers discovered that doctors and nurses were spreading diseases and hospitals developed the solution of having staff wash their hands more thoroughly and wear sensors that the issues were addressed and the harm significantly reduced. Similarly, just because someone improves their diet and eats only organic food does not mean they are not obese, will lose weight, or will lose weight and then gain it back several months later.

Correlation is something that everyone is looking to find, but that does not necessarily mean cause and effect. This concern is frequently found in the sports world as a team might sign a new coach or star player. If the team does well is it because of the new coach or star? Could it be the opponents are not as strong, could it be that the coach has a phenomenal impact regardless of who they have on their roster? Could it be the support players who rally around the new star? Many people will postulate they know what caused the team to do well, but it is hard to prove that any one element in fact made the difference. The same issue applies to companies marketing products that might sponsor a NASCAR team and undertake numerous other marketing efforts. If the products sell very well which exact campaign or combination of campaigns resulted in the increased sales? This is the question that marketers often examine to determine if there is correlation between various strategies and what might increase sales. In the obesity context, some of the states with the highest obesity rate are in the southern United States, giving some the idea that obesity is directly tied to poverty. Likewise, some of the healthiest states appear to be states with higher average incomes. Does this mean that if someone is wealthy they will not be obese? Of course the answer is no. Just because there might be a correlation between obesity numbers and income or geographic locale does not mean there is cause and effect.

Any correlation can be examined in light of the numbers. Sports are components of a winning culture, and a winning culture keeps score and measures results. A team could measure the number of three-point shots made or the time of possessions as examples of thousands of data points that could be examined. The issue is – are those the right data points? If a team's goal is to win, then those numbers might not be as relevant as the win–loss record. That is where framing the question comes into play. Hypothesis generation is not that difficult. What is more difficult is to rigorously test the hypothesis with data. The process starts with identifying the problem or question, examining the data, and then identifying possible solutions. Through collecting and analyzing data a researcher can try to find potential answers. The researchers then have to present and act on the results. This can best be accomplished by having the data tell a story to stakeholders to get them to take action. The process seems quite simple, but there are numerous questions associated with the data from the first step of framing the question until the results are presented to stakeholders. Some of these questions include:

- What was the source of the data?
- How well does the sample represent the broader population (or does the data encompass the entire population of data)?
- Does the data distribution examine outliers? How do outliers affect results? Are you attacking the noisy part of the problem that captures everyone's attention or the real underlying issue?
- What assumptions are behind the analysis and what if the assumptions are wrong?
- Which analytical approach was used and why was that approach used over other options?
- Is the model (algorithm) used to examine the data appropriate for today and the future?
- Will the data benefit one element of the organization or be a benefit to the entire enterprise?
- How likely is it that independent variables are actually causing the changes in the dependent variables?

These questions should help lead to the truth. Data should not be used to prove a point or support a given objective, but to lead to the truth. Researchers should put forth data and analysis, not opinion. Once the data is presented then stakeholders can try to develop opinions from the results. This approach helps eliminate the process of reaching an opinion and then trying to find the data that will support that opinion (Davenport & Kim, 2013).

In the obesity context, and as highlighted above, there is a lot of data out there. That data can be confusing, counter-intuitive, or even outright wrong (whether manipulated intentionally or calculated inaccurately). Also, with so many different government and private entities all fighting for money to address the issue, there is a financial benefit to keeping the obesity crisis alive and in the spotlight. It is sad to think of people's lives being used as pawns in a game of greed, but the reality is that powerbrokers exist everywhere in the world and data can help them sell a solution. Thus, some people have blamed fast food restaurants for the obesity crises and some have gone on to sue such restaurants claiming they are the culprit in the crises. Some cities/states in the United States (such as New York City) have tried to outlaw large drinks and other obesity causing foods and requiring menus to indicate the nutritional value of meals. Such efforts have not been really successful, but customers voting with their wallets has been effective. Numerous restaurants have changed their menu not from political pressure, but from customers going elsewhere. The data in the US and United Kingdom showed that fast food chains voluntarily agreed to make their food healthier and have taken some steps to improve the quality of meat, limit sugar, and reduce saturated fat. However, the results did not improve for milk/dairy and sodium. In total, the effort to be healthier actually failed for most fast food chains. The eight chains analyzed (McDonald's, Burger King, Wendy's, Taco Bell, Kentucky Fried Chicken (KFC), Arby's, Jack in the Box and Dairy Queen) failed to raise the nutritional value of their dishes in 14 years, in spite of pledges to offer healthy choices, according to a 2013 study (Boseley, 2013). Value menus offering huge meals are just one culprit, but more chains are starting to offer salads, basic grilled chicken, low-sodium meals, and other options to drive revenue growth which has been flat at many chains. Consumers are also driving change with a greater demand for gluten-free, allergy free, locally sourced fresh food, grain-fed beef, free range chickens, and related options. Rest assured, the data drives decisions made by major corporations. The data also shows that government efforts to change school lunch eating habits have had mixed results. While government-run lunch programs are trying to encourage kids to eat more fruits and vegetables (to some success if few other options are made available), kids are throwing away over 25 percent of their lunches each day (primarily in fruits and vegetables) and the total cost of wasted lunch food is estimated at over $2 billion a year (This Lunch Rox, 2011).

There are no easy answers to address the obesity crises. Solutions start with knowing what to ask and the goals of the different entities trying to address the crises. Obesity is just one of numerous possible issues that can be examined and analyzed using data. The key for any in-depth research to solve a potential problem is to identify the problem and frame the problem to better conduct research and develop possible solutions.

Let's take a look at how an issue can be framed. The example we will use is competitive eating. In 2001 Takeru Kobayashi (aka Kobi) transformed the famous Nathan's Hot Dog Eating Contest competition and the world of competitive eating. The record prior to 2001 was 25.5 hot dogs and buns. That would be an impressive number for any competitive eater. However, a new breed of competitive eater came about with Kobi. A relative unknown, Kobi shattered the world record by downing 50 hot dogs in 12 minutes. Opponents raised numerous allegations about Kobi cheating through taking muscle relaxants or expanding his stomach with stones. These rumors turned out to be unfounded. So how did Kobi not just win, but destroy his competition? The Japanese eater introduced advanced eating and training techniques that transformed the landscape of competitive eating.

According to an in-depth analysis of Kobi's career by Levitt and Dubner (2014), prior competitors ate similar to average people, but just shoved as many hot dogs and buns into their mouths as possible in the short time frame. Kobi decided to break down the competition and examine ways to more effectively eat. Competitors were asking how could they eat more hot dogs? Kobi framed his analysis of the problem around how he could make hot dog eating easier. This is an example of taking a problem, undertaking some research, developing a new model, and then examining the data (results) to determine if the proposed solution will help address the problem. This is the approach advocated in this text and in Davenport's and Kim's (2013) *Keep up with Your Quants* – develop a model (framing) >> examine past practices/findings >> solve the problem with data (creating a model, finding the necessary data, and then analyzing the data) >>> develop and act on the results.

Using this approach (even if he did not intend to follow a specific analytical model) Kobi broke with tradition and decided that he would cut each hot dog in half rather than eating the traditional way from one end to the other. He then went to work on the bun and started separating the hot dogs from the buns. He would eat his broken-in-half hot dogs and then after eating several of them he would eat the buns. He then tinkered with the buns and started dunking them in water and squeezing out the excess liquid. This made it easier to eat the buns and also allowed Kobi to take in some liquid while eating – thus minimizing his need to take time to drink liquids while eating.

He not only changed the way eaters competed, he changed the way they trained. He started videotaping his training sessions and recorded the data in spreadsheets. This information was used to find potential inefficiencies. His detailed research examined everything from what was the best pace to pursue, to how much sleep he needed to perform at his best. He even figured out that he could make more room in his stomach by dancing while eating. This strange but effective dance came to be known as the Kobayashi Shake (Levitt & Dubner, 2014). It should be noted that Kobi's competitors were so focused on surpassing 25.5 hot dogs that they in fact created a barrier since they were hoping to reach 26, 27, or even 28 hot dogs. Kobi in contrast decided that the record was an artificial barrier and that he would focus not on the number, but how he ate them.

Since the early 2000s, other competitors have burst onto the competitive eating scene. The current record is held by Joe Chestnut who finished off 69 hot dogs/buns in ten minutes in 2013. Chestnut also holds records for eating pork ribs (13.76 pounds in 12 minutes) and Twinkies (121 in six minutes). Matt Stonie, who beat Chestnut in the 2015 competition (with 62 hot dogs/buns) also holds several eating records including bacon (182 strips in five minutes), birthday cake (14.5 pounds in eight minutes), and frozen yogurt (10.5 pounds in six minutes). Competitors can earn significant income from appearance fees and competitions. Mr. Chestnut reportedly earned around $230,000 in 2014. The eaters are not the only champions. Nathan's Hot Dog has been the primary beneficiary. Their competition attracts 40,000 fans every year and the event has been broadcast on ESPN since 2003. The competition has propelled Nathan's hot dog sales from 250 million in 2003 to over 1 billion in 2014. Likewise their publicly traded stocks have increased from $6 a share in 2004 to $53 a share in 2014 (Peter, 2015). Eaters and

PHOTO I.1   Nathan's Famous hot dogs

the food manufacturing company each have a different framework for what they consider success, even as it relates to the same event. This example helps highlight how various entities might have different goals/objectives (the problem being framed) and data can be used as a tool to measure whether each has met their respective goals/objectives.

This same approach can be used in the sport business context. Just because an approach has been used in the past does not mean that it is still an appropriate approach. This can be seen in the framing context as it relates to ticket sales for sporting events.

In the good ole days, there were limited ticket options. A person could buy a season ticket (at a discount price based on a per game price), buy an individual game ticket at a set price, obtain a ticket as a gift, or buy a ticket from a scalper. With the growth of the secondary ticket market (with companies such as StubHub and TicketNetwork) teams had to re-examine how they sold tickets. Not every game was the same. This was noticed by Stanford University, an early adopter of dynamic ticketing. They might have a regular ticket price for a game against Arizona or Oregon State, but everyone wanted the tickets for the UC Berkeley game. Thus, they increased the ticket price for that game. Similarly, many teams knew that tickets for their best games were in hot demand, while tickets for weak opponents drew very little interest and often resulted in low attendance numbers for the perceived poorer quality games. This led to the development of mini-ticket plans over the past 20 years where someone would need to buy 3–4 tickets to weaker games in order to purchase a ticket for a hot demand game. It was hoped that a fan would at least attend several of the weaker games with the tickets they had. In reality, many of the weaker tickets flooded the secondary market and teams started putting limits on tickets to prevent selling on certain secondary markets or developed their own secondary market outlet.

The issue (framing) became how to maximize ticket revenue without upsetting fans. Nothing could make a fan more upset than paying $200 for a ticket and then having someone sit right next to them who bought their ticket for only $20. Dynamic pricing had been used for years in the airline, hotel, and related industries to sell remaining inventory. However, the process was very complex as there was so much data and it took time to communicate price changes effectively. With the growth of computers, what used to take days could be accomplished in seconds. The real growth in the sports field started in baseball as a Major League Baseball (MLB) team had an inventory of over 81 games to sell compared with an NFL team that had only around 8–9 games a year and fewer individual game tickets (i.e. more season tickets sold). Dignonex, a company which develops and provides software to several pro-sports teams, including the Minnesota Twins, developed an algorithm that allows it to examine about 40 variables for every game on a team's schedule and come up with a suggested price for tickets in each section of a stadium. Among the variables examined are weather, historical sales trends, current standings, pitchers, the day of the week and the demand in the "secondary market" – tickets resold by sites such as StubHub (Williams, 2012). Ticket pricing may change hundreds of times from several weeks before a game, to a week before a game, to even an hour before the game begins. The prices reflect the value the consumer puts on that ticket which can be impacted by both external variables (team standings, pitcher, weather) to internal variables (the consumer's wallet, desire to get out of the house, etc.). Since a team cannot anticipate all the various variables throughout a season, they have to examine what they can in fact control. That would normally be the cost charged to season ticket holders. Season ticket holders are a team's lifeblood and deserve the best deals. If the price of a seat in a season ticket package is $18, for example, and $25 for a single-game purchase, the cost under dynamic pricing could climb above that $25 level or drop down to $18, but should never go below $18. That is the incentive for customers to buy season tickets.

Flexibility and customization are the keys to keeping customers happy. To provide its football fans with more ticket buying options, Washington State University created a 48-Hour Pack for the 2015 season. The plan (which costs $165 and allows fans to attend three games) allows fans to wait until individual game times are announced by the conference to decide if they want to claim a ticket for that game. Fans do not have to pick which games they want to attend before the season starts. Instead, when each game's start time is announced by the Pac 12 conference (normally 12 days before the game) fans will receive an email from the ticket office notifying them of the kick-off time. Fans will then have a 48-hour window in which to claim a ticket to that game (New plan for Washington State football tickets, 2015). Based on declining attendance numbers at schools such as Iowa and Michigan, providing flexibility to fans who might be time sensitive with work schedules provides fans with options.

Ticket sales are covered in greater detail in the marketing chapter. However, it is relevant in the context of framing to show that numerous data points are being used to change how tickets are being sold. Just because tickets were sold one way years ago does not mean that new approaches should not be used leveraging the latest technology. Going back to the four elements highlighted by Levitt and Dubner, we can see that:

- Fans like a reward, such as being able to buy a ticket at a great price or even to pay a higher price to get the best ticket they want.
- Teams need to know what to measure and dynamic pricing algorithms can measure a good number of data points over a significant time period to help generate the best possible price for customers.
- Conventional wisdom was geared to treat each game the same, but every game is different. Data can help show that difference and can more effectively determine what should be the best price points.
- Correlation can help examine numerous pricing, game, weather, team, and other variables to determine what should be the best price point. There is no perfect price point, but if a customer feels happy buying a ticket at a set price because of the variables most important to them then the cause (variables associated with the game impacting the ticket price) results in the effect of them buying a ticket.

So far we have examined various data issues associated with the sport and fitness industry. These examples are designed to highlight how data impacts every facet of the sport industry. But the examples also show that data can be similar to peeling an onion. The more the numbers are exposed, the more issues that might arise. That is what we hope readers will take away from this book. Numerous numbers and data points will be explored. Sport organizations live by the numbers but just throwing numbers out does not give the entire story and that is where we will explore various functional areas within a sport entity and across various sport organizations to produce a comprehensive view of how data will continue to transform the industry. Through using this text a reader will hopefully be able to appreciate what data might be able to help them make more appropriate decisions and how data can also lead them in the wrong direction.

We hope you find value in the way we are approaching using data and that you can leverage data to advance your careers and make critical decisions to help the sport, fitness, and recreation industry grow. This text will not cover all aspects of analytics and will attempt to blend the ever evolving area of business analytics with the specialized sector of sport analytics. While sport analytics is a very specialized area, it is a strong growth area with the potential for significant future growth. One study in 2014 concluded that sport analytics had a market size of $125 million and it was estimated that by 2021 that number could grow to $4.7 billion (Sport Techie, 2015). It will be hard to imagine such a huge growth, but when the study examined all cloud, tablet, and phone traffic associated with sports then it became clear that the broader sport technology area, including analytics, will grow significantly over the next couple years.

References

Averkamp, S. (2015). Gym statistics: Members, equipment, and cancellations. Retrieved from www.fitnessforweightloss.com/gym-statistics-members-equipment-and-cancellations/

Boseley, S. (2013, May 7). US fast food chains "failing" healthier menu test. Retrieved from www.theguardian.com/lifeandstyle/2013/may/07/us-fast-food-fail-healthy-menu-test

Center for Disease Control (2010, July). Strategies to improve the quality of physical education. Retrieved from www.cdc.gov/healthyyouth/physicalactivity/pdf/quality_pe.pdf

Center for Disease Control. (2012). Childhood obesity facts. Retrieved from www.cdc.gov/obesity/data/childhood.html

Data analytics: Go big or go home. (2015, July 27–August 2). *Bloomberg Businessweek*. S1–6.

Davenport, T., & Kim, J. (2013, July–August). *Keep up with your quants*. Boston, MA: Harvard Business Review Press.

Fairclough, S. J., & Stratton, G. (2005). Physical activity levels in middle and high school physical education: A review. *Pediatric Exercise Science, 17*, 217–18.

Freedman, D. (2011, February). How to fix the obesity crisis. Retrieved from www.scientificamerican.com/article/how-to-fix-the-obesity-crisis/

Gym membership statistics (2015, April 27). Retrieved from www.statisticbrain.com/gym-membership-statistics/

Hyman, M. (2014, November 30). Four ways other countries are successfully tackling obesity. Take note, America. Retrieved from www.huffingtonpost.com/dr-mark-hyman/four-ways-countries-obesity_b_5845336.html

Jesdanun, A. (2015, July 16). Like gym memberships, enthusiasm for fitness trackers drops. Retrieved from http://health.wusf.usf.edu/post/gym-memberships-enthusiasm-fitness-trackers-drops

Levitt, S., & Dubner, S. (2014). *Think like a freak*. New York, NY: Harper Collins.

Levitt, S., & Dubner, S. (2015). *When to rob a bank and 131 more warped suggestions and ill-intended rants*. New York, NY: Harper Collins.

Matilda, B. (2014, May 29). Dramatic increase in obesity rates globally, study. Retrieved from www.scienceworldreport.com/articles/15045/20140529/dramatic-increase-in-obesity-rates-globally-study.htm

New plan for Washington State football tickets. (2015). Retrieved from http://athleticmanagement.com/content/new-plan-washington-state-football-tickets?referer=4573e5bbfd5eae7515915e9d691d2170

Penn, M. (with Zalesne, E. K.). (2007). *Microtrends: The small forces behind tomorrow's big changes*. New York, NY: Twelve (Hachette Book Group USA).

Peter, J. (2015, July 22). *Playing a dangerous game*. USA Today. 1C.

Reed, K. (2014, March 10). Overall youth sports participation rate continues to decline. Retrieved from http://leagueoffans.org/2014/03/10/overall-youth-sports-participation-rate-continues-to-decline/#sthash.tPquPOLa.dpuf

Shemkus, S. (2015, April 17). Fitness trackers are popular among insurers and employers – but is your data safe? Retrieved from www.theguardian.com/lifeandstyle/2015/apr/17/fitness-trackers-wearables-insurance-employees-jobs-health-data

Sport Techie. (2015, August 8). Universities need to focus on training students in sports analytics. Retrieved from www.sporttechie.com/2015/08/09/universities-need-to-focus-on-training-students-in-sports-analytics/#comment-274137

The White House. (2010, May 11). Childhood obesity task force unveils action plan: Solving the problem of childhood obesity within a generation. Retrieved from www.whitehouse.gov/the-press-office/childhood-obesity-task-force-unveils-action-plan-solving-problem-childhood-obesity-

This Lunch Rox. (2011, September 14). Waste not. . . . Retrieved from http://thislunchrox.com/2011/09/waste-not/

UnitedHealthcare. (2015). Fitness reimbursement program. Retrieved from www.uhctogether.com/uhcwellness/16181.html

Williams, D. (2012, April 23). Dynamic pricing is new trend in ticket sales. Retrieved from http://espn.go.com/blog/playbook/dollars/post/_/id/597/dynamic-pricing-is-new-trend-in-ticket-sales

PART I
Data 101

1

AN INTRODUCTION TO ANALYTICS AND DATA

Ceyda Mumcu

Introduction

In the introduction section of this textbook, you read about how data are used in different situations, what data might be and how we come across data, and many examples from obesity to competitive eating to ticket sales and pricing. In this chapter, you will be introduced to more technical concepts, such as analytics, data, data types, some key concepts and various statistical analyses to develop a baseline, before moving to the chapters covering application of analytics in functional areas of sport. Please remember that this chapter is not developed to replace a statistics textbook. It is, rather, a brief summary of some relevant statistical concepts and key analyses. If needed, please refer back to statistics textbooks for more detailed information.

Analytics and its importance in the sport industry

Every organization would benefit from executing their business with efficiency, and sport organizations are no exception. Due to the saturated market, it is especially important for sport organizations to function with maximum efficiency and to make smart business decisions. Today, business decisions are not done with hunches; but they are based on analytics. Davenport and Harris (2007) defined analytics as "the extensive use of data, statistical and quantitative analysis, explanatory and predictive models, and fact based management to derive decisions and actions" (p.7).

The sport organizations with the analytical mindset generate and collect data through various internal and external sources, and analyze business performance to derive insights and make fact-based decisions to create competitive advantage, and increase the effectiveness and efficiency of the organization. Sport organizations could utilize analytics in certain functional areas or organization-wide. Most commonly, sport organizations use analytics to:

- analyze athlete performance to make decisions on the starting line-up, game plans and which players to sign/draft/trade;
- predict and prevent player injuries;

- assess value of athletes to their brand;
- examine effectiveness of various marketing activities;
- segment existing fans and estimate their value;
- predict retention of fans; and
- develop an incident prevention model based on past incidents.

While the benefit of analytics to a sport organization is obvious, what "data" is might not be so clear to all. Let's turn our focus to understanding what data is and some important concepts about it.

What is data?

Data is information in a variety of forms such as numbers, words, pictures, video, measurements, observations, and so on. It can be raw and unorganized, or also transformed into a format that is useable. Today, sport organizations have access to a vast amount of data including transactional data (e.g. sales, cost and inventory), non-operational data (e.g. industry sales, macroeconomic data) and meta-data (e.g. data definitions) (Frand, n.d.). In order to achieve benefits from analytics and make good decisions, organizations should begin the process by asking questions about data before jumping into data collection, and should utilize systematically assembled data (Davenport & Harris, 2007):

1 Data relevance – what data is needed?

This will be dependent on the objectives of the organization and the questions they want to answer in the pursuit of achieving their objectives. Every organization sets business objectives to gain a competitive advantage in the market place, and these objectives are based on the current status of the sport property in the market, what they want to accomplish, and their resources and competencies. Based on these components, organizations set functional objectives and identify operational metrics to measure their performance in achieving the objectives. For example, if a fitness facility aims to have a set number of active memberships monthly, they can simply count the number of memberships. While the number of memberships shows if they met their goal or not, this might not provide enough information to the administrators especially if the facility didn't meet the goal. Looking at retention rate for current members and the number of new memberships acquired would provide more detailed insights on why they failed to meet their goal. As you see a variety of data is relevant in answering one question, and data will provide insights only if you start with a question and collect relevant data.

2 Data source – where can this data be obtained?

Based on the type of data needed, the source of data will change. Sport organizations can obtain data both from internal sources and external sources. Internal data could be gathered from finance, manufacturing, research and development, and human resources departments. Marketing departments can also provide internal data such as Return on Investment (ROI) metrics of advertisements (more details are provided in Chapter 4). External data could be gathered from suppliers and customers, and also could be purchased from a third party such as Nielsen TV ratings or Scarborough customer data.

3 Data quantity – how much data is needed?

Once the type of data needed and how to acquire it are decided, the next question to tackle is how much data is needed? The answer to this question is "it depends." In some cases, a sport organization might have data of an entire population, whereas in other cases they can only access a sample. How much data one needs is especially important when analysis is done with data collected from a sample that requires power analysis to identify adequate sample size. In addition to sample size, representativeness of the sample is also an important concern for the accuracy of findings. These concepts will be covered in more detail in the "Some key statistical concepts" section of this chapter.

4 Data quality – how can the data be made more accurate and valuable for analysis?

The next step that requires attention is the quality of the data. A large data set is not always the answer. Quality data is needed to achieve valid and reliable results. Some of the important aspects of data quality are completeness, accuracy, consistency, and currency.

- Completeness: Availability of all necessary and relevant data.
- Accuracy: Reflecting real-life situations and being precise.
- Consistency: Being consistent between systems with common definitions and standardization, and avoiding duplicate records in data.
- Currency: Being updated periodically – daily, weekly, monthly.

Types of data

Most often data is extracted from its source in raw format, and needs to be cleaned by removing incorrect, incomplete and duplicate information and then transformed to be useable. Once data goes through the cleansing and transformation processes and is stored in a database, it becomes ready for analyses. Here, understanding the type of data becomes important, because the type of data and the level of measurement dictate the type of analyses one could perform. Data could be qualitative (descriptive information) or quantitative (numeric information), and quantitative data could be further classified as discrete or continuous. Discrete data can only have certain values (integers), and negative values and decimals are not possible. On the other hand, continuous data can have infinite possibilities with no gaps (e.g. 1.1, 1.135, 1.2, and 2.367) (Lomax, 2007). For example, the number of tickets sold would be an example of discrete data due to ticket sales numbers being integer numbers, and height of athletes or time in a race would be examples of continuous data.

Another important concept to understand about the quantitative data is the levels of measurement which are classified in four levels:

- Nominal: At nominal level of measurement, numbers are used to classify data. Most of you are familiar with this type of data in classification of genders such as assigning 1 to males and 2 to females in your data set. In this type of classification, numbers do not mean anything other than showing a classification and do not have an order. If we go back to our example of classification of genders, 2 is not higher or better than 1 in any way and numbers are used solely to classify groups.

- Ordinal: This type of scale displays some type of order between the numbers with respect to the characteristic being measured. For example, at a road race, the runner who completes the course in the shortest time would be ranked as first, and the others finishing the race following the winner would be ranked second, third and so on based on their time. Although rank order of 1, 2 and 3 seem to have equal distance between them, the differences between the numbers are approximate and unequal. Going back to our example, the difference between the time of first and second runners is not expected to be the same as the difference between the time of second and third runners, and so on. Therefore, an ordinal scale communicates an order; but does not claim equal distance between the points on the scale.

- Interval: Similar to ordinal scale, interval scale orders the measurements, but it also provides equal distances between the points on the scale. One of the common examples of interval scale is IQ scores. Average IQ score is 100, and the difference between IQ scores of 80 and 90 is equal to the difference between scores of 100 and 110. In addition, lower scores show lower IQ levels and higher scores show higher IQ levels. One important aspect of an interval scale is not having a true zero point which means a zero on an interval scale does not indicate an absence of the property that is being measured. Therefore, it cannot be said an individual with an IQ score of 140 is twice as smart as another individual with an IQ score of 70.

- Ratio: The ratio scale carries all characteristics of interval scale and also has a true zero which indicates the absence of the quality being measured. Going back to the runner example, at the beginning of the race, the clock is set to zero minutes and seconds, and if the winner finished a 5-kilometer road race in 18 minutes, he could be said to be twice as fast as a runner who finished the race in 36 minutes.

Some key statistical concepts

Before moving into various analyses, it is important to remember some key statistical concepts. Statistics in general is divided into two types, descriptive statistics and inferential statistics. Descriptive statistics summarize and describe data via frequencies, central tendency, measures of dispersion and distribution characteristics. Some examples from the sport world would be batting average in baseball, number of turnovers or steals in basketball, demographic characteristics of a team's fan base in percentages or counts, and so on. These statistics could be calculated based on a sample or could be calculated for an entire population and would be called parameters. A sample is "a subset of a population," and a population is defined as "consisting of all members of a well-defined group" (Lomax, 2007, p.6). Traditionally, analyses often rely on a sample and inferences are made about a population from the sample data via inductive reasoning, which is called inferential statistics. In this process, how the sample is acquired is extremely important as inferential statistics are based on the assumption that sampling is done randomly. Simple random sampling is selecting a sample from a population with a process that gives each observation an equal and independent chance of being selected (Lomax, 2007). The importance of simple random sampling relies on the idea that the sample will be representative of the population and the results of inferential statistics will be generalizable to the population. For example, if we were to ask our season ticket holders about their experience at our games, we could reach out to all season ticket holders or survey a sample of them. For the sake of this example, let's assume that we decided to collect data from a sample of season ticket holders who were randomly selected from the entire season ticket holder pool. If our sample was large enough, then the results derived from the sample would be generalizable to all of our season ticket holders. This brings us to the topic of adequate sample size and limitations of small sample size in inferential statistics. The main idea is as sample size increases, we are sampling a larger portion of the population and therefore the sample becomes more representative of the population (Lomax, 2007).

Hypothesis testing is another concept to cover before moving into types of analyses. Hypothesis testing is a decision-making method where two competing decisions, which are known as null hypothesis and alternative hypothesis, are weighed with statistics (Lomax, 2007). A null hypothesis about a population parameter is tested with a sample by computing a test statistic along with a p value. If the p value is less than the significance level (α) set for the statistical analysis, which is usually set as 0.05 for social sciences, the null hypothesis is rejected whether it is about point estimates of mean scores, relationships or probability of an event to take place and we say the results are statistically significant. Let's continue with the season ticket holder example from the previous paragraph. If the goal was to understand the quality of the experience at our home games for the season ticket holders who attend the majority of the homes games versus those who attend less than half of the home games, we would compare the mean scores of these two groups on quality of experience at our home games. The null and alternative hypotheses could read as follows:

H_n: There is no difference between the quality of experience at games for season ticket holders who attend the majority of the home games versus those who attend less than 50 percent of the games.

H_a: There is a difference between the quality of experience at games for season ticket holders who attend the majority of the games versus those who attend less than 50 percent of the games.

The alternative hypothesis could also express the direction of the difference if the researcher has an expectation such as season ticket holders who attend the majority of the home games will report a higher quality of experience than the season ticket holders who attend less than 50 percent of the games. This example is based on mean scores and the analysis would report if the mean scores of the two groups are statistically different from each other or not. When a statistically significant result is derived from a large random sample and results report small standard errors with narrow confidence intervals, we trust the results more. However, not every statistically significant result is practically important, and practical significance should be considered when interpreting results and making decisions. Although there are many more topics to cover, we will turn our attention to various analyses for the rest of the chapter. Please refer to statistics textbooks for more detailed information.

Data analysis

Regression analysis

In regression analysis, we are interested in predicting an outcome variable with a set of explanatory variables. A regression analysis can be a simple regression or a multiple regression based on the number of predictors in a model. A simple regression explains a relationship between an outcome variable (also known as criterion variable) and a predictor, while a multiple regression explains the relationship between an outcome variable and a set of predictors. In reality, more than one factor relates to an outcome variable; therefore multiple regression analysis is used more commonly than simple regression analysis.

In the field, most of the modeling involves linear regression models, where the regression equation is written as follows and "y" indicates a criterion variable, Xs indicate predictor variables, bs are parameters to be estimated and e is the error of prediction (Stevens, 2009).

$$y = b_1X_1 + b_2X_2 + \ldots + e$$

An example of regression analysis could be seen in a situation where a sport team tries to predict the number of ticket sales for a game. The number of tickets to be sold would be input in the equation as the criterion variable (y) and quality of the opponent, day of the week, time of the game and time in season along with many other variables could be incorporated as the predictor variables (Xs). As we see in the industry, post-season games, games against top teams and rivals, and teams with star players attract more interest from the spectators, and as a result ticket prices for those games are set accordingly. By conducting a regression analysis, any sport team or organization can predict the number of ticket sales, and the importance of accurate sales prediction to any sport organization is undeniable.

Logistic regression analysis

On many occasions, analysts try to estimate the probability of an event occurring, whether it is ticket purchases, clicking on an email campaign, or an athlete getting injured, and occurrence of these events could be based on several predictors. These types of situations call for logistic regression analyses where the criterion variable is a dichotomous (binary) variable. A dichotomous variable can only take two values and they are often coded as zero and one. Logistic regression analysis estimates the probability of the criterion variable taking the value of one or zero based on a combination of predictors, and it is essentially a classification method.

In logistic regression, the probability of an event occurring can be written as follows and z is a linear combination of predictors and their coefficient estimates (Stevens, 2009):

$$\text{Prob(event)} = 1 / 1 + e^{-z};$$
$$z = b_0 + b_1X_1 + b_2X_2 + \ldots + b_pX_p$$

A logistic regression could be applied to identify which season ticket holders have a higher probability to renew their tickets next season. Although various factors could be input in the model, for the sake of the simplicity of the example, we can assume season ticket holders' ticket usage for the current season, recency of their attendance, and dollar amount spent during their attendance are the predictors of the probability of their season ticket renewal. It should be mentioned here that predictors of a propensity model could vary from team to team, and logistic regression is not the only way to answer this question.

Another example of where logistic regression could be used is predicting the likelihood of injuries in athletics. Medical scientists developed mathematical models based on logistic regression to predict the likelihood of injuries and identified the risk factors for a variety of injuries (Cruz-Marquez *et al.*, 2012). This method has implications in the industry as well. AC Milan examines many physiological, orthopedic, and psychological factors to identify the risk factors of injuries, predict the risk of getting injured for each athlete, and then attempt to prevent these injuries (Davenport & Harris, 2007). There are also sports injury predictors available online for fantasy sport participants.

Decision trees

Decision trees are a type of multi-variable analysis. They can substitute for traditional statistical analyses, such as multiple linear regression, and data mining techniques, such as neural networks, and can also supplement various analyses in business intelligence ("Decision trees," n.d.). These tree-shaped structures can be used for classification or prediction. Decision trees as a classification model generate rules that distinguish between objects of different classes, while as a predictive tool decision trees predict the class label of unclassified records ("Classification," n.d.).

A decision tree has three types of nodes and two types of branches ("Classification," n.d.; "Introduction to decision trees," n.d.):

- Root/Decision node: This is a point where a decision needs to be made, and a root node doesn't have an incoming branch, but has one or more outgoing branches.

    o Decision branches: These are the branches extending from a decision node and connecting to an internal node. The number of branches extending from a decision node depends on the exhaustive list of possible events which are mutually exclusive.

- Internal/Event (chance) node: This is a point where uncertainty is resolved, and an internal node has an incoming branch and could have one or more outgoing branches. The decision tree model must present all possible events with a node (exhaustive) and these nodes must be mutually exclusive.

    o Event branches: These branches connect an event node to a terminal node, and the number of event branches is dependent on the number of possible outcomes.

- Leaf/Terminal node: This is the end of the decision tree model that is shown as the end of a branch, and indicates the outcome.

Now that we know the components of a decision tree model, we can direct our attention to how to build a decision tree. Decision tree models are developed based on algorithms, which are formulas taking into account various variables. Algorithms make decisions on which variable to use for splitting the data with the goal of identifying the best way to split the data into subsets. In sport industry, a decision tree model could be utilized to

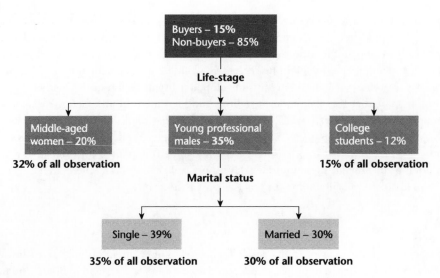

FIGURE 1.1   Sample decision tree

analyze the outcome of a marketing campaign and profile target customer groups to pursue when the campaign is repeated in the future. Let's assume Gym X implemented a marketing campaign to acquire new members and the campaign resulted in a 15 percent overall sales rate, and the algorithm resulted in the decision tree model depicted in Figure 1.1 (this example is adapted from Laursen (2011) with modifications).

The interpretation of this model would be as follows: The sales rates for young professional males, middle-aged women and college students are 35 percent, 20 percent, and 12 percent respectively. Instead of targeting various customers at different life stages, if Gym X targeted young professional males only, their sales rate for the marketing campaign would be 35 percent. We could dive deeper and examine a subset of young professional males as either single or married. If the gym targeted single young professional males, their sales rate would have risen to 39 percent. Therefore, if the gym administration decides to repeat the same campaign in the future, they could increase the number of new memberships by approaching single young professional males.

Time series analysis

A time series is a measurement of variables in sequence over time. If a time series contains only one variable, it is known as a univariate time series, and recording of more than one variable is termed as multivariate time series (Adhikari & Agrawal, 2013). In time series, variables are either measured every possible occasion or periodically in time, and data are arranged chronologically. Once a time series is developed, several components of the series should be investigated prior to fitting a model to the data ("Overview of time series," n.d.; Senter, n.d.). Time series example includes:

1.   Trend in time series. A trend is a long term pattern in time series, and the data should be screened to identify whether values of the variable increase, decrease or stay stable over time.

2. Seasonality in time series. Data should be evaluated for any systematic variation during different times within a year. The important factors causing seasonal variation for each industry could be different. For instance, if the overall value of merchandise sales for collegiate athletic departments is under investigation, we would see an increase in March due to "March Madness."
3. Cyclic variation in time series. In addition to seasonal patterns, time series could demonstrate cyclic variations caused by circumstances that repeat in the medium term.
4. Irregular variation in time series. Finally, time series should be examined for any irregular variations by investigating if the variance is constant when abrupt changes and/or outliers are present.

While time series could be used to identify any pattern in data whether it is seasonal, cyclic or long term, time series could also be used in forecasting, predicting future values of the time series. Fitting a model to a time series and estimating the parameters in the model by using the known data values is called time series analysis (Adhikari & Agrawal, 2013). Once the pattern in time series and the relationship among the variables are identified, a model with an adequate fit is developed to predict future values of the time series. During the model development process, several competing models with an adequate fit could be identified. In this case, model parsimony should be considered. In other words, the simplest model should be chosen. For more information on time series analysis and various forecasting models (AR, MA, ARIMA, SARIMA), please refer to textbooks on time series such as Box, Jenkins and Reinsel (2008) and Hamilton (1994).

Before moving to the next analysis, let's take a look at an example. Every business is interested in projecting sales, attendance, concession sales, ratings, and so on. Managers make decisions early in processes without exact numbers, which requires them to utilize time series analyses to forecast the future numbers. A common goal of time series analysis is extrapolating past behavior into the future. Let's think about the ratings of Super Bowl games and how it can be used in selling and pricing commercial spots for the game. As you all know, commercial spots are sold prior to knowing exact TV ratings for the particular year's Super Bowl game. Therefore, the television network, that has the rights to the game, predicts ratings of the upcoming game via time series based on the trend in past TV ratings. Time series analyses of TV ratings for major sport leagues in the US could be used in explaining the differences in broadcasting rights fees earned by each league. Historical data allows media corporations to predict future TV ratings for each sport league, which assists them in their negotiations with the sport leagues and assigning value to the deals. As you read the case study titled "Data management for a professional team" in Chapter 2, you will see another example of forecasting via time series. Here, it is important to point out that forecasting and future predictions could be done with linear regression analysis, as well. One difference between time series analysis and linear regression analysis is the auto-correlation nature of time series. Data is collected on the same variable at different times and the value of the variable at a time is correlated to its value from a previous time. Therefore, observations are not independent of each other which would violate the independence assumption of linear regression analysis.

Cluster analysis

When analysts are interested in identifying homogenous groups of observations (individuals, objects, accounts, and so on) within data, they can conduct cluster analysis. In sport industry, the most common use of cluster analysis is in market segmentation. As it is not practical to target each customer individually, marketers divide existing customers into groups to provide them with relevant marketing tactics. In sport industry, the common practice is segmenting sport fans based on their product usage and expected product benefits which results in value-based and need-based segmentation, respectively. In performing cluster analysis, a series of steps are taken:

1.   Choose the characteristics on which the grouping will be performed.
2.   Decide on the clustering method (hierarchical, k-means, and two-step).
3.   Interpret the clusters.

Hierarchical clustering starts with each observation being its own cluster, and then combined with another case in each step based on similarities, which are measured in distance metrics. This process goes on until all of the observations are clustered together, and the clustering is performed based on an algorithm. For example, assume the Gym X has 1,000 members. In hierarchical clustering, at the very beginning there would be 1,000 clusters. In other words, every individual would be a cluster. The second step would be combining the members into clusters based on a variable such as use of exercise programs offered (yoga, kick boxing, Pilates, step-aerobics, etc.). The next step could be further grouping these clusters based on the frequency of use, and the process goes on. In this type of cluster analysis, the analyst decides on the number of clusters to retain, whether to collapse clusters further or keep them separate (Mooi & Sarstedt, 2011).

In k-means clustering, the number of clusters is specified prior to the analysis, and the algorithm assigns observations into the clusters by minimizing the variation within clusters (Mooi & Sarstedt, 2011). An example could be segmenting sport fans of a team as heavy, medium and light users based on their attendance frequency. Prior to performing the cluster analysis, it is known that the goal is to identify three clusters based on the frequency of attendance. The k-means clustering is the recommended method for moderate sized data sets and when the number of clusters is known.

The two-step clustering is the combination of the two previous methods. In the first stage, a number for clustering is set and performed, which is followed by a hierarchical clustering in the second step. This type of clustering is recommended for large data sets with continuous and categorical variables (Norusis, 2011). If we continue with the aforementioned season ticket holder example, the first step would be once again identifying three clusters as heavy, medium and light user segments. The following steps would be hierarchical clustering. One can identify further clusters for the main three clusters based on demographics such as gender, age, marital status, who they attend with, and so on. Once the clusters are formed, the final stage is the interpretation of the clusters and examination of managerial relevance based on being substantial, differentiable, actionable, stable, and parsimonious (Mooi & Sarstedt, 2011). By evaluating the fan segments identified via cluster analysis, the sport team can develop a persona for each segment and use it in acquiring new fans.

Sentiment analysis

Sentiment analysis has been used in the political science field frequently during presidential elections for years. Similarly, movie reviews have incorporated sentiment analyses. Today, sport consumers are engaged, outspoken and eager to express their opinion and feelings freely. An abundance of information is available in emails, text messages (SMS), forms, surveys, customer reviews, social media, and so on. Therefore, text analytics has become an important area in sport analytics, and via sentiment analysis, it is possible to identify individuals' opinions, feelings, emotions, and attitudes.

Sentiment analysis is based on the idea of opinions having binary oppositions. For instance, an individual might be for or against an idea, like or dislike a product, or perceive an issue as good or bad. Sentiment analysis aims to extract, identify and classify the sentiment content as positive, negative or neutral, and can utilize several different approaches (natural language processing, bag of words, or machine learning). Some of the questions one can answer via sentiment analyses are whether a product review is positive or negative, a customer expresses satisfaction or dissatisfaction in their email, public perception of the sport organization is positive or negative, sport fans are in favor of a trade of an athlete, and so on. Understanding individuals' opinions would allow a sport organization to improve their weaknesses, correct their wrongdoing, communicate better and emphasize their strengths.

There are many examples in this area. IBM has been analyzing Super Bowl fan sentiments to understand how consumer sentiments change, and John Squire – IBM's Director of Digital Marketing and Analytics – said "By applying analytics in social media settings we can identify nuances – positive, negative, irony, snarky vs. sincerity, in real-time. That's enough time to help an organization or a professional athlete to adjust their comments and actions to impact their brands" (2012). Analyzing customers' sentiments during crises could be very useful to sport organizations and any affiliated corporation. For example, when the FIFA corruption case exploded in 2015, the media blew up with news and FIFA partners felt pressure and had to evaluate how the crisis would impact their organization's images. Similarly, when the NFL was shaken with domestic violence cases in 2014, social media was taken over by fans and CoverGirl felt the adverse effects of the issue as the NFL's official beauty sponsor.

CASE STUDY: MANAGING A YOUTH SOCCER ORGANIZATION'S DATA

Name: Evan Dabby
Title: Executive Director
Current employer: New Jersey Youth Soccer
Brief work history: Throughout my career, I have analyzed data to identify trends, interpret information and leverage facts to make better decisions. These tasks became increasingly important working at Major League Soccer, and the same approach aids my current work as the Executive Director of New Jersey Youth Soccer.

PHOTO 1.1
Evan Dabby

During my 16-year tenure at MLS, I was responsible for game operations, sports medicine, team travel, security and supporter relations. In each of these areas, data analysis helped us answer fundamental questions which, in turn, allowed us to chart a new course or validate an existing approach.

Security

MLS often faced the stigma of "hooliganism" anytime we experienced an altercation in the stands. Media was quick to draw a parallel to the destructive culture that plagued international soccer in the late twentieth century. To dispel those perceptions, we engaged in the lengthy process of recording every single ejection and arrest that occurred at an MLS game. Over the course of 12 months, and then again after 24 months, we were able to provide true statistics to counter claims that "hooliganism" threatened MLS.

Sports medicine

Over the last decade, concussions and head injuries have been headline news. In 2012, MLS created and implemented a concussion evaluation and management protocol to provide state-of-the-art professional care for MLS players. Our key strategy involved analyzing every game to collect data on each documented concussion to understand the mechanism of injury. These data allowed us to answer the following questions:

- What actions or events cause concussions? Head to head contact? Head to ground? Head to ball?
- How often do concussions occur? Is the number of concussions increasing year over year?
- Who is suffering the most concussions? Forwards? Defenders? Goalkeepers?

Answers to these questions allowed us to educate players, coaches and referees to create safer playing conditions.

Team travel

With ten plus games a week across the country, 200 plus people and 30 plus weeks per season, MLS spends millions of dollars on travel (airfare, hotel and ground transportation). Each season, we analyzed costs to assess how we performed against industry standards to answer questions like:

- Are we effectively negotiating hotel rates?
- Are our service providers beating industry standards?
- Are we budgeting effectively?

Supporter relations

The fan culture of MLS distinguishes the League among other professional sports. The passion, authenticity and commitment of supporter groups has been a driver of the League's success. Unfortunately, passion sometimes gets out of hand, and we inquired into a relationship between supporter groups and stadium security. After tracking misconduct, statistics showed that a highly disproportionate number of incidents occurred in the stadium section that hosted the visiting supporters. This statistic led MLS to create a specialized training program to educate stadium security staff about supporter culture. Equally important, ongoing tracking of misconduct in these visitor supporter sections demonstrated a reduced number of incidents over time, which, in turn, validated the training strategy.

Game operations

Live televised events adhere to an extremely strict timeline. With large broadcast deals driving team and League revenues, games must start on time, which is largely a function of game operations. We tracked the number and severity of kick-off delays and distinguished whether these delays were caused by players or the broadcast team. This data allowed us to evaluate these issues and chart the best course of action:

- If numerous kick-off delays result from players being late out of the locker room, should we increase team fines?
- If numerous delays result from broadcasting, should we start games before the signal from the telecast?

Almost two years ago, I began my current role as Executive Director of New Jersey Youth Soccer. New Jersey Youth Soccer, a 501(c)(3) organization affiliated with US Youth Soccer and the US Soccer Federation, is composed of more than 100,000 players aged 5 to 19 years old, more than 40,000 coaches, and thousands of volunteers. Members collectively support the sport of soccer through training, practice, competition and good sportsmanship. The association features recreational and travel programs at multiple skill levels; the Olympic Development Program; tournaments including the National Championship Series and Presidents Cup; coaching education and certification programs; and TOPSoccer, a program for children with special needs.

Although NJ Youth Soccer's staffing and marketing resources are a fraction of MLS's, we employ the same methods of database and market research to make informed decisions. We are fortunate to have a dedicated Board of Directors committed to improving the youth soccer landscape. Here are a few examples of how NJ Youth Soccer relies on statistical information to guide us forward:

Social media

Facebook and Twitter provide easy-to-read statistics that demonstrate the effectiveness of a social media campaign. For example, we capitalized on the FIFA Women's World Cup to send a simple NJ-centric message, and Facebook supplied us with data confirming that our message reached more than 30,000 people:

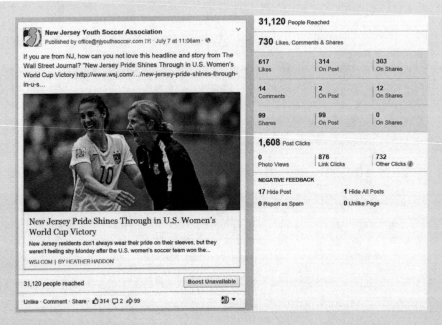

FIGURE 1.2 Screenshot of NJYS social media reach

Surveys

We utilize surveys to gauge customer satisfaction. We sent a short survey to approximately 800 parents of Olympic Development Program players and received a statistically relevant number of responses conveying their impression of topics such as program costs, quality of communication and quality of facilities. We invited anonymous responses to encourage feedback because our priority was volume of data.

Annual awards dinner

Statistics also help NJ Youth Soccer understand patterns and behavior. In tracking registration for our annual awards dinner, we monitored the numbers weekly. This data collection helped us learn which marketing promotions were most successful. Looking ahead to next year, we will be able to evaluate if we are ahead or behind past performance in terms of numbers of registered attendees.

Olympic Development Program (ODP)

Data mining, the process of examining large quantities of data to hopefully find patterns and commonalities, was employed to learn about the pool of players signing up for our Olympic Development Program (ODP) tryouts. In the past year, we tried some new techniques to promote the tryout process. We sampled digital advertising and analyzed the click through rates to determine the customer acquisition costs. Specifically, we examined how many people clicked through to our registration page as a result of those digital placements.

ODP largely takes place in one location, centrally located in NJ, so that players from all over the state can access the program. We researched players' home towns to geo plot our customer base and identify trends such as:

- which areas of NJ participate in ODP;
- are there areas of NJ that are not participating.

With this information, we can then take the next step of trying to learn why these trends are occurring. Is it a geographical issue? Is travel time preventing participation? Is it a communications issue? That is, are players in select areas not aware of or not understanding our programming?

Mining the data also helps us learn which clubs and towns have a large and small concentration of players in our program. This information allows us to understand where we need to spend more of our time promoting programs.

Executives and board members want and deserve proof to validate theories and proposals. They want to be convinced that a new direction or strategy has merit before they back and endorse it. The same likely applies to your professors and future employers. For example, you may be convinced that team X is not investing enough on player development but how can you prove that? What information can you provide to make your argument credible? Without question, data and statistics are one such way to make a convincing argument.

Conclusion

This chapter aimed to refresh your memory on some key statistical concepts and analyses, and to build a baseline for the upcoming chapters covering applications of various analytics in functional areas of sport. There are numerous other statistical analyses that the reader should explore such as Bayesian theory and economic modeling. An in-depth understanding in statistical analyses, modeling, and data visualization are extremely important to the newly developing sport analytics field. Complementing this skill set with experience in database management, information systems and using various software packages would make one a valuable asset to any sport organization.

References

Adhikari, R., & Agrawal, R. K. (2013). An introductory study on time series modeling and forecasting. Retrieved from http://arxiv.org/ftp/arxiv/papers/1302/1302.6613.pdf

Box, G. E., Jenkins, G. M., & Reinsel, G. C. (2008). *Time series analysis: forecasting and control.* Hoboken, NJ: John Wiley & Sons, Inc.

Classification: Basic concepts, decision trees and model evaluation. (n.d.). Retrieved from www-users.cs.umn.edu/~kumar/dmbook/ch4.pdf

Cruz-Marquez, J. C., Cruz-Campos, A., Cruz-Campos, J. C., Cueto-Martin, M. B., Garcia-Jimenez, M., & Campos-Blasco, M .T. (2012). Prediction of sports injuries by mathematical models.

In K. R. Zaslav (Ed.). *An international perspective on topics in sports medicine and sports injury.* Rijeka, Croatia: InTech. Retrieved from http://cdn.intechopen.com/pdfs-wm/28457.pdf

Davenport, T.H., & Harris, J.G. (2007). *Competing on analytics: The new science of winning.* Boston, MA: Harvard Business Review Press.

Decision trees – What are they? [SAS Paper] (n.d.) Retrieved from http://support.sas.com/publishing/pubcat/chaps/57587.pdf

Frand, J. (n.d.). Data mining: What is data mining? Retrieved from www.anderson.ucla.edu/faculty/jason.frand/teacher/technologies/palace/datamining.htm

Hamilton, J. D. (1994). *Time series analysis.* Princeton, NJ: Princeton University Press.

Introduction to decision trees [Educational Sources]. (n.d.). Retrieved from http://treeplan.com/chapters/introduction-to-decision-trees.pdf

Laursen, G. H. (2011). *Business analytics for sales and marketing managers: How to compete in the information age.* Hoboken, NJ: John Wiley & Sons, Inc.

Lomax, R. G. (2007). *An introduction to statistical concepts* (2nd ed.). Mahwah, NJ: Lawrence Erlbaum Associates, Inc.

Mooi, E., & Sarstedt, M. (2011). *A concise guide to market research.* Berlin, Heidelberg: Springer.

Norusis, M. (2011). *IBM SPSS statistics19 guide to data analysis.* Upper Saddle River, NJ: Prentice Hall.

Overview of time series. [Online course content]. (n.d.). Retrieved from https://onlinecourses.science.psu.edu/stat510/print/book/export/html/47

Senter, A. (n.d.). Time Series Analysis. Retrieved from www.sfsu.edu/efc/classes/biol710/timeseries/timeseries1.htm

Squire, J. (2012, February 2). Super Bowl analysis takes us beyond the Tweets. Retrieved from http://asmarterplanet.com/blog/2012/02/super-bowl-analysis-takes-us-beyond-the-tweets.html

Stevens, J. P. (2009). *Applied multivariate statistics for social sciences* (5th ed.). New York, NY: Routledge, Taylor & Francis Group.

2

THE DATA ECOSYSTEM

Gil Fried

This chapter is a multifaceted chapter. The entire information technology infrastructure within, and now outside (such as cloud computing), a company needs to be continuously monitored and evaluated. The technology infrastructure requires more than just storage space, it needs significant computer equipment to gather, process, and analyze the data necessary for sport analytic decision-making. A good way to think about this is whether or not a person wants to upgrade their current smart phone to a new smart phone. Their phone might be working fine or it could be that there are now faster microprocessors or better screens. It could also be that the phone was dropped and the screen was shattered. One issue is whether or not to update the phone. The other issue is all the information on the phone. Will any data or photos transfer? What about the tap to pay feature or any other applications that might contain sensitive information such as credit card numbers. The decision to switch phones becomes an issue of both equipment and data – similar to the multifaceted way to examine information technology for a company.

The decision for a sport organization is obviously much more complex than the phone example. Larger sport organizations have invested millions of dollars in hardware platform, databases, software (often referred to as ETL – extraction, transformation and loading – which is what the software does to the data), business intelligence dashboards, advanced analytical tools, equipment maintenance contracts, system upgrades, storage systems, and other elements customized for the organization's needs (Davenport & Dyche, 2013). Such a system will be very expensive to build and maintain.

This chapter will examine some of the computer and information technology issues that should be considered by anyone in sport analytics. It should be noted that technology is ever changing so computer systems purchased today are often obsolete in a couple years. Similarly, new companies are launched on a regular basis which provide better, more efficient, or just different ways to analyze data. While Microsoft Excel has been around since 1985, and is the most well-known spreadsheet system on the market, over the past ten years there have been numerous new software systems that have flooded the market (such as SAS, Oracle, IBM, Tableau, for example) with different systems to analyze big data and present findings in a more effective manner. There will be further change as time progresses, so it would not be as prudent to analyze these software systems as any such analysis might become obsolete in a matter of months.

How to get the best system

The DeLone and McLean Information Systems Success Model (DMSM) (DeLone & McLean, 2003) is one of the most well-regarded tools for examining how elements within the information system environment interact with each other. The basic DMSM model incorporates the following elements:

- information quality;
- system quality;
- service quality.

Information quality focuses on the information that the information system is able to store, deliver, or produce. Bad data or a user's inability to leverage the data reduces information quality. The quality of information can be measured by number of errors, time to make more usable, satisfaction of those who use the data, and related metrics.

System quality refers to whether the information system is able to deliver what users need when they need it. If the system keeps shutting down, breaks down, requires too much time, and related issues (which all can be measured) then the system might not be functioning as desired.

Service quality directly impacts usage intentions and user satisfaction with the system. What was the system supposed to do when it was designed and does the system deliver what was promised? System users are often surveyed to determine if they like the system, what they like about it, what they would like to change, etc. to gauge their satisfaction with service quality.

Each one of these three areas will impact user satisfaction, usage intention, and net benefits of the system. Quality is the key and having low quality, wherever in the process, will limit the value of the data derived through the process.

In the sport context, DMSM should be analyzed as a complex system with various components and parts. For example, the Leicester Tigers – an English Rugby Union club – require their players to wear equipment during training that captures statistics like heart rate as well as the forces absorbed by rugby's frequent jarring hits. Data are uploaded to the team's database, where IBM's modeling software looks for patterns. Additional info is drawn from player questionnaires that could provide insight into their stress levels and injury history (Team AnalyticpediA, 2012). Thus, the system requires gear on the athletes, data from such gear, data from the athletes, a computer system, software to process the data, and then personnel at various points to collect the data and then interpret the data. The concern though is often how much data needs to be analyzed. Rogers Arena in Canada has a facility management system called EOS that monitors everything from the heating system to lights and uses monitors throughout the building to help operate more efficiently. That system sends over 5 million pieces of data to the clouds every day. Computers then process the information and directives are sent (based on pre-programmed variables) back to the facility for equipment that automatically adjusts such as lights shutting off or temperature zones changing based on area occupancy. This example is only being highlighted to help show the amount of data that needs to be processed and that systems need to be compatible with the type and volume of data.

Compatibility

Data volume and tools have evolved over the years and will continue to evolve. Similarly, how information is collected, stored, and analyzed has evolved. This process can be seen in many companies, and more specifically governments, which have numerous computer systems in place that either cannot talk with one another, or require significant effort and money to work. The process normally started with one division of a company buying one computer system and software system while another unit bought a different operating system and software. Each division might have a significant amount of data and equipment and they do not want to lose it, so for years they operated separately. Now with more data needs, these companies end up having computers that do not talk with each other, incompatible data, and none of the divisions want to give up their system for the good of the entire organization. Many government agencies cannot have their computers talk to one another and the problem with having data in some very old systems can lead to significant failures. In a massive data breach of United States Federal Government employee information in 2015, government officials had to admit that their systems were not able to encrypt (protect) data because they were too old. Thus, while some government systems were secure, many more were not and some could not even deploy firewalls to help protect data and systems (Bennett & Diersing, 2015). If a sport business cannot analyze data cross-functionally, then decision-makers will be stuck in their individual silos. If a software package cannot measure the lifetime value of a season ticket lead because data from the marketing platform cannot intersect with the CRM system then the team can lose a sale. Even if a team has great data, if the systems cannot share the data effectively and in an appropriate manner then there are real consequences – inefficiency, lost time, and lost revenue.

Processing data

To more effectively manage all the data and technology necessary for effective decision-making there needs to be a data pipeline. One way to look at the data pipeline is as a recipe. The data are the ingredients. Good ingredients make a great meal. No matter how good the pots and pans are or the oven is, if the ingredients are poor or not added in the correct amounts or at the right time, the meal will suffer. A chef will possibly have some processed ingredients they can purchase from others. The chef might also grow some of their own ingredients. Lastly, the chef might have some raw ingredients they need to process before using them. Similarly, data might come in various states and are funneled through a process to make them appropriate to use. Some of the ingredients might not be used and others will be mixed together and then processed to make the final meal. The same process is used with data. Various forms of data (and from different sources such as databases, third party vendors, or the clouds) are processed at various times and in different ways so that the data can more effectively be compared and analyzed. Some of the raw data can be analyzed with a program such as Hadoop. Other data will be cleaned for ease in analysis. The data then goes to a data warehouse where it can be analyzed using different software packages.

Once again, referring back to the cooking example, services are available where all the ingredients can be purchased and all the chef has to do is mix and cook. A chef also has to take precautions to avoid food contamination and other safety related precautions while cooking. Similarly, data needs to be cleaned, processed, and all contamination (such as bugs and viruses, and also incorrect data) needs to be removed. Scale is important for chefs. It is one thing to prepare a meal for two people, but a completely different beast when cooking for 100 people. With data, pre-packaged programs can be bought off the shelf to make the process easier. Data also needs to be protected, whether through encryption, firewalls, or limiting access so the information is only available to pre-approved individuals. Scaling is critical with data, as it is much easier to review ten pieces of data compared with 1 million.

One of the key points of this process is data warehousing. A data warehouse is a central repository of integrated data from multiple disparate sources used for reporting and analysis (Setting the data strategy, n.d.). When examining such storage it is important to differentiate between data stored in a transactional manner, such as cash register receipts or ticket purchase orders, and data stored for analytics. Analytic databases are purpose-built to analyze extremely large volumes of data very quickly. An analytic database has a column-based structure, where each column of data is stored in its own file and this allows for data compression (allowing easier storage and processing). Transactional databases can be added and averaged without much difficulty, but more complex analysis requires data stored in an analytic manner. The best data is raw data as it provides the greatest opportunity to manipulate the data without losing any information. If the data has already been scrubbed, some information might be missing. Furthermore, the more the data is modified or converted, the greater the likelihood of an error. With the growth of big data (both structured and unstructured data), there needs to be a way to move data for ease in processing and storage. Figure 2.1 is an example of a big data stack.

There are various systems that help analyze data. One of them is Hadoop which is a framework that allows for the distributed processing of large data sets. Hadoop is best for larger projects such as recommendation (music or video choices), facial recognition systems, and large search engines such as Bing. Hadoop is not typically used for data analysis and visualization of businesses and their customers. Thus far, we have explored how analytic data can be aggregated into a single central repository (which needs to be updated automatically as a business evolves) and the data is housed in a platform that allows programs to analyze the data. Data in many systems can be queried using SQL, the dominant language of data. For more advanced statistical analysis researchers can use R, SAS, and Matlab as just some example programs. SQL – Structured Query Language – is universally regarded as the primary language used to interface with databases. SQL uses an English-like syntax that allows non-technical researchers the ability to more easily query large amounts of data without having to know significant computer programming skills. Other more advanced statistical software systems are available for those interested in doing more in-depth data analysis. One way to understand the different systems is as follows: A spreadsheet will help tell the director of marketing how many tickets were sold last season; in contrast a statistical tool will help a researcher determine the impact of a branding campaign on ticket sales.

The tools listed (p. 37) represent a discreet workflow, where a researcher asks a question and the tools give an answer that leads to another question. Tools can help deliver value by speeding up the process of answering questions. The future is with tools that can

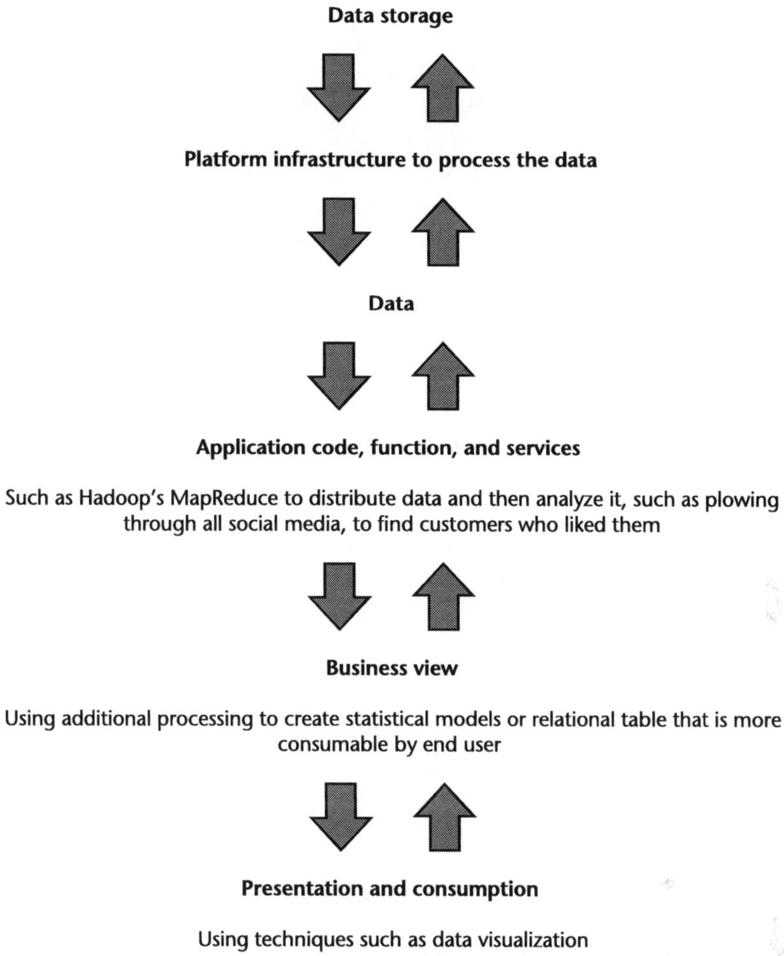

Data storage

Platform infrastructure to process the data

Data

Application code, function, and services

Such as Hadoop's MapReduce to distribute data and then analyze it, such as plowing through all social media, to find customers who liked them

Business view

Using additional processing to create statistical models or relational table that is more consumable by end user

Presentation and consumption

Using techniques such as data visualization

FIGURE 2.1   Big data stack flow diagram

Note: The arrows represent data and processes flow both ways.
Source: *The Big Data Stack* (Davenport & Dyche, 2013).

anticipate the future questions which need to be asked. This is often referred to as machine learning and can be found in major systems such as IBM's famous Watson program, which appeared on the game show *Jeopardy*. Using complex computers and artificial intelligence these systems are very powerful and used by the largest businesses with huge amounts of data looking for anomalies or other issues that might be missed by humans.

No matter how data is analyzed, it is very difficult to comprehend millions of pieces of data. That is where visualization and data dashboards can help present the data in an easier to understand manner. Thus, whether it is ten pieces of data or 1 million, the system needs to be able not just to gather and process the data, but provide useful information that management can understand and act upon. While in a perfect world it would be easy to have enough computer equipment and software to handle all foreseeable needs, the big constraint for most businesses will be costs.

Cost

The cost to develop a data pipeline is significant. If one engineer was deployed to develop a pipeline the cost would probably start around $10,750 a year for set-up ($6,000 in time for data extraction, $750 for warehousing, and $4,000 for data warehousing). This is only the start as the yearly minimum cost to continue a data pipeline is around $110,000, with the bulk of that cost being dedicated to personnel for analysis and system engineering costs (Setting the data strategy, n.d.). Because of this significant cost, smaller companies will usually outsource data pipelines as long as they have the ability to have access to their data in a secured manner when they need it.

The cost for obtaining the data can be very expensive. Many companies obtain primary data from their own surveys or sales data. While this might seem like an inexpensive option, the data collection and entry process can take time (and money) from developing the survey instruments, administering it, entering the data into a database, analyzing the data, and then reaching some conclusions can be very costly. Even if fans complete an online survey or form, there is still a cost – albeit reduced. Many sport businesses also use an outside compiler to validate their primary data. These external compilers collect data from numerous sources and then cross-reference data the sport business might have. These external data companies are needed for several reasons – primarily low survey response rates and many people lie on surveys/forms. For example, a fan named Jane Doe completes a form to be put into a raffle. The team might process the form and then cross-check the information with a compiler (normally in large batches). The compiler might come back with information that Jane gave the wrong street address, and then from public records, such as driver licenses, can tell the sport business how old Jane is, if she has children, what car she drives, and lots of other information they might have in a database. One company offering this service is Acxiom (www.acxiom.com/data-packages/).

Data storage is rapidly changing with a move to the clouds. Amazon Web Services generated a $687 million profit in 2015 on $2.4 billion in cloud storage sales. These numbers will only increase as more companies, such as Google, try to enter into the data storage market. This will hopefully lead to lower costs. One concern with moving so much data to the clouds is the vulnerability such services might face if hackers or others can access the information in the clouds. If data will be stored in-house, for whatever reason (such as security/sensitivity), a 20–40 TBs (terabyte) system could cost around $500,000. Furthermore, if a company wants to develop its own data warehouse the process can take from six months to a year (Goolsby, 2012). Other cost comparisons have estimated the cost of storing one terabyte of data for a year to be around $37,000 while a database appliance and Hadoop cluster would be significantly cheaper (Davenport & Dyche, 2013). It should be noted that equipment is only part of the costs. Along with the primary expense of personnel, there are costs such as back-up electrical systems (to keep data flowing during an emergency), dedicated air conditioning systems (to keep the equipment from getting too hot), and special fire-retardant systems (so the electrical system does not get destroyed by water).

Servers are needed for data processing. Servers are utilized by every computer and help with everything from mouse movement, to speakers, printers, webpage access and numerous other functions. A server is designed to share data as well as to share resources and distribute work across a computer system. Using a client–server model, the

PHOTO 2.1 Servers such as this can replace what used to be a room full of servers and a stack similar to this can cost close to half a million dollars

server serves data to clients (programs). This is normally accomplished through a request and response system where data is requested and then a response sought. Basically the server is the one who connects the data with a program and allows the process to work. A system needs data, hardware, and software, and data processing servers allow the flow between these parts.

Software is another cost. Numerous systems such as Tableau, SPSS, SAS, R, Python, and others can be purchased (R is available for free) with costs varying depending on the size of the purchaser (i.e. how many licenses they are purchasing), and what features they want.

Data analysis also costs money. Someone needs to look at the data and find ways to massage the data. For example, some teams break down groups by percentages and then that percentage is also broken down even further so they can take a fractional look at the data. A team/league could have up to 1,000 different pieces of data they can explore for ticket buyers. No team can ever examine all these data points so they look at the top several keys/traits of their ticket buyers (or customers) such as clusters of fans who might show some correlation between their traits and buying pattern. This can help identify which season ticket holders are more likely to renew. To clear the key data from the fog takes time and money.

It should be noted that volume has been the focus of data for years, but more emphasis is being placed on variety as more and more information can be analyzed from various sources such as videos, text, photos, voice, and related data. For example, bankers have stored the voices of over 50,000 people who are known bank scammers into a database and then when someone applies for a suspicious account they can compare voices to see if they are a known threat.

Speed of delivery

Over the years, there has been exponential growth in how fast computer systems have evolved. A computer today has about a million times more power than a computer 40 years ago. This speed, along with cheap memory, has enabled people to do more with computers than ever before. International Business Machine's (IBM's) Watson computer system is more than just a chess or *Jeopardy*-playing computer system. The question answering system utilizes machine learning to become an expert in a given field, often utilizing unstructured data to help answer questions. Watson can process 500 gigabytes, the equivalent of a million books, per second. Such power is great, but it can also represent that speed is changing an industry.

For example, ESPN used to be the world leader in sport broadcasting through its Sports Center program, which provided more in-depth and more frequent sport news stories for the avid fan. But fans have access to data anytime and anywhere, so they can look up a game or score immediately without relying on watching the evening news or Sports Center. This has forced ESPN to respond, but the same speed issue applies to all sport organizations. Ticket sellers cannot wait minutes to order tickets, when robo-calling ticket brokers can purchase thousands of tickets during the same time period. Speed is king, and sport companies need to be able to get out information in an accurate and expedient manner.

Coordination of various systems is another major focus of any information system. For example, a manufacturing plant with numerous robots would need the robots connected to a central system to monitor their actions. Monitors throughout the plant and in each robot can be connected through the clouds to monitor issues such as temperature in the factory to when a robot might fail. This can provide an ideal environment for preventive maintenance that could be applied at any time rather than during production downtime – which is how issues were dealt with in the past.

More complex data systems can entail numerous technological components that need to be coordinated to work effectively. For example, a baseball field data collection company, such as MLB's Statcast, utilizes multiple radar guns, CCTV cameras, and an artificial intelligence system to provide constant data about player and ball speed, movement, and location. Multiple systems and components can also be inserted into a grass turf to measure humidity, acidity, moisture, nitrogen and other elements of a field. These probes need to be connected with a watering system and data management system to identify where and when sprinklers need to come on or when more fertilizer might be required.

System operation

Whichever system or combination of components is used, it has to accomplish its intended job. A point of purchase system might be a great place to find concession related data, but if the system cannot process payments, miscalculates totals or does not help track inventory then the system is not as effective as possible. Similarly, an online store cannot function by just putting up a webpage with items to sell. There needs to be a complete back-end system that will make sure the inventory is present, process payments, make sure items are shipped, track customer satisfaction, process returns/refunds, and then restock items. Each one of these points can be measured. How many items have been returned and for what reason? How long does it take to process an order? How many orders are stopped before the checkout cart and for what reason? These just represent some of the measurable points to evaluate if the online store is operating effectively.

The same issue can apply to any ticketing system. Hiring a customized ticket processing system can help remove some of the potential hurdles, but such an effort will not resolve all issues. Any order processing system should offer the availability of support technicians, at least for a period of time after implementation, to make sure those who are working on the back-end know what they are doing and how to handle more complicated transactions.

A common concept to all issues with system operations is scalability. It is hard to start with buildings full of computers for a small sport business. Most sport organizations start their analytics journey with personal computers and once they start getting more data and need more power to process data, they need to start buying better computers, data processing capabilities, and larger storage options. That is scalability – how they can grow their needs without losing data, time, and money.

When all the components are put together they can process a lot of data and produce results. One non-sport example to show scalability is the package movement company UPS. The company has been tracking packages since the 1980s. The company tracks 16.3 million packages a day for 8.8 million customers. This results in an average of 39.5 million tracking requests from customers each day and produces 16 petabytes of data (Davenport & Dyche, 2013). While those numbers are impressive, the company is making huge progress from telematics sensors in over 46,000 vehicles. These sensors compile data such as vehicle speed, direction, braking, and drive train performance. This data is collected and analyzed to monitor daily performance and also how to more effectively structure driver's routes. Utilizing third party online map data, the system can coordinate UPS's data with the maps to better structure delivery routes in real-time. In its first year the project saved over 8.4 million gallons of fuel and cut 85 million miles off of daily delivery routes. Such a project requires deploying data collection tools, collecting the data, processing the data, sending out results based on pre-set criteria, and then monitoring the results. Data and equipment are required at all stages along with the personnel to develop and implement such a project. The end results were phenomenal savings and running a more energy efficient company.

Scalability can also be found at the league level for professional sports. Microsoft helped NFL teams in 2014 by developing a customized Surface 2 pro for every team. In 2016, MLB and Apple teamed up to have iPads in every team's dugout. Each tablet is customized with the MLB Dugout app that allowed each team to harness scouting information, analysis, and videos. In the future the system will support Apple Pencil usage and video annotation. For fairness the tablets will not be connected to the internet or stream live videos. Thus, all information needs to be added in the offseason (Snider, 2016). This example helps show how baseball has evolved from keeping score via pencil and paper to tracking every facet of the game and preserving that information in a readily accessible format to use during games.

CASE STUDY: DATA MANAGEMENT FOR A PROFESSIONAL TEAM

Name: John Morris
Title: Executive Director of Business Intelligence and Analytics
Current employer: New York Mets
Brief work history: Prior to joining the Mets in 2011, I worked as a senior consultant at Deloitte and as a systems engineer at Northrop Grumman. I hold an MBA in finance from New York University, an MS in Applied Mathematics from Rensselaer Polytechnic Institute, and a BS in Applied Mathematics from Columbia University.

PHOTO 2.2
John Morris

In 2015, the New York Mets created a new department to assist with the analysis and presentation of data in business operations – Business Intelligence & Analytics. We're a group of four people who help identify and solve business problems using analytics – putting numbers behind how the company is performing and finding ways to optimize those metrics.

We each have analytical backgrounds – we all studied math or economics in college, but none of us were experts in analytics before (or after) the formation of the department. The most important thing we have in common is a familiarity with numbers and a desire to learn about the systems and processes that make the business work. By studying how the business operates, we're able to deliver recommendations on improving it.

Our work touches all non-baseball departments, including Ticketing, Marketing, Sponsorship, Accounting, and Finance.

We seek to:

- provide a complete and concise analysis of business operations to the executive team;
- increase revenue by optimizing ticket sales efforts and supporting corporate sponsorship sales;
- reduce costs by automating and optimizing business processes.

At the highest level, our team spends much of its days reducing large amounts of data into actionable information. For example, which prospective client should a sales rep call? How should sales reps be commissioned for group sales? How much can the organization expect a particular customer to spend?

At the lowest level, answering these questions requires approaching data from disparate sources methodically and without bias, and to use tools to quickly separate the useful from the extraneous. To that end, we turn to a handful of software tools: a database, a statistical modeling system, and a graphical display system.

In our database, we store information on ticket sales, weather, team performance, and our fan base. Holding this information in one place allows us to ask and answer questions on as broad a base of topics as possible, and to find connections between seemingly unrelated conditions.

In addition to our strategic work reporting metrics on business performance, our group acts as an internal consulting team within the Mets organization, seeking to understand and improve how the business operates. In conducting regular assessments with the staff of each department, we ask five basic questions:

- What data do you currently need to complete your job?
- What data do you deliver to other people as part of your job?
- What process(es) has you repeating the same task on a regular basis?
- What does your data look like?
- Where do/did your reporting requirement come from? When was the last time this requirement was reviewed?

These questions help us identify and address issues that department staffers are unaware of. Often, processes in place came into existence organically – at some point in the past, a need was expressed for a particular bit of information, or information in a specific format, and a routine was built to deliver that information. Changes and enhancements – demands for additional information, format changes, etc. – are added piecemeal, often turning a trivial task into a day's work for an employee. Other times, reports and metrics become obsolete over time – products are discontinued or the business changes substantially – but the reports continue to be generated, consuming the time and energy of employees that can be better put to use elsewhere.

After conducting an assessment, the Business Intelligence team will meet to discuss our findings, reviewing how the department stores, transforms and delivers its data. After the first meeting, there are usually a few pieces of "low-hanging fruit" – problems easily solved using existing infrastructure or the Microsoft Office Suite.

An example of a problem with a solution that leverages existing infrastructure, is the matter of our Free Shirt Friday promotions. On Fridays throughout the season, all fans passing through the turnstile receive a complimentary t-shirt, courtesy of the Mets and a naming rights sponsor. By guaranteeing t-shirts to all patrons, the organization creates two optimization problems: order too many shirts, and the organization wastes money printing, shipping and storing the surplus; order too few, and the organization wastes money printing and shipping extra shirts that are issued via rain-check voucher after t-shirts run out on the night of the game. While we could take this problem on as a standalone issue, the business intelligence team was able to share its forecast attendance metric for each of the 81 scheduled games in the baseball season. This model is based on several factors, including day of week, month of year, scheduled opponent, scheduled promotion and the historic attendance records for every game played at Citi Field since it opened in 2009. While factors like roster strength and team record no doubt impact attendance, the t-shirt order must be placed in December, before any baseball is played, so such factors are excluded from the model. As forecasts are updated through the season, the impact of team performance on attendance is included in the updated models.

The attendance model is one of several key pieces of reporting infrastructure the Business Intelligence department has built to serve the organization. Joining the attendance model are models projecting revenue, concession and merchandise sales of future games.

The flipside to predictive modeling is accurate recording and reporting on historic data. Every ticket sold is classified as one of a season ticket, group ticket, or single game ticket, and attributes describing each event are recorded as they become available (day of week, month of year, starting pitchers, team records, game result, weather on the day of the event, game pricing classification, time of first pitch). This data allows us to rapidly deliver responses to ad hoc requests – if someone is curious about the attendance at Tuesday games when the temperature was lower than 70 degrees, the answer is quickly searchable.

Other services provided by the Business Intelligence group include cash-flow reporting and forecasting. With access to the ticket system, we can record payments made as they occur, as well as anticipate future payments based on pre-configured payment plans, scheduled invoices and collection of past due receivables. Historic trend analysis contributes to these models, and so does team performance. (You might expect ticket sales to be slower once the team has finished playing for the season, or that going to the World Series is good for business – and you'd be right!)

In addition to tickets to Mets games, the ticketing system facilitates the sale of tickets for two minor league affiliates, our Spring Training facility, any concerts hosted at Citi Field, along with fees for tickets, orders, deliveries, and suite rentals. The organization maintains separate bank accounts and settlement routines for each of these entities, and we work continually with Accounting & Finance to identify new events and classify them for reconciliation purposes. In doing so, we monitor and report on the health of all Mets businesses, not only the one we are most well-known for: the 81 regular season games we host each year.

One business process we were able to improve quickly was the internal parking request system. Previously, guest names were emailed and called down to a central location in the security center, and a physical list was generated and run out to guard booths on game days. This system had outgrown its usefulness as time went on – the team improved, attendance increased, and relaying names to the guard booth was on its way to being a full-time job. After meeting with the staff at the security center and at the parking lots, we were able to identify requirements and design a system that both captured the old needs as well as providing additional functionality. After our meeting, the requirements were as follows:

- Mets employees should be able to add approved guests (vendors, VIPs, members of the press) to the parking lists throughout the day.
- The Building Command Center should know who is on the list for a given game at any time.
- Departmental Vice Presidents should know who has been added by members of their staff.
- Adding/removing a name should be straightforward.

Using online spreadsheets and handheld wireless devices, we were able to build a system that not only met these requirements, but also one that informed staff of the approval status of a given request, computed any associated cost (security, tax, etc.) and displayed usage statistics – most popular games, most frequent requestors, and most frequently repeating guest.

If there's a downside to becoming a data-driven organization, it's that it's only easier to find ways to improve. The first data model takes tremendous effort to build, understand, optimize, and roll out to operation, but as time progresses and the collective skill set of the organization improves, there's no end to what can be improved. As more staff comes on, the mindset of the organization can change, to a point where employees are no longer seeing themselves confined by the reports available to them, but rather as empowered by the tools at their hands.

Keep it simple

While technology can be complex, sometimes it is the simplest matters that can cause all the headaches. In Chapter 8 the issue of a St. Louis Cardinals employee pleading guilty to hacking is mentioned. What is not mentioned there is how the employee was able to "break in" to the Houston Astros' system. The breach involved a database generated by Astros' general manager, Jeff Luhnow, who used to work with the Cardinals and ran a similar database for them. Luhnow supposedly used the same passwords in both places, leaving the database open to anyone with simple system knowledge to break into the Astros' system without much effort (Kalaf, 2015). Even if the most expensive firewalls are used, a simple failure to regularly change passwords can make such a firewall almost worthless.

To help prevent hacks, whether from outside sources or internal personnel (such as an employee trying to commit a crime, simple mistakes, or a former employee trying to cause harm), steps can be taken to minimize access to information. One approach is to store sensitive data in the clouds with limited access. Private clouds can be found that are password protected and can have encrypted service. Such an approach is especially critical when health care related information might be involved. This could be for a fitness club with some customer health information, a team's medical information on players, or even regular employee files that might contain some medical information (which should always be kept separate from regular employment information typically found in a personnel file). Other information that needs protection includes scouting reports, sales and other projections, credit card information, access to databases, and other proprietary/confidential information. Besides carefully monitoring the computer hardware/software, a sport organization can try to develop additional protection through requiring employees to sign non-disclosure agreements, regularly changing access passwords, and vigorously prosecuting anyone who tries to break into the system.

Conclusion

This chapter has attempted to convey that data does not magically morph and analyze itself. Data needs a system by which it can be entered in, needs hardware for storage, software for analysis, and people at every stage of the process. To effectively manage a big data system, a manager needs to know the various moving parts as well as the latest trends. This does not mean a manager needs to know all the various operating systems or software, but needs to know the basic moving parts of the system and how to effectively manage them to help grow the analytics system in a scalable and economical manner.

References

Bennett, B., & Diersing, C. (2015, June 16). Hacked federal files couldn't be encrypted because government computers are too old. *LA Times*. Retrieved from www.latimes.com/nation/la-na-government-data-breach-20150616-story.html

Davenport, T., & Dyche, J. (2013, May). Big data in big companies. SAS. Retrieved from www.sas.com/resources/asset/Big-Data-in-Big-Companies.pdf

DeLone, W. H., & McLean, E. R. (2003). The DeLone and McLean Model of information systems success: A ten-year update. *Journal of Management Information Systems, 19*(4), 9–30. ME Sharpe Inc. Retrieved from www.tandfonline.com/doi/abs/10.1080/07421222.2003.11045748

Goolsby, K. (2012, July 9). *Big data doesn't have to cost big money*. Retrieved from http://sandhill.com/article/big-data-doesnt-have-to-cost-big-money/

Kalaf, S. (2015, June 6). *Report – FBI investigates St. Louis Cardinals for hacking*. Retrieved from http://deadspin.com/report-fbi-investigates-st-louis-cardinals-for-hackin-1711673515

Setting the data strategy for your growing organization [Free resource] (n.d.). Retrieved from https://rjmetrics.com/resources/guide/setting-your-data-strategy

Snider, M. (2016, March 31). MLB teams with Apple for iPads in the dugout. *USA Today*, 5B.

Team AnalyticpediA (2012). Sports analytics, injury and IBM. Retrieved from http://analyticpedia.com/sports-analytics-injury-and-ibm/

PART II

Analytics in functional areas

3

THE DATA GAME: ANALYZING OUR WAY TO BETTER SPORT PERFORMANCE

Maria Nibali

The world of professional sport: from big business to big data

In 2015 the global sport industry was estimated at USD $1.5 trillion, with the US market share comprising USD $498.4 billion (Sports Industry Statistics, n.d.). The 2015 ranking of "The World's Highest Paid Athletes" published in *Forbes Magazine* in 2015 listed the top 100 athlete salaries and (or) winnings from #100 James Harden (Basketball) at USD $14.8 M to #1 Floyd Mayweather (Boxing) at USD $285 M. When you factor in remunerations from endorsements, the overall earnings of top athletes are staggering, making them highly valuable commodities. It is not surprising then, that professional clubs are seeking every means possible to protect their investment – ensuring the welfare of the athlete and a high level of competitive performance is paramount!

Today's innovation and technology driven markets are enabling sport scientists, conditioning staff, and coaches to monitor athlete and competition performance like never before, as they endeavor to enhance performance and mitigate the risk of injury. Wearable technology allows monitoring of all aspects of an athlete's physical and physiological status during training and competition, providing rich spatio-temporal, biometric, and neuro-muscular performance data. Advancements in optical tracking technology and machine learning techniques have made it possible to monitor every movement of every player, for every second of every game in sports like basketball and football (i.e. soccer), producing millions of data points that need to be processed, analyzed, and interpreted in a meaningful way. The incredible volume of data that is generated and the vast amounts of information that is now available to sport practitioners have propagated the rapid growth of sport analytics in recent years. The emergence of analytics in today's era of professional sport is so dominant that the global sport analytics market is forecasted to increase from USD $125 million (2014) to USD $4.5 billion by 2021 (Custiss & Eustis, 2015).

In this chapter, we will discuss the application of analytics for the enhancement of sport performance. Firstly, we will discuss the evolution of sports analytics, and consider how advancements in data management systems and technology have affected its evolvement and subsequent competitive value. Secondly, we will explore the driving forces behind the emergence of sport analytics and discuss how these data-driven technologies are affecting the decision-making of high-performance staff and coaches. Specifically, we will discuss the contribution of 1) sophisticated data management systems; 2) pertinent technologies in the non-invasive measurement of sports performance – ranging from force plate technology and wearable sensors such as global positioning systems (GPS), to "smart" clothing and equipment, and optical tracking, and 3) computer vision (pattern recognition) and machine learning. Lastly, we will examine how cutting-edge research in predictive analytics is providing compelling insights into sports performance, and briefly discuss the concept of actionable intelligence.

The evolution of sport analytics

The systematic analysis of sports performance is nothing new; sport scientists have long endeavored to discern the characteristics that dictate and, ultimately, predict athletic performance and competitive success. However, such analyses have traditionally been performed under experimental conditions designed to simulate real-world sporting performance, with findings delivered *post hoc*. So what's changed? Advancements in innovation and technology have fueled the emergence of non-invasive measurements of sports performance, facilitating a shift in sport science and performance analysis from the restrictive confines of laboratory-based testing to the new frontier of field-based monitoring. This shift has given rise to the ability of sport practitioners to gather vast amounts of data on athletes during training and competition, providing real-time or near real-time insights into various aspects of sports performance; thus allowing them to make data-driven, evidence-based decisions related to athlete management and (or) game strategy "on the fly." Add to this the advancements in computer science and machine learning of recent years, and we now have the ability to capture and monitor performance, efficiently process vast volumes of data, and subsequently predict athletic and competitive performance prior to or during the event.

We have moved along the sport analytics continuum from traditional retrospective analyses that provide low-to-moderate-level insights to the high-level competitive advantage afforded by predictive modeling and machine learning (see Figure 3.1).

The driving forces of sport analytics

Data management

As data volumes continue to increase in concert with advancements in technology and monitoring capabilities, there is an increasing need for sporting organizations to effectively manage and subsequently analyze this information. On a daily basis, high-performance staff are inundated with data arising from athlete welfare and performance monitoring, including:

1. wellness (e.g. mood state, sleep quality, muscle soreness);
2. physiotherapy and medical screenings;
3. anthropometric profiles (e.g. body mass, skinfolds);
4. neuromuscular status (e.g. force plate profiling);
5. nutrition and recovery status (e.g. protein intake, hormonal and hydration markers);
6. GPS (e.g. training and competition); and
7. performance analysis (e.g. game/competition statistics).

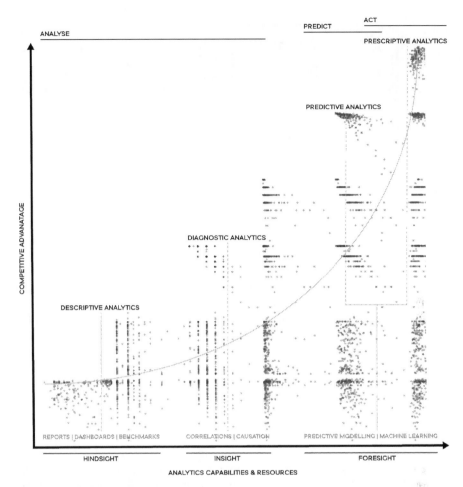

FIGURE 3.1 The sport analytics continuum. A graphical representation of the evolution of sport analytics from retrospective analyses to predictive modeling.

Source: MODUS PERFORMANCE SCIENCE (with permission).

Whilst we are quick to embrace new technologies and eager to monitor every aspect of an athlete's physical, physiological, and technical status, the deluge of information arriving from these disparate data sources is often mismanaged. The multidisciplinary nature of the information collected means it is often gathered by numerous staff and inevitably ends up quarantined in data silos (i.e. stored and managed by individual departments and (or) staff), thus impeding analysis. The advent of sophisticated data management and athlete monitoring systems allows the integration of all athlete data into a centralized hub. Eradicating data silos and facilitating the coupling of structured (e.g. GPS) and unstructured data (e.g. medical and treatment notes) make identification of associations and relationships that are present between and within the data possible.

Organizations are building in-house data management systems or adopting commercially available software that can be customized to their needs. Smartabase (Fusion Sport, Queensland, Australia) is a completely customizable athlete data management system with

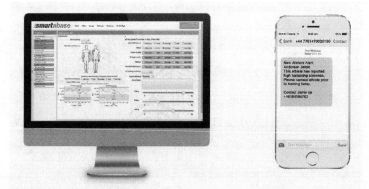

FIGURE 3.2 SMARTABASE athlete and data management software

Source: Fusion Sport (with permission).

comprehensive API for third party integration of data sources such as heart rate (HR) and GPS files (Figure 3.2). Live custom dashboards and reports are set up to deliver key information and alerts to high-performance staff and coaches, providing a multidisciplinary overview of an athlete's or team's performance at any given time. In addition, data can be seamlessly exported as a CSV file for subsequent analyses using more advanced analytical software (e.g. *R* and *Python*).

Sport technology

The intersection of technology and sport has undoubtedly revolutionized the way we monitor athletes and assess training and competition performance. The vast and rich data arising from this technology is enabling sport scientists and coaching staff to push the boundaries of athletic performance, making real-time or near real-time decisions from insights gained via the analyses of this technology-driven data. In this section, we will look at some examples of pertinent technologies that are driving the data game and optimizing performance.

Force plate technology

The assessment of vertical jump (VJ) performance via force plate profiling is a useful tool in the routine monitoring of athletes. The direct measurement of VJ kinetic and kinematic variables provides valuable insight pertaining to 1) the neuromuscular strategies employed to achieve maximal jump performance, thus reflecting the movement efficiency of the athlete; 2) the neuromuscular status of athletes in response to training and competition, thus intimating the presence of adaptation or fatigue (and potential risk of injury); and 3) the lower-body explosive qualities of the athlete, thus highlighting areas of deficiency to better direct training program design (Nibali, Tombleson, Brady, & Wagner, 2015). Traditionally, force plate assessments have generally been adopted in research-based settings, yet the emergence of portable force plates and commercially available data acquisition and analytical software, has made the adoption of force plate profiling a viable option for the routine monitoring of athletes in their daily training environment.

SpartaTrac is proprietary software (Sparta Performance Science, California, United States) that is designed to analyze the "movement signature" of athletes, providing information on lower-body strengths and weaknesses, risk of injury, and adaptations to training. The movement signature is based on the ratio of three key kinetic variables: 1) *Load* (i.e. eccentric rate vertical force); 2) *Explode* (i.e. average vertical concentric force); and 3) *Drive* (i.e. concentric vertical impulse). The value of this software lies in its ability to provide an overview of the quality of the movement, focusing on variables that depict the execution of the movement, rather than focusing on outcome-focused variables such as jump height or peak power. This is important as the neuromuscular strategy employed by athletes will differ under situations of fatigue or in response to training (i.e. positive or negative adaptations), yet their peak power output and (or) maximal jump height may remain unchanged. This is evident in the repeat scan profile of a female basketball athlete taken over a six-week period at the commencement of the season (Figure 3.3). The second scan demonstrates a substantial decline in *Load*, which indicates a reduced capacity to brace and create stiffness, which is crucial during change of direction movements that require rapid deceleration followed by acceleration. The magnitude of the change in *Load* over the six-week period is a "red flag" for conditioning staff, highlighting that the athlete is at increased risk of injury. On January 1, 2013 (the day following the second force plate scan), this athlete sustained a torn anterior cruciate ligament (ACL) injury. This insight enabled conditioning staff to modify the training loads for this athlete in response to similar observed declines in *Load* in subsequent seasons.

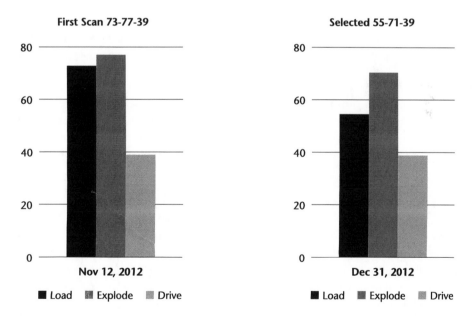

FIGURE 3.3 Example of the change in an athlete's movement signature over a six-week period. Note the substantial decrease in *Load* on the scan to the right (Dec. 31, 2012); the athlete suffered a torn anterior cruciate ligament (ACL) the following day (Jan. 1, 2013).

Source: Sparta Performance Science (with permission).

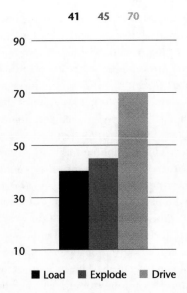

FIGURE 3.4 Example of a "movement signature" that is related to the incidence of ulnar collateral ligament injury in professional baseball players. *Load*: eccentric rate vertical force; *Explode*: average concentric vertical force; *Drive*: concentric vertical impulse.

Source: Sparta Performance Science (with permission).

Additional research, examining the relationship between force plate scan metrics and the incidence of ulnar collateral ligament injuries in professional baseball players, has found that elbow injuries are more likely to occur in athletes who display a movement signature in which greater jump heights are achieved via an over-reliance on momentum (i.e. *Drive*) rather than explosive strength (i.e. *Load* and *Explode*) (Hawkins, 2015) (Figure 3.4). Such insight is invaluable to conditioning and medical staff, as it enables a more directive approach to the conditioning and management of athletes, allowing them to prescribe exercises that specifically address areas of concern, thus mitigating the risk of injury.

Wearable technology

The proliferation of wearable technology in sport has opened the door to athlete monitoring during training and competition, providing a wealth of data that is ripe for real-time or *post hoc* analysis to support the decision-making of conditioning staff and coaches. Wearable devices such as global positioning system (GPS) units and radio frequency identification (RFID) technology are having profound impact in the areas of:

1. athlete load monitoring and management (i.e. modifying training loads, injury risk assessment, in-game substitutions); and
2. performance analysis (i.e. understanding the physical and physiological demands of training and (or) competition).

In 2015, the NFL introduced RFID technology (Zebra Technologies, Illinois, United States) to the game, inserting RFID chips in the shoulder pads of every player that enables location and accelerometer data to be relayed to a number of receivers placed around the playing field in real-time. Currently, the data is only used for broadcasters to provide in-game statistics to viewers, but there exists the opportunity for NFL clubs to access this information in the future to gain better insights into the movement patterns and physical demands of the game.

Whilst US team-sports have been slow to embrace wearable technology, other professional sports, such as rugby union, rugby league, and Australian Football, have reaped the advantageous insights afforded by this technology for many years. GPS units (Catapult, Victoria, Australia) are worn by players in training and competition, providing a rich source of objective information on player external workloads and movement patterns. In addition to location-based (x–y co-ordinates) and distance–time (speed) data, GPS units are fitted with accelerometers, gyroscopes and magnetometers, providing data on accelerations, decelerations, change of direction movements, and vertical jumps (height and frequency) performed. Conditioning staff can use this information to assess the external loads imposed on players during training and (or) competition, allowing them to modify training accordingly (whether that be participation in specific training drills, or an increase/decrease in the intensity and volume of training), or inform in-game substitutions and player rotations. This serves the dual purpose of minimizing the risk of injury that occurs when player workloads are mismanaged (Drew & Finch, 2016; Gabbett, 2016; Hulin, Gabbett, Lawson, Caputi, & Sampson, 2015), and confirming that the workloads prescribed for specific training drills are in fact accomplished, ensuring correct adaptation to training and optimal fitness (refer to the case study on p.56). Furthermore, the physical demands of competition can be assessed using GPS and accelerometer data (Gabbett, Jenkins, & Abernethy, 2011) to better direct the prescription of training loads and the position-specific requirements of players (Austin & Kelly, 2013). The outcome is a more sophisticated approach to player monitoring and improved decision-making in the management of athlete training and game loads.

"Smart" Clothing and Equipment

"Smart" Clothing and Equipment is the latest emerging technology driving sport analytics, and much like the introduction of GPS some years ago, "smart" technology is set to revolutionize the way we monitor athletes and sports performance in the field and in-game. Smart compression garments (SCG) that are fitted with pressure sensors and integrated with piezoresistive materials, offer a low-cost solution capable of measuring muscle activation loads and joint/limb positioning in the real-world training environment of elite athletes. This offers exciting opportunities for conditioning coaches and medical staff, as it provides information on muscle activation and loads, highlighting potential risk of injury from asymmetrical or overload straining of the muscle (Belbasis, Fuss, & Sidhu, 2015). Similarly, sensors are being integrated into a compression sleeve to assess baseball pitchers biomechanics and the load experienced by the ulnar collateral ligament (UCL) (The Associated Press, 2016) that is a common site of injury in pitchers. Furthermore, football in-soles can be fitted with pressure sensors (Tan, Fuss, Weizman, & Troynikov 2015) to determine the on-field force loads experienced by athletes. This serves the dual purpose of measuring left versus right load asymmetries and the overall workload performed by the athlete, facilitating a more directive approach to load monitoring and prescription of training loads, and the assessment of injury risk. Pressure sensors are also being fitted to football footwear to detect the magnitude of impact forces between the foot and ball during kicks (Weizman & Fuss, 2015). Kicking forces and measurement of the center of pressure (COP) of the boot during impact is then correlated with kicking accuracy to provide feedback on kicking efficiency in a practical setting; a task previously confined to a laboratory setting, and thus arguably lacking construct validity.

Similarly, the instrumentation of cricket balls with high-speed gyros and electronic equipment for wireless data transfer to a laptop or smart phone (Doljin & Fuss, 2015) is facilitating the on-field performance analysis of bowling technique in cricket. Bowling kinematics and aerodynamics are assessed, providing key insight into the biomechanics of different delivery types and styles to improve technique.

CASE STUDY: USE OF GPS TO PREDICT TRAINING LOADS IN PROFESSIONAL AUSTRALIAN FOOTBALL

Name: Michael Rennie
Title: Conditioning Coach and Sport Scientist
Current employer: Sydney Swans Football Club
Brief work history: My experience in professional sport started during my undergraduate degree when I volunteered at several organizations in Sydney, Australia, to develop an understanding of how to design and run an elite program. I quickly fell in love with the science, training, monitoring and injury prevention processes that are integral to a high-performance department and decided to complete an honors research study with the University of Technology, Sydney (UTS) and the Sydney Swans Football club. During the 2012 season, I spent mid-week working on my research at the club and the weekends working with performance analysis staff during matches, which

PHOTO 3.1   Michael Rennie

involved collecting statistics during the game and then reporting these to the coaches. Following a very successful year at the football club, I was offered a PhD scholarship to study with UTS and continue my research at the Sydney Swans as a conditioning coach. My PhD topic aims to identify the contribution of physical performance to match performance and the analysis of movement profiles during successful periods of play. My job role initially involved monitoring training loads, recovery, and wellness measures. As my PhD progressed, my initial role grew and it is now focused on rehabilitation and sport science within our high-performance department. Since completing my undergraduate degree I have lectured at UTS and in vocational education in a variety of areas in strength and conditioning and exercise physiology.

How do think data helps influence your industry segment?

In the sport science industry, the majority of data collection and use pertains to injury prevention, enhancing recovery, or attempting to identify factors that affect performance during competition. An abundance of research exists in all areas and each has benefited from data as it provides a foundation for evidence-based decision-making. Applied sport scientists are typically pragmatic in their approach, i.e. they work on things that have real-world practical application and thus the data that is typically collected has a real impact on our day-to-day operations. Sport is often highly emotional (at the end of the day we are all just fans); however, sport science and sport analytics offers a degree of objectivity. The movie *Moneyball* is the most widely renowned example of how data can help performance. The Oakland A's general manager Billy Beane used data science methods known as sabermetrics (developed by a statistician named Bill James) to identify opportunity and value in baseball that otherwise had not been fully explored. His methods were then adopted by the Boston Red Sox, who went on to win the 2004 World Series and break the "curse of the bambino." In essence, Billy's methods used historical data to create a team of players that, statistically, possessed the qualities required to win a World Series. Similar methods are now used by many sporting teams throughout the world in a pursuit to identify ways of improving a team's performance.

The use of data to predict an outcome has become extremely common in the last decade and is likely to be the way of the future. Over the last ten years the Sydney Swans Football Club has utilized a neural network system to identify injury risk in players, and since its inception, the club has recorded one of the lowest injury rates in the Australian Football League (AFL). A neural network identifies a set of conditions via assessing the interaction of numerous different variables that suggests an increased likelihood of injury risk. Medical and conditioning staff can then make the necessary modifications to the training session that leads to a reduction in injury risk (e.g. reduce training duration, modify participation in a drill, etc.).

What example can you share regarding the use of data to help make a decision?

The majority of my experience has been within the football department, which consists of coaching, sport science, and medical staff. We have collaborated on numerous projects that have multi-factorial applications and many of our projects have utilized data that assists in the planning of training. One system that is heavily used by many sport organizations is global positioning system (GPS) data that is collected during training sessions and games. Each player wears a small unit, roughly the size of a mobile phone, that collects information such as distance covered, speeds, and accelerometer data. The sport science staff can see this information in real-time on the side of the field using a data receiver and laptop computer, and subsequently use the information to modify training as the session progresses.

One of the common uses of GPS data is to report the workloads completed during specific drills or training sessions designed and selected by the coaching staff. Over the last four years, we have collected in excess of one million data points pertaining to player movements in various skills and conditioning drills. We can now use this information to predict what will be involved in specific training sessions, depending on the drills the coaching staff select, the time spent performing each drill, and consequently the training loads likely to be experienced by each player. Over the past five years, we have developed an interface that we use to create and predict the load for each individual player based on the choices of drills made by coaching and conditioning staff. This information is then compared to the player's most recent training loads to determine the appropriateness of the planned session.

The problem

Historically, training loads were estimated by conditioning coaches using their previous experience and expertise. While experience and expertise are clearly vital, objective measures of exercise intensity make the prescription of training far more robust. GPS systems have allowed conditioning staff to strategically design their running progressions using historical data. When designing training programs, coaches aim to prescribe the correct mode of exercise (the type of exercise via specific drills), the right intensity (how hard) and volume (how much), which all equate to the correct dosage of exercise. In essence, this aims to ensure that athletes are exposed to an appropriate stimulus and, thus, adapt in response to the training session. The challenge with training prescription is the need to suit the training session to the physiological state of the athlete at a specific moment in time. Because the physiological state of the athlete is highly dynamic and affected by a myriad of factors (such as recent training loads, injury history, and current levels of muscle damage) the prescription of appropriate training loads is clearly very challenging. Furthermore, all staff has an input into the planning and execution of training. The coaching staff aims to optimize the development of the player's technical and tactical abilities. Secondly, the fitness staff wants to ensure that the training loads are adequate in order to achieve the desired fitness adaptations. Lastly, the medical staff wants to make sure that the players stay healthy and injury free. Inherently, all departments work together to design training sessions that not only move the team in the right direction, but cater to individuals who require particular modifications based on their specific needs (such as injury or load management, improving specific fitness or skills, etc.).

Initially, GPS data was used to report on training sessions *post hoc* and was not used in the planning of training sessions. However, historical data presents an opportunity to build and plan training sessions. For example, if a player participates in five different drills, for ten minutes each, how many meters will the player run? How many high-intensity running efforts will they complete? How many skill efforts will they execute? In order to prescribe the correct dose, we need to be able to build their training session and determine what the player's likely output will be. Initially, the drills were selected and implemented without the use of technology to measure the physical metrics, and without sophisticated analysis systems to interpret the data – the resulting workloads and the appropriateness of these workloads for the individual athlete were therefore largely unknown (Figure 3.5).

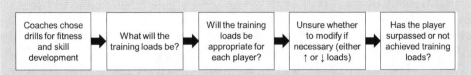

FIGURE 3.5   Inefficiencies in the planning and execution of training prior to the adoption of GPS technology and the development of workload predictors

Planning of training

Time is often the most easily managed variable with regard to training. Time spent training can be easily modified according to a player's fatigue or fitness levels. However, a progression of this planning includes the composition of the activity the athlete is performing during this training time. For example, what total distance does the player run? How many high-intensity running efforts will the athlete complete? Furthermore, coaches are mindful that acute increases in weekly training loads may place athletes at risk of soft tissue injuries, and conversely, chronically low training loads involve a high level of risk due to deconditioning. Generating data that predicts a player's upcoming session (i.e. acute workload) can be used to ensure that the player is not put at risk compared to their recent training loads (i.e. chronic workload).

Designing a pre-season training program

A typical pre-season initially involves a high fitness load and a low skill load. Then as the pre-season progresses, time spent performing fitness work decreases and the time spent performing skills increases (Figure 3.6). It is relatively easy to progress in time (i.e. spend

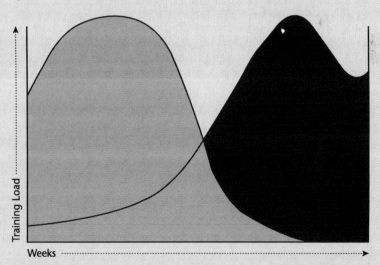

FIGURE 3.6   GREY represents a model of progression for fitness work and BLACK represents the progression of skills. Manipulations can be made to the model based on how much time the coaching staff dedicate to fitness work or skill development.

10 minutes on day 1, 20 minutes on day 2 etc.); however, it can be a challenge progressing high intensity running, stop/start running movements and tackling. The use of a prediction model can help the coaching staff ensure that there is an appropriate progression of all movement metrics such as high-intensity running, stop/start movements and the number of tackles within the drills that are chosen.

Rehabilitation

Injury prevalence in professional Australian Football is approximately 150 missed games per season per club; on average, players miss 3.5 games each season because of injury. Rehabilitation plays a major role in returning players to full health and match-ready fitness. Typically, players progress through various stages of rehab, which may include jogging, fast running, sprinting, agility progressions, and then a gradual return to team skills. However, prior to the development of training prediction models we have previously been unable to numerically illustrate the progression of speed and agility progressions to ensure athletes are, in fact, progressing.

The analysis

All GPS data was collated into a large database and was converted into per minute of training time. For example, the number of tackles likely completed per minute of time spent in a specific drill.

The specific information included:

1. time spent participating in various drills (minutes);
2. time spent performing fitness or skill work (minutes);
3. skill pressure (open or closed skill, rating of pressure [high, moderate, low] – manually coded by coaches);
4. skill load (number of technical skills executed [number of kicks, handballs, tackles] – manually coded by coaches);
5. drill type (open or closed skill – manually coded by coaches);
6. distance covered (meters);
7. high-intensity running (time, distance and number of events);
8. change of direction profile (number of acceleration and deceleration events);
9. work and recovery ratios (time spent performing high-intensity activity divided by time spent performing low-intensity activity);
10. repeated sprint efforts (defined as three sprint efforts within a 21-second duration);
11. average and maximum heart rate (beats per minute).

Drill selection

The next task was to create the interface for the session builder. Firstly, the coach selects the players that will participate in the session. A drop-down box was created using the data validation function in Excel, which allows the coach to click on the dropdown box in order to select the drill from the database. The coach then enters the amount of time for the drill. The sheet will look up the typical movement profile of the drill for each player and extract the average work rate for the drill using the index and match functions in Excel. We can then generate information on how much distance the player will cover, the amount of high intensity activity performed, and the number of acceleration and deceleration events. All drills can also be manually coded by coaches to provide specific information about ratings of physical contact, how often players can perform a technical skill, and how much pressure players experience while performing these technical skills.

Individual player predictions

When the drills are selected for the players participating in the full session, the session builder generates a prediction for each individual player that is based on their previous participation in those drills (or of a similar position if the data does not exist for a particular athlete). Using a set of specific thresholds that highlights abrupt changes in training load (from their 2-, 3- or 4-week rolling average), a red flag system identifies that if players participate in the planned training session it would violate the "safe" thresholds range. In an adjoining sheet, calculations are made that automatically suggest modifications to the players' training loads to reduce the risk of injury (Figure 3.7).

Rehabilitation

This database and predictive format allowed us to assess the progression of our commonly used rehabilitation progressions. For example, following a knee injury, players are slowly introduced to various activities in order to rehabilitate the injured site and return them to pre-injury fitness. The GPS predictor can be used to choose the correct drills that involve an appropriate movement profile that matches the player's current level of fitness. For example, following a knee injury a player will undertake a progression of agility drills. Over time, we have been able to profile the stages of rehabilitation to ensure that the workloads are in fact progressive, and make modifications to the rehabilitation progressions if an issue is identified.

The end result

The data provides the basis for designing the running loads for our training and rehab sessions. Our conditioning staff work alongside our coaching and medical staff to select the specific drills and time spent performing each drill in order to determine the amount of activity the players will likely perform. Our medical staff can also use the prediction model to identify specific drills that players in rehab can complete, either during the early stages of their rehab or closer towards periods of returning to full training and competition. The training data is then compared to the player's recent training data to ensure that the training progression does not put the player at risk. Furthermore, with the assistance of real-time movement data, we can make modifications during training to ensure that our athletes' training loads are optimized (Figure 3.8).

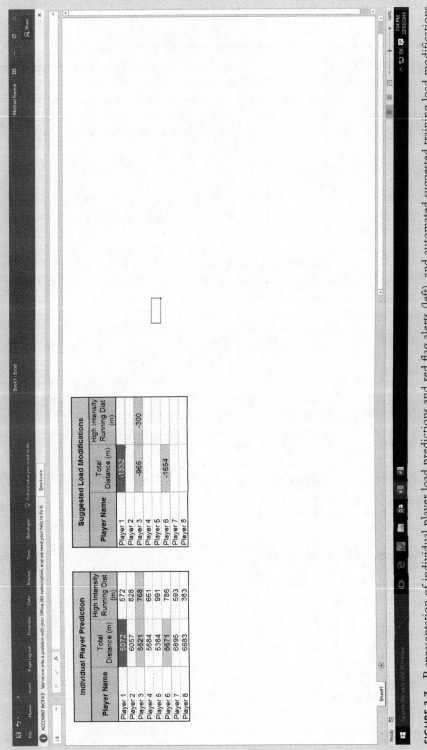

FIGURE 3.7 Representation of individual player load predictions and red flag alerts (left), and automated suggested training load modifications (right)

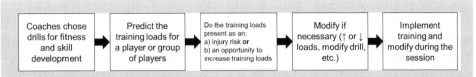

| Coaches chose drills for fitness and skill development | Predict the training loads for a player or group of players | Do the training loads present as an: a) injury risk **or** b) an opportunity to increase training loads | Modify if necessary (↑ or ↓ loads, modify drill, etc.) | Implement training and modify during the session |

FIGURE 3.8   The current process for planning and implementing player training loads

What lesson did you learn from the process?

First and foremost, the data that is collected needs to be valid and reliable. It needs to measure accurately the construct that you are attempting to measure and it must produce the same result when measured repeatedly in the same conditions. This will result in clean and accurate data. If there are any issues at this fundamental stage of data collection, the resulting information and decision-making are likely to be flawed.

The biggest practical lesson I learned is to develop systems that can be easily adopted by a variety of different departments. Data analysis can be extremely complex and it's not everyone's area of expertise. To take something highly complex and design a robust and simple tool for coaching and medical staff to use has been a rewarding experience. The best users of data are the people that have a vision for the type of information they want and how the resulting system is going to be used. It is important to have a clear question or goal and to determine if your current data sets can answer these questions for you.

What suggestions do you have for students about data in your discipline?

I would encourage students to spend time learning the basics. Creating databases in Excel is an easy way to begin. The basic functions and optional add-ons provide a solid platform to learn the fundamentals of creating a database, mining the data, and then creating reports. Data really becomes cool and exciting when you use numbers to provide evidence and, hopefully, answer some questions. Therefore, it is vital to be pragmatic and hypothesis driven so that you have a clear vision of the type of analysis you are going to perform.

I would also suggest that once you become relatively proficient; try to stay up to date with developments in data science. There are also some really exciting areas that are becoming increasingly common, including the use of multi-level modeling and non-linear mathematics for the prediction of risk that will become more prominent over the next decade.

Optical tracking

Advancements in optical tracking technology and computer vision have enabled automation of the previously laborious process of manually tracking player and ball movements and coding game event statistics. This improves both the accuracy of the data and the speed at which it is delivered. It also opens the door for more sophisticated analytics in the domain of performance analysis, providing an additional layer of insight to performance analysts and coaches.

Recently, the NBA introduced the optical tracking system SportVU (STATS LLC, Illinois, United States) across all stadia. SportVU utilizes a six-camera installation (originally designed to track missiles) to capture player location and ball trajectories in real-time at a rate of 25 times per second (STATS LLC, 2015). Sophisticated algorithms are applied to produce spatio-temporal data, which consists of *object trajectories* that capture the x, y, z position co-ordinates of the players and ball, and *event logs* that record the time-stamped location of game events (e.g. passes, shots on goal, rebounds) (Gudmundsson & Horton, 2016). Thus spatio-temporal data provides a plethora of in-game statistics that are then relayed in real-time (within 60 seconds) to sport broadcasters and professional teams for analysis.

Whilst *object trajectory* and *event log* data represent discrete aspects of play and can individually be used to assess sport performance, when used in combination they provide a rich, contextual overview of the game (Gudmundsson & Horton, 2016). The application of sophisticated analytics to game-generated data allows identification of the most pertinent elements of performance that dictate a winning outcome. More importantly, analytics facilitates a better understanding of how the relative importance of these "key" elements changes in response to varying game situations, and in turn, influences the likelihood of success; for example:

1. low versus high points differential games (i.e. close versus open scoring games);
2. different opponents and player combinations;
3. game strategy (e.g. offensive and defensive tactics, team formations); and
4. different locations (e.g. home advantage versus travel).

Much of the work arising from optical tracking technology and *object trajectory* data is in defining regions of value in a playing area and computing a players' ability to control or "dominate" that space. As some regions are more valuable than others, the dominant region a player occupies largely dictates the strategic options available for a given possession for both the player (and team) in possession, and the defense (Cervone, Bornn, & Goldsberry, 2016). The analysis stems from the concept of Voronoi cells in computational geometry. At any given point in time, the playing area is subdivided into regions based on the computation of a player's dominant region, which is based on their position, speed, and acceleration (Gudmundsson & Wolle, 2014); the control or "ownership" a player has over this playing area is inversely proportional to their distance from this space (Cervone *et al.*, 2016). The application of Voronoi diagrams in the modeling of spatio-temporal data is advantageous as it reveals behavioral patterns that provide insightful information on 1) the influence that individual players exert on the game; 2) the effectiveness of offensive and defensive plays and team formations; and 3) player selection and game strategy. For instance, it is possible to determine the value of off-ball events (i.e. those occurring by players who are not in possession of the ball) that lead to a scoring opportunity by calculating the dominant regions that have been freed up for their teammates to occupy as a result of their movements (e.g. running a particular line that draws in defenders and opens up space). Conversely, a player's and team's ability to relegate the offense to a region of low value on the playing field highlights the impact of individual players on the game, and the effectiveness of defensive strategies. The generation of new metrics derived from this information is invaluable to coaches and performance analysts as it can be used to explain a performance outcome, and thus offers evidence-based support in future player selection and formulation of game strategies on a per opponent basis.

CASE STUDY: ANALYTICS AT THE 28TH SOUTHEAST ASIAN (SEA) GAMES 2015

PHOTO 3.2   From left to right: Joash Ng, Nicole Chua and Benoit Ammann

The following executives work at the Singapore Sports Institute

Benoit Ammann, Deputy Director

Benoit joined the Singapore Sports Institute (SSI) in 2014 to lead the High Performance Sports Analytics and Technology team. He is currently leading the development and implementation of a complete integrated Athlete Data Management System across all SSI departments with a new platform that provides a central database for collecting and sharing athletes' data and videos. This project contributes to building analytics capacities, to impact on objective decision-making and efficient sport organization management, while engaging the entire sport community in Singapore. Prior to this position, Benoit has developed a very strong expertise in performance technology and video platform solutions by leading the northern Europe sales of Dartfish video solutions. This led him to successful collaborations on technology projects with the British Olympic Association (BOA), the English Institute of Sport (EIS) and many other Sports Governing bodies in the UK and across Europe. He holds a postgraduate Master's degree in Advanced Studies in Sport Administration and Technology from the AISTS in Lausanne, during which he researched

B-to-B distribution opportunities of Olympic content for the International Olympic Committee (IOC).

Joash Ng, Executive

Joash joined the Singapore Sports Institute (SSI) in 2014 as part of the High Performance Sports Analytics and Technology team. He is currently working with the team to develop and implement an integrated Athlete Data Management System, providing a centralized database for analysis of athlete data and video content. This project would greatly enhance the analytical and technological capabilities within the Sports Institute and the various National Sports Associations in Singapore. He holds a postgraduate Masters of Science (MSc) in Sports Management from New York University, during which he researched professional and college sport operations and the impact of negative publicity on sports sponsorship.

Nicole Chua, Executive

Nicole Chua joined the High Performance Sports (HPS) department within Singapore Sports Institute in 2013. She supported the team throughout the launch of the Sports Excellence Scholarship (spexScholarship) which provides enhanced level of support for athletes within the HPS pathway. With her knowledge in performance analysis gained during her time with HPS, she was transferred to the newly formed High Performance Sports Analytics department in 2014. The HPS Analytics Team are currently working on several projects and initiatives that will impact the overall HPS ecosystem with enhanced analytical capabilities. Nicole is a graduate of the University of Western Australia with a Bachelor's degree in Science (Sport Science).

The Southeast Asian (SEA) Games is a biennial multi-sports event that involves the 11 Southeast Asian nations: Brunei, Cambodia, Indonesia, Laos, Malaysia, Myanmar, Philippines, Singapore, Thailand, Timor-Leste and Vietnam. The SEA Games is widely considered as the most important multi-sports event for all Southeast Asian nations, ranking just beneath the Olympics and Asian Games in terms of significance.

The recent SEA Games was hosted by Singapore from 29th May to 16th June 2015. This edition of the games was especially significant as it was Singapore's first time in 20 years hosting the region's largest multi-sports competition. The 11 SEA nations competed across 36 sports and disciplines in 402 events. The athletes and teams competed for a total of 402 gold medals, 402 silver medals and 522 bronze medals. The contingent size for Team Singapore was 747 athletes, which was the largest contingent ever sent for the SEA Games.

Who is HPS analytics?

The High Performance Sports (HPS) Analytics, Technology and Education department was formed within Singapore Sports Institute (SSI) in August 2014 as a central pillar to support the high-performance ecosystem in Singapore. The department serves a key purpose in enhancing the analytical capabilities of the sport ecosystem and further developing inexpensive and easy-to-use technology within the various National Sports Associations (NSAs).

Specifically for the SEA Games, the department's role was to provide video and data analysis of Team Singapore athletes' performance to better enhance and add value to training preparations prior to the Games. During the Games itself, the department was tasked to capture video footage of Singaporean athletes and their competitors, analyze the footage and upload the footage onto a secured online platform in as short a lead time as possible. In addition, the department also worked on producing daily reports to provide context and perspective on the Singaporean athletes' performance.

Objectives for the SEA Games

With regard to the SEA Games, the department set out to accomplish two key objectives:

1. Exposure of video analysis and ecosystem to NSAs.
2. Build a video database/repository of region's top athletes.

As a relatively new department, one of the first projects the department embarked on was developing a well-rounded video management system that was intuitive and easy to use. The video ecosystem developed needed to integrate seamlessly the various processes involved, from the capture of video footage to analyzing the video content to the sharing of the analysis. Thus, being a multi-sport competition, the SEA Games represented an invaluable opportunity to expose this newly developed video management system on a large scale to the National Sports Associations and Team Singapore athletes.

The other key objective the department sought to accomplish was to build a video database of the region's top athletes. The SEA Games serves as a gathering of all the elite as well as up-and-coming athletes from each Southeast nation and provided the perfect platform to start building a video repository, collecting crucial information and video content of Singapore athletes as well as regional competitors.

Preparing for the SEA Games

Prior to the start of 28th SEA Games in 2015, Singapore Sports Institute produced a Pre-Games Report on the Medal Projections and Simulations for Team Singapore. The report contained an analysis of where Singapore's best chances of medals were going to come from, from which sport, and drilled down to which specific individual athlete and formulated through the tracking of results and performances of Singaporean athletes as well as regional competitors over a 12-month period.

Leading up to the SEA Games, the HPS Analytics Team also worked closely with Team Singapore athletes and coaches on their preparation. The department developed tagging templates based on the coaches' feedback, which were specific in only tagging events that the coaches wanted to highlight and collate information on. These tagging templates were then used to analyze the videos and were further refined along the way. After the tagging was completed, the video analyses were then uploaded to a secured cloud platform to which only coaches and athletes had access and were utilized during their film sessions. With the ecosystem set up, athletes were also able to access the video analysis on the cloud platform.

During the Games

Management of video ecosystem

The mission of the team during the SEA Games was to collect video and data of Team Singapore athletes' performance, and in some cases of competitors/opponents, in order to analyze and provide reports and video analysis to scientists, coaches, athletes and other stakeholders.

The HPS Analytics Team used the video platform for athletes and coaches to conduct video analysis of their competitors and themselves within the shortest lead-time possible. For example, when an athlete had completed competing in his event, the HPS Analytics Team would process the relevant video footage and upload it onto the online video platform, where the athlete and coaches had exclusive access via web browser or specific mobile app provided by Dartfish solutions.

How does the video ecosystem work?

First, the video footage has to be captured, through either on-site cameras or the broadcasted feed. Once the video content is captured and analyzed, it is uploaded onto a secured online video platform. The tagging files and video analysis are then assessed by coaches, athletes and sport scientists. The videos can also be downloaded for offline viewing, which allows the coaches to show their athletes specific highlights of their game performance during training sessions by referring to the specific tags, rather than watching the full game. At the same time, athletes can view the content before or after training to better prepare themselves for upcoming training sessions or competitions. The display screen is highlighted in Figure 3.9.

For example, Figure 3.10 shows the synchronization of the tagging templates used with video footage capture. Each point won or lost by the Team Singapore Badminton Doubles team was time-stamped on the tagging template. This helped to give the athletes an overall statistical analysis of the match they just played as well as review specific points with their coaches for feedback and learning.

How did we do it?

During the SEA Games, the HPS Analytics Team was supported by three permanent staff and two interns. There were two locations where the team set-up the necessary equipment: a) Second level of the West Wing within Games Headquarters (Games HQ) and b) HPS

FIGURE 3.9 Layout of cloud platform

FIGURE 3.10 Match analysis of a badminton match

Analytics Room within SSI Office. All captured videos were tagged by using markers and key worded in order to create structured and enriched online video archives.

Throughout the duration of the Games, there were at least one or two people stationed at Games HQ to capture all videos produced by the SEA Games Host Broadcaster.

These video feeds were transferred from the International Broadcast Centre via optic fiber cables. Time shifts were organized in order to cover all broadcasted sports from 8:30am to 11:00pm on a daily basis. All video from any single broadcasted event has been captured in MPEG-4 H264 HD quality, and uploaded onto a private video platform during the day after completion of the event.

Two staff members worked the HPS Analytics Room within SSI Office to capture the video feeds which were connected to the fixed cameras within the Kallang Cluster venues, i.e. National Stadium, OCBC Aquatics Centre, Singapore Indoor Stadium and OCBC Arena Hall 1. This alternative provided additional raw videos, which could give better angles for performance analysis purposes. One of the angles included a top down view of the basketball court. This angle was critical for the basketball team in analyzing their off-the-ball movement and positioning on the court.

The result was the creation of a video database with 1,297 videos, 745 hours of footage covering 19 different sports. Each video was labeled with relevant keywords and meta data to ensure users were able to retrieve specific videos efficiently.

TABLE 3.1 The Sport Analytics Continuum

Total number of. . .	Quantity
Sports covered	19
Videos	1,297
Hours of videos	745

During the Games

Daily report of Team Singapore's performance

In addition to the management of the video ecosystem during the Games, the department assisted in tracking the performances of Team Singapore athletes. Working together with the HPS team, daily reports of Team Singapore's results were delivered. The reports were relayed to key stakeholders and senior management and helped put performances and results into context, enabling them to make objective assessments of how Team Singapore had performed.

Throughout the day, the HPS Analytics Team also provided an hourly update on Team Singapore's results and the overall medal tally. This information was also used to update an online reporting and visualization platform, which was one of the Games' sponsors, Qlik.

Reports were then compiled at the end of each day with data visualizations about Team SG's results. They consisted of information on how Team Singapore was performing in relation to the targets set and drilled down to key information regarding the individual athlete, such as the level of support the athlete received and whether the athlete was a debutant athlete. In addition, performances were compared with historical results to provide greater perspective. For example, Figure 3.11 shows the historical results of the women's discus throw event. The position of each individual athlete is plotted across

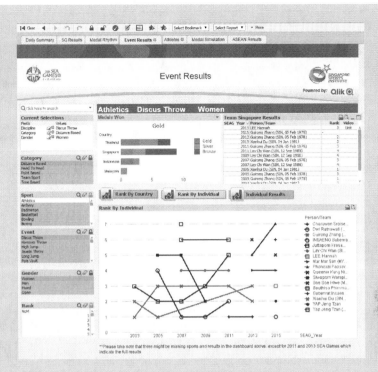

FIGURE 3.11 Historical results of discus throw (women)

the various editions of the SEA Games in chronological order. This helped the stakeholders to judge an athlete with greater perspective and help understand if the athlete has maintained a certain level of performance over a period of time and whether she is in career ascendancy or decline.

Impact of analytics

At the conclusion of the Games, the department looked back to assess if the objectives set were met. In many ways, the Games proved to be the ideal platform to increase exposure of the video ecosystem that the department developed to the relevant parties. Coaches and athletes were able to experience first-hand the potential of analytics in aiding their preparation especially in a time-sensitive environment. For example, the Singapore football team actually received captured footage of their competitors every evening, analyzed the footage through the night and had reports ready by the next morning during the team's training session.

Another outcome of the department's efforts at the Games was the creation of a well-organized central depository of videos that were key worded and easily retrievable. National Sports Associations (NSAs) also started seeing the value of the proper management of a video ecosystem and started actively engaging the department to help develop their own video analytics system as well.

What does the future hold?

The SEA Games in essence represents the first steps in the development of an integrated video ecosystem for Singapore sport. The platform we developed generated significant buy-in from each National Sports Association. The challenge now is to integrate all NSAs within the analytics ecosystem and facilitate sharing of information and knowledge across sports. In addition, using analytics in a time-sensitive environment, such as during major Games, will help give Team Singapore athletes a competitive edge – thus making analytics a true game changer.

Machine learning

Machine learning evolved from the study of pattern recognition and computational learning theory in the 1950s; it is a division of computer science that utilizes a class of algorithms to identify and learn from patterns in data to make predictions without the need to be explicitly programmed. Advancements in computational power have seen a phenomenal increase in computer vision and the complexity of pattern recognition that is possible. In turn, the predictions made and the problems that machine learning can solve are rapidly growing, providing exciting opportunities and applications in the field of sport analytics.

The advantage of machine learning is that it can accomplish tasks that are impossible for humans to perform. Machine learning can deal with vast volumes of granular data that require the efficient processing of numerous complex neural networks and decision-making in real-time. This makes it ideal for processing of in-game data to inform decisions such as game strategy and player substitutions. Another exciting application of machine learning in sports, is its ability to automate game event classifications such as good or poor passes in football (Horton, Gudmundsson, Chawala, & Estephan, 2015) to more complex events like a pick-and-roll in basketball (McQueen, Wiens, & Guttag, 2013). US-based company Second Spectrum (California, United States) is at the forefront of leveraging the power of machine learning and pattern recognition to derive insightful information from spatio-temporal data (provided by the optical tracking system SportVU by STATS LLC, Illinois, United States). They analyze movement patterns and identify key aspects of the game that are vital to winning and losing, providing further insight to coaches on how to structure or defend against such plays. More information detailing the application of machine learning in sport analytics is available by viewing the 2015 TED talk "The math behind basketball's wildest moves," presented by Second Spectrum co-founder Rajiv Maheswaran (Maheswaran, 2015).

The future of sport: predictive analytics

It is critical to note that technology is only part of the solution; how the data arising from this technology is interpreted and applied is what determines its value. The true value of sport analytics lies in its predictive capabilities and the competitive advantage they afford. Imagine the competitive advantage gained by athletes and teams if they are able to predict the likely location of shots on goal, or in knowing the likely decision a player in possession of the ball will make based on the team formation at that time, or the likelihood of a particular serve in tennis based on the opponent they are playing, or the foresight of knowing what type of baseball pitch will be thrown and when. Well the time for imagination is over; the future of sport has arrived, and it is all about predictive analytics.

In a previous section, we discussed some of the analytical work arising from optical tracking technology. Now, let's take it to the next level and look at how optical tracking data is being used to evaluate the decision-making of players and to predict points scoring (Cervone, D'Amour, Bornn, & Goldsberry, 2014; Wei, Lucey, Morgan, Reid, & Sridharan, 2016). At the core of this work is the concept that players will systematically make decisions and employ tactics to maneuver their opponents to their advantage; as such, the "key" move likely occurred several events prior to the actual scoring of points. Therefore, quantifying the movement patterns and understanding the strategy employed prior to the scoring of points rather than the event of scoring itself is what derives real value. In the sport of basketball, this concept led to the computation of a new metric called *expected possession value* or EPV (Cervone *et al.*, 2014). EPV is the "quantitative representation of a whole possession that summarizes each moment of the possession in terms of the number of points the offense is expected to score" (Cervone *et al.*, 2014). The EPV is calculated by fitting a probabilistic model that assumes the decision-making of the ball-carrier is influenced only by the spatio-temporal configuration of the players on court at that time (Cervone *et al.*, 2014). Whilst the analytics behind the computation of the EPV are complex, the outcome is relatively straightforward. For each moment of possession, the EVP assigns a point value to every tactical option available to the ball-carrier. For example, passing to a teammate who is heavily guarded near the basket results in a lower EPV compared to passing to a player who has been left in open space near the basket (Cervone *et al.*, 2014). The ability to apply a framework for the value of decision-making opens up avenues of deeper insights into the game of basketball, allowing coaches to make more informed decisions surrounding offensive plays and game strategy.

Similarly, spatio-temporal data has been used to accurately predict shot outcomes in tennis (Wei *et al.*, 2015; Wei *et al.*, 2016). The analysis examines the contextual behavior patterns (i.e. shot combinations) employed by players to establish dominance over their opponents, and groups players who display similar strategies known as *style priors*. When combined with match context (e.g. opponent) and player characteristics (e.g. fast serve) data, the prediction accuracy of the model is enhanced (Wei *et al.*, 2015). The researches provided an example of the serving behavior of high-ranking opponents against renowned tennis player Roger Federer. Rafael Nadal typically prefers to serve to Federer's backhand (49 percent likelihood this serve type will be played), whilst Bernard Tomic and Andy Murray typically serve a forehand shot (50 percent and 37 percent likelihood, respectively). Interestingly, Nadal boasts a superior winning record against Federer compared to his competitors. It is evident that the ability to predict the type of serve typically selected by a particular player in varying match contexts offers invaluable information in the formulation of opponent tactics, thus improving the likelihood of a winning outcome.

In baseball, the sport that grandfathered sport analytics, machine learning is being leveraged to predict the pitching behavior of players to better inform in-game decision-making. Ray Hensberger, a baseball-loving analyst, used Major League Baseball (MLB) data to develop a model that can predict "what" a pitcher will throw and "when" the pitch will be thrown, with an accuracy of 74.5 percent (Hensberger, 2014). Factors such as the type of pitches thrown by particular pitchers/teams, number and position of players on base, ball-strike count, and number of innings played were incorporated into the model. The result was a model that could determine upcoming pitches using real-time game statistics.

Conclusion

The primary goal of sport analytics is to *save time* and *provide unique, actionable information* for decision-makers (Alamar, 2013). The challenge for sport scientists and data analysts is to present the information derived from analytics to athletes and coaching staff in a manner that is meaningful and provides context for interpretation. Sport analytics is as much about telling a story with data as it is about the complex algorithms and machine learning techniques applied to the data. The world of professional sport is a highly charged, highly dynamic and fluid environment, in which daily training schedules, team selection, and game strategy can change at a whim for a myriad of reasons. As such, the ability to immediately extract and deliver information on player monitoring data, injury risk status, training drills, team tactics, etc. is paramount. Consideration must be given to how the information is delivered – often a dynamic (i.e. live data refresh) interactive dashboard that allows high-performance staff and coaches to derive a multifactorial snapshot on any given athlete at any given point in time is your best bet. When suited to the data, "a picture is worth a thousand words" and can convey layers of data and insight that would be lost in tabular or written format. As such, the importance of data visualizations in this process cannot be underestimated.

References

Alamar, B. (2013). *Sports analytics: A guide for coaches, managers, and other decision makers.* New York, NY: Columbia University Press.

Austin, D. J., & Kelly, S. J. (2013). Positional differences in professional rugby league match play through the use of global positioning systems. *The Journal of Strength and Conditioning Research, 27*(1), 14–19.

Belbasis, A., Fuss, F. K., & Sidhu, J. (2015). Muscle activity analysis with a smart compression garment. *Procedia Engineering, 112,* 163–68.

Cervone, D., Bornn, L., & Goldsberry, K. (2016). *NBA Court Realty.* Paper presented at the MIT Sloan Sports Analytics Conference, Boston, MA, USA.

Cervone, D., D'Amour, A., Bornn, L., & Goldsberry, K. (2014). *POINTWISE: Predicting Points and Valuing Decisions in Real Time With NBA Optical Tracking Data.* Paper presented at the Proceedings of the 8th MIT Sloan Sports Analytics Conference, Boston, MA, USA.

Custiss, E.T., & Eustis, S. (2015). *Sports analytics executive summary.* Wintergreen Research. Retrieved from http://www.wintergreenresearch.com/sports-analytics

Doljin, B., & Fuss, F. K. (2015). Development of a smart cricket ball for advanced performance analysis of bowling. *Procedia Technology, 20,* 133–37.

Drew, M. K., & and Finch, C. F. (2016). The relationship between training load and injury, illness and soreness: a systematic and literature review. *Sports Medicine, 46*(6), 861–883.

Gabbett, T. J. (2016). The training-injury prevention paradox: should athletes be training smarter and harder? *British Journal of Sports Medicine, 0,* 1–9.

Gabbett, T. J., Jenkins, D. G., & Abernethy, B. (2011). Physical demands of professional rugby league training and competition using microtechnology. *Journal of Science and Medicine in Sport, 15*(1), 80–85.

Gudmundsson, J., & Horton, M. (2016). Spatio–Temporal analysis of team sports–a survey. *arXiv:1602.06994*.

Gudmundsson, J., & Wolle, T. (2014). Football analysis using spatio-temporal tools. *Computers, Environment and Urban Systems, 47*, 16–27.

Hawkins, S. (2015). *Force plate metrics predictive of UCL injuries* [Blog]. Retrieved from http://spartapoint. com/2015/12/14/force-plate-metrics-predictive-of-ucl-injuries/

Hensberger, R. (2014). *How sports data analytics is upsetting the game all over again*. Retrieved from www. fastcompany.com/3033324/how-sports-data-analytics-is-upsetting-the-game-all-over-again

Horton, M., Gudmundsson, J., Chawala, S., & Estephan, J. L. (2015). A Method for analysis of passing performance in football matches. *ACM Transactions on Spatial Algorithms and Systems, 1*(1), 1–26.

Hulin, B. T., Gabbett, T. J., Lawson, D. W., Caputi, P., & Sampson, J. A. (2015). The acute: chronic workload ratio predicts injury: high chronic workload may decrease injury risk in elite rugby league players. *British Journal of Sports Medicine, 50*, 231–236. doi:10.1136/bjsports-2015-094817.

Maheswaran, R. (2015, March). *Rajiv Maheswaran: The Math Behind Basketball's Wildest Moves*. [Video File]. Retrieved from https://www.ted.com/talks/rajiv_mahreswaran_the_math_behind_basketball_s_wildest_moves? language=en

McQueen, A., Wiens, J., & Guttag, J. (2013). Automatically recognizing on-ball screens. Paper presented at the 7th MIT Sloan Sports Analytics Conference, Boston, MA, USA.

Nibali, M. L., Tombleson, T., Brady, P. H., & Wagner, P. (2015). Influence of familiarization and competitive level on the reliability of countermovement vertical jump kinetic and kinematic variables. *The Journal of Strength and Conditioning Research, 29*(10), 2827–35.

Sports Industry Statistics and Market Size Overview [Statistics Report]. (n.d.). Retrieved from https:// www.plunkettresearch.com/statistics/sports-industry

STATS LLC. (2015). SportVU. Retrieved from www.stats.com/sportvu/sportvu-basketball-media/

Tan, A. M., Fuss, F. K., Weizman, Y., & Troynikov, O. (2015). Development of a smart insole for medical and sports purposes. *Procedia Engineering, 112*, 152–56.

The Associated Press. (2016, April 2). *Putting data science on a player's sleeve*. Retrieved from www. nytimes.com/2016/04/03/sports/baseball/putting-data-science-on-a-players-sleeve.html?_r=0

The World's Highest-Paid Athletes. (2015). *Forbes*. Retrieved from http://www.forbes.com/pictures/ mli45Fdide/1-floyd-mayweather-jr#52597c946bc7

Wei, X., Lucey, P., Morgan, S., Carr, P., Reid, M., & Sridharan, S. (2015). Predicting serves in tennis using style priors. Paper presented at the 21st ACM SIGKDD International Conference on Knowledge Discovery and Data Mining, Sydney, AUS.

Wei, X., Lucey, P., Morgan, S., Reid, M., & Sridharan, S. (2016). The thin edge of the wedge: Accurately predicting shot outcomes in tennis using style and context priors. Paper presented at the 10th MIT Sloan Sports Analytics Conference, Boston, MA, USA.

Weizman, Y., & Fuss, F. K. (2015). Development of instrumented soccer footwear for kicking analysis and training purposes. *Procedia Engineering, 112*, 157–62.

4

STRATEGIC TALENT MANAGEMENT ANALYTICS

Khadija Al Arkoubi

Introduction

As the world becomes more interconnected and volatile, the organization of the twenty-first century is faced with the challenge of transforming itself into a more proactive, forward thinking and innovative entity. No organization, however, can reach this goal without its most valuable talents and without finding ways to utilize its talents' data in an effective and efficient manner.

Big data, data science, business intelligence, data mining and analytics are all concepts frequently used nowadays since they play a critical role in all domains of life from football, to consumer behavior, to talent management decisions. The power of analytics has been recognized by many professionals and academics who argued that it guides decisions, facilitates forecasting and predictions, improves practices and processes and adds value to business (Galagan, 2014; Harris, Craig, & Egan, 2010; Harris & Mehrotra, 2014).

Talent Analytics according to Harris *et al.* (2010) is a relatively new management discipline and only a few leading companies manage their talent as a strategic resource.

This chapter focuses on Strategic Talent Management Analytics (STMA). It provides first an overview of Strategic Talent Management (STM) and its evolution. Secondly, it defines analytics, describes its types and explains its growth globally. Thirdly, it explains the applications and uses of STMA in an organizational context and finishes with the implications of this discipline for the twenty-first-century organization.

What is Strategic Talent Management (STM)?

The origins of Talent Management (TM) go back to the Human Resource (HR) planning movement that emerged in the 1980s and 1990s with the hope of making staffing a strategic HR function (Scullion, Vaiman, & Collings, 2016). The focus was on recruitment, career development, talent pools and succession planning as key areas in the responsibilities of the HR strategic business partner. Progressively, talent started to be perceived as a strategic resource (Silzer & Dowell, 2010).

The concept of "Strategic Talent Management" (STM) became more known as the strategic deployment of talent by the end of the last decade (Scullion *et al.*, 2016). According to Scullion and Collings (2011), four factors helped reshape this field and increase its relevance. Firstly, the change of the global economy has led to a talent shortage globally (the war for talent). Secondly, technology has transformed our lives and the work design at global level. Thirdly, the increasing need for valuing the different types of global workforce diversity. Fourthly, the changing demographics, especially the ageing workforce that has accrued the talent scarcity in developed countries.

During the past two years, scholars have devoted a growing attention to TM and STM leading to multiple definitions of these terms (Gallardo-Gallardo & Thunnissen, 2016). In this chapter, STM is defined as "the systematic attraction, identification, development, engagement/retention and deployment of those individuals with high potential who are of particular value to an organization" (Talent Management, 2006, 2008). STM is tightly aligned with the strategic goals and values of the organization (Farndale, Scullion, & Sparrow, 2010; Kim & Scullion, 2011). It is key to competitive advantage in domestic, international and global settings. Moreover, STM is perceived here as an integrated and comprehensive framework that contributes to organizational strategic decision-making.

What is analytics?

Analytics is the analysis of data using advanced techniques and technology to derive insights that serve for better decision-making. According to Grillo and Hackett (2015), there are three types of analytics that reflect three levels of complexity and sophistication. These are: descriptive, predictive and prescriptive. Descriptive analytics, while basic and focused on the past, transforms the data into information and creates the foundation for the predictive analytics. The latter emphasizes advanced forecasting and modeling that is focused on the future. The prescriptive type is ranked at the top in terms of seeking prospection and meaningful interpretation of data that will lead to a course of actions. The following story describes the three types of analytics pre-mentioned in a simple way (Lytle, 2016):

> A consultant who worked for a multinational company on multiple varying levels of turnover, was able to determine the factors that forecasted whether an employee would leave the company and to identify how to retain him. Working on projects perceived by employees as interesting turned out to be a big motivator, so the company applied that insight to retain the employees most probably to move on.

Analytics is deemed to be the most desired technology by businesses all over the world and one of the priorities of top executives (Gartner, 2009). It relies on people skills, technologies, applications, and business processes. According to Kapoor (2010, p.21):

> The technologies and applications include data management methods for planning, collecting, storing, and structuring data into data warehouses and data marts as well as analytical tasks for querying, reporting, visualizing, generating online active reports, and running advanced analytical techniques for clustering, classification, segment-ation, and prediction. Data warehouse focuses on enterprise wide data, and data mart is restricted to a single process or a department, such as Human Resources Department.

One of the key challenges for the HR department like any other department is the explosion of data. It is in fact estimated that by 2020, the amount of data generated every year will reach 35 zettabytes (1 zettabyte = 1 billion terabytes, 1 terabyte = 1,000 gigabytes)

FORMULA FOR AN HR ANALYST

HR data analysts are hard to come by because the field is still new and the demand is high. If only HR departments could create their own data analysts.

Here's what they would need:

- Shot of statistics. Analysts need to know a regression analysis from a double-blind experiment.

- Tall tube of storytelling. What good are the numbers if you can't explain why they matter?

- Beaker of business background. If analysts don't understand how the company works and makes money, they won't ask the right questions.

- Cup of curiosity. It may kill cats, but it sure helps in thinking about what's working and what's not – and why – in a company.

- Carton of collaboration. Working with other departments in the company helps uncover workforce challenges and relevant data.

- Heaping helping of HR knowledge. Analysts need to understand what drives attraction, engagement, retention and performance management in their organization.

FIGURE 4.1 Formula for an HR analyst

Source: Lytle (2016)

(*The digital universe decade*, 2010). This exponential growth suggests a critical need for data/ HR/Talent analysts.

> "Analysts" can be defined as "workers who use statistics, rigorous quantitative or qualitative analysis, and information modeling techniques to shape and make business decisions – a broad range of activity"

(Harris et al., 2010, p.15)

In reality, a survey by Deloitte on Global Human Capital trends (2015), indicated that 35 percent of companies were already engaged in developing data analysis capabilities within HR. Yet, less than 9 percent had a good team in place.

CASE STUDY: CAN NUMBERS TELL THE WHOLE STORY ABOUT AN EMPLOYEE

Name: Brian Smith
Title: Senior Vice President of Human Resources
Current employer: A Sport Marketing Company
Brief work history: I attended Ithaca College in Ithaca, NY, as an undergraduate and was a psychology major. I knew I didn't want to get into clinical psychology but it was my senior year, so I took a course called industrial psychology and found it very interesting. As many psychology majors know, you cannot do a whole

PHOTO 4.1 Brian Smith

lot with psychology without your master's degree, so I went to Farleigh Dickinson University in New Jersey and received my master's degree in Industrial Psychology. When I graduated, I really wanted to join what was then Anderson Consulting and their change management group, but they only recruited from large schools such as Cornell and Columbia, not Farleigh Dickinson. I then was scanning the newspaper and found a posting for an HR assistant for a company in the city and realized there were a lot of similarities between HR and what I had gone to school for, so I took the position in 1999. I worked with that firm for about two years, then went to Mercer HR Consulting and did internal HR consulting for that company and learned a great deal. I then moved to Porto Novelli, which is a PR company, and was their HR manager. I moved again to a company called WRC media, which was a holding company for the *Weekly Reader* and *World Almanac*, and was their HR director. They were merged with Reader's Digest and since WRC media was a smaller company, they let us go. I then came across a posting for my current company and I had known the recruiter for some time, so I ended up here and that was about eight years ago.

The main responsibilities of my current job include: oversight of the entire HR process, which includes payroll, benefits and recruitment. There are directors of each of these areas whom report directly to me. The two areas I enjoy the most are employee relations, and specifically learning and development. Employee culture and working with international workers (Visas, etc.) are also included in my responsibilities.

How do you think data helps influence your industry segment?

I am not a traditional HR person, meaning I don't go home and study HR publications or go to a lot of Society for Human Resource Management (SHRM) meetings. My style of HR is to sit down with employees and have personal contact. Now I share this with you because I think there is a tremendous place for analytics in HR, and if you would go to a company like GE or Mackenzie, you would see a very analytics driven HR system. My current company uses a different approach to HR. We have foundations in data, but it is not as detailed as some other corporations, which makes us no less but just a bit different from the norm. We are also different because of our size; other big corporations have the resources to have very detailed analytical HR systems and processes. With that being said, there is a tremendous need and use for metrics in this segment. Specifically, metrics are used for compensation and especially when employees are up for performance reviews. Our performance reviews are done on a scale; employees can receive Met Expectations, or they can be evaluated on either side of that (Failed to Meet Expectations or Partially Met Expectations; Exceeded Expectations or Significantly Exceeded Expectations). What we have done is created a compensation structure that assigns a specific percentage based on the rating you get in your performance review. If you Met Expectations, you will typically get a 3–4 percent raise, and the rest of the percentages are based off those numbers.

Another example of where analytics is used in HR would be in recruiting practices. Throughout the year, we will go through the demographic data on recruitment and look at how many people applied to jobs, how many were interviewed, and how many were hired. Of those people interviewed and hired, how many were African American, Hispanic,

Asian, etc. We really need to keep an eye on this data and keep checking how many people are diverse. If we have 100 people apply to a job and only three are African American, it helps to tell us that we are not reaching the target market and our job listings are not getting out to a wider audience. This is important because not only do we want to do the right thing, but diversity at a company is so important for culture and business. We work a lot with brands to create a program for the end consumer, and we have to have an understanding of the general population. If we don't have employees that are from different cultures and backgrounds, we will not be able to reach certain segments and that will not make us successful marketers.

What example can you share regarding using data to help make a decision?

The issue

At our firm, we have different levels of employment. Our first level is an Account Executive, and our second is a Senior Account Executive. Within the Senior Account Executive position, there are three levels of salary ranges. If you are an Account Executive and are promoted to a Senior Account Executive, you are going to fall into the first tier of the salary range. The second tier is 1–2 years of being an SAE, and the third tier is 2–3 years of being an SAE and looking towards a higher level.

The analysis

Analytics are used during performance reviews to help decide compensation for SAEs and how they are going to move within the three salary ranges. If an AE is promoted, they are automatically going to be in the first tier of the SAE salary. Upon their performance review and based on whether they met expectations, exceeded expectations or partially met expectations, they will either stay in their salary tier or move up. This is the same for all SAEs.

The end results: Which level of compensation they will receive as well as how much percentage their raise will be pending the completion of the performance reviews.

What lesson did you learn from the process?

From this process, I learned that you need to use data and numbers to set the base for almost anything. If I am trying to initiate a program, whether it be a trainee program, a recruitment program, or a compensation program, I need to come with a proposal and that proposal needs to be steep with data and numbers. Otherwise, why am I doing this? Having data and analytics is necessary to back up claims and help explain how these things are going to benefit the company.

As it relates to using numerical metrics for candidate selection, we currently don't have a formal numerical-based rating process. In the past, I have worked for companies that have utilized such systems, but we currently don't use one. While I can see value in such systems, our approach is more than the numbers; in terms of rating each job qualification category and assigning a numerical value to it, we focus on the bigger picture and a big piece of that is cultural fit. Numbers don't always tell the entire story. Some recruiters would stay away from that statement because of the increasing demands on quantitatively proving why you did or didn't select someone. However, our approach has been a more holistic one. Certainly, we identify the key components of a job and make sure our interview process focuses on identifying if a candidate has demonstrated or has the ability to exhibit the behaviors of those key components (behavioral based interviewing), but we don't assign a numerical value. Our expectation is that our hiring teams come together after a candidate has completed the process and they openly discuss the strengths and weaknesses of a candidate and come to an agreement on which candidate will best meet the needs of the position. Again, I understand the perspective of assigning numerical value to each component of the job (including cultural fit), but our approach is more open and has strength in that the interview teams are providing their qualitative input into the decision.

Similarly, we don't have a numerical approach to our performance management process. We have a three step process whereby the focus is on making sure the employee, who is not performing up to the standards of the role, is given clear feedback on the areas of concern with specific examples. This involves two verbal discussions, the first with the manager and the employee and the second (if needed) with the manager, employee and HR. If performance doesn't improve after that, we move to a formal sit down with the manager, employee and HR during which a formal written memo is provided to the employee. At that time, the employee will have a certain amount of time to improve and if they don't, we look to terminate. Here again, we don't assign numerical weighting to the specifics of the job. Rather, we have a baseline for what we consider meeting standards for each job. Those expectations are included in the job description as well as included in documentation for each skill set level. For example, we have a clear outline of what is expected of an Account Executive for verbal communication and a clear outline for what is expected of a Senior Account Executive for verbal communication, so on and so forth for each level. These expectations are very specific and clear so that there is no question as to whether someone is meeting the expectation or not in any of those 11 skill sets. For that reason, we don't need to assign numbers to employee performance.

What suggestions do you have for students about data in your discipline?

My suggestion would be to get comfortable with numbers and understand how to read and use them. It is not uncommon for a head of HR to report to a CFO, which is actually who I report to. A CFO is very analytical, and I have had to adapt my communication style and how I approach things so that I can report it to my boss because I know what she is going to ask. When I want to give an employee a raise she is going to want to know the history behind it, what is the percentage, how long have they been there, and what level do they work at, so being able to talk numbers is extremely important. Also, being a business partner you have to know your business, which means understanding revenue and how we get it, understanding operating income before net profit and understanding taxes. I know we are talking about analytics but I am relating it to financials because a good HR person understands the business and knows that how well the business operates is going to affect the types of programs you are able to do. Being in HR you don't need to be a mathematician, but you need to understand how numbers affect your department as well as the business as a whole.

Applications of strategic talent management analytics

Leading organizations such as Google, Best Buy, Sysco, and others are progressively embracing analytics rather than relying on assumption or gut instincts to attract, retain, enhance talent engagement and improve performance across the organization (Davenport, Harris, & Shapiro, 2010). STM in these organizations relies heavily on analytics using hindsight, insight and foresight perspectives. Below, we describe how some STM practices use analytics to gain a competitive advantage.

Talent planning

Talent planning is a critical HR function since it is a systematic process by which organizations forecast their talent needs while gaining insights into the internal and the external labor environments of the organization. This practice is instrumental in identifying talent planning gaps and specifying effective strategies to avoid talent shortage or surplus.

According to Grillo and Hackett (2015), there are three steps that facilitate this process from an analytics stance:

1. Talent Data Collection and Analysis (Hindsight): Data collection and analysis, described as *"hindsight"*, enables talent analysts to develop a comprehensive understanding of the internal labor market of the organization as well as the most relevant talent practices such as attraction, hiring, development, promotion, geographic or functional assignments, mobility and retention. The data to be collected include job types, employee demographics, termination rates, transfers and recruitment strategies. The mapping of the Internal Labor Market provides a compelling picture on employee movements that serves for forecasting and discussions of talent philosophy and strategy (Shen, 2011).
2. Talent Supply and Demand Forecasting (Insight): This step is described as *"insight"* and aims at predicting the number of employees with the needed competencies for future organizational success. It also forecast if the supply will meet the organizational needs. For instance, Shen mentions Kaiser Permanente (KP), a health care provider who designed a thorough supply and demand forecast model in collaboration with the Center for Health Professions at University of California San Francisco (Shen, 2011). The new model provides flexible scenarios on the internal and the external drivers of supply and demand. To predict the number of pharmacists needed, KP conducted analytics using pharmacy operations data of the numbers of prescriptions filled.

"The firm made assumptions based on demographics of patient age and acuity, and patient population growth. The pharmacy forecast then factored in trend data about how prescriptions for medications are filled and delivered, in-person versus mailed, big-box store versus hospital or local pharmacy. The large health care provider also factored in improvements in business systems, team staffing and the new mail-order process." (Shen, 2011, p.55)

3. Predictive Talent Analytics (Foresight): This step results in educated predictions in areas like future talent acquisition, performance (based on past behaviors and trends), retention, motivation, etc. The upcoming two decades in the US will witness the retirement of millions of baby boomers who will be replaced by a cohort of millennials. This cohort will assume different jobs requiring different competencies. Talent acquisition teams are making industry employment predictions using five and ten years projections to assess if the current market will offer sustainable talent pipelines (Ferguson, 2015). The results of predictive talent analytics can inform training, development and education programs needed to prepare the millennials for the next stage of their lives and the companies for the challenges of the future.

The role of predicative talent analytics in organizations can be drastic. Ferguson (2015, p.39) reports that "Johnson & Johnson reversed a three-year policy of favoring experienced candidates over recent college graduates." The company falsely believed that it would be hard to retain new graduates and that they may not perform as well as employees with experience. Nonetheless, the analysis of data pertaining to nearly 47,000 employees showed that recent graduates' performance was as good as the group with a few years of experience and that they tend to stay longer than the comparative group.

Interestingly enough, predictive analytics revealed that hiring policies that eliminate job hoppers or applicants with employment gaps on their resumes are misleading and have no impact on the talent pool (Ferguson, 2015).

Talent engagement and retention

Analytics are heavily used to predict turnover, engagement and retention strategies. For instance, a company in China, after analyzing past employee turnover data, found out that compensation was not the primary reason of turnover. Instead the company needed to focus on retention initiatives with high impact (Grillo & Hackett, 2015).

Also, Davenport *et al.* (2010, p.5) reported that Google's vice president of people operations, Laszlo Bock, said "It's not the company-provided lunch that keeps people here. Googlers tell us that there are three reasons they stay: the mission, the quality of the people, and the chance to build the skill set of a better leader or entrepreneur. And all our *analytics* are built around these reasons."

Another company cited by Davenport *et al.* (2010) is JetBlue. This organization has initiated employee-satisfaction metrics around its talent's willingness to recommend the company as a place to work and is monitoring employee engagement monthly. Hence, this approach is serving JetBlue's organizational reputation well. It has also used metrics to examine compensation changes and calculate executive bonuses. Employees are asked annually on their hiring date if they would recommend the company, so JetBlue can effectively monitor employee engagement monthly.

In the same vein, the adoption of analytics by Sysco enabled managers to enhance retention especially among delivery associates whose retention rate moved from 65 to 85 percent, saving the company close to $50 million in hiring and training costs.

Similarly, Cognizant, a US-based professional services firm with many employees in India, conducted an analysis of social media contributions, particularly blogs. It discovered that bloggers were more engaged and satisfied than others and performed about 10 percent better, on average (Davenport *et al.*, 2010).

HR analytics can also be used for numerous areas around engagement or termination. For example, what if employees were falsifying records or incorrectly documenting sales in order to increase their commission? Through analytics, employment fraud and mistakes, which can be very costly from both a business and regulatory perspective, can be spotted. Health clubs have regularly examined the issue of whether fitness trainers should be classified as independent contractors or employees. The difference might seem minimal, but the cost and legal challenges are very significant when workers' compensation, taxes, and other issues are examined.

CASE STUDY: CATCHING MANAGERIAL ISSUES USING ANALYTICS

Name: Brian Anderson, JD, MBA
Title: Chief Human Resources Officer
Current employer: ECP-PF Holdings, Inc.
Brief work history: I graduated from law school and moved to Boston to oversee Parent and Youth Services for the Urban League of Eastern Massachusetts, where I cut my teeth in Human Services and Human Resources. After completing my MBA I spent time working in Human Resources for Stop and Shop Supermarkets in Massachusetts; Top's Markets, in Buffalo, New York; for two hospitals in the Kaleida Health system in Western New York and Duke University Hospital in Durham, North Carolina.

PHOTO 4.2
Brian Anderson

In my recent role as the Chief Human Resources Officer for a private equity company operating in four different states and Canada with 650 plus employees, there are several data requirements that I have to maintain in my role to ensure the legal obligations regarding employment are met in order to safeguard the organization. The myriad of labor law requirements associated with the employer/employee relationship that are fraught with data obligations that I have to juggle in this role include the following:

- providing the Federal Office of Child Support Enforcement data on each employee to ensure child support regulations are met;
- maintaining health and wellness benefits for all employees whether new or experiencing a qualifying event;

- ensuring that all eligible full-time employees, as outlined by the Affordable Care Act, are offered benefits and that whether they accepted or waived benefits is documented;
- maintaining recruitment, onboarding and orientation process for all employees aligned with specific pay scales and each state's minimum wage.

The field of Human Resources is a highly regulated profession as Federal and State agencies outline rules and regulations for the management of employees making the maintenance of data vital.

How do you think data helps influence your industry segment?

Human Resource professionals think of the process that begins with recruiting to the conclusion of the employee's tenure as moving across a lifecycle: the Lifecycle of the Employee. The lifecycle of an employee involves the following stages: Recruitment and Selection, Orientation and Onboarding, Training – Development and Performance Management.

Recruitment and Selection

The Recruitment and Selection process is not only the starting point to ensuring the creation of a strong team of employees, but it is also burdened with regulations and the need to ensure that data is utilized to validate consistency in decisions. The major concern during the recruitment and selection stage is that of consistency throughout the process. Inconsistency in the hiring and recruitment process could create liability for an organization. Maintenance of data is vital to ensure consistency. Ensuring that all applicants are asked the same questions and endure the same application and hiring process while maintaining the data and documents associated with the process are key.

Orientation and Onboarding

The Orientation and Onboarding process for new employees is the process of creating a connection with new employees that builds engagement and creates employees who can be productive quicker. Orientation is normally a one to two day process where the new employee is presented with a myriad of data that includes information on benefits, parking, employee perks and the history of the organization. Onboarding, however, is the process that lasts for a year that involves acculturation. During the onboarding process, the gathering of data on new employees is essential in the prevention of costly employee turnover. Gathering data from your new employees during their 30, 60 and 90 days along with constant feedback during the first year, is crucial in the onboarding process for new employees.

Training – Development and Performance Management

Training and Development and Performance Management are important aspects in any organization as they are the tools necessary to create the next level of talent in successor planning. While it is a choice for companies to search for new employees from outside of the company, there is considerable value for companies to choose to promote qualified current employees into vacant positions. In order to objectively select those internal employees who would be a good fit for a position in the organization, the data gathered through utilization of metrics is analyzed to measure employee performance.

Companies that utilize a performance management process in conjunction with promotional guidelines, will often create metrics to gauge employee performance in accordance with success in next level roles. The data that is extrapolated to measure success is so important in validating decisions around selection, possibly limiting potential claims of nepotism or favoritism in the process.

The reliance on data, as well as the maintenance of the data within performance management, is not only vital when it comes to promotions, but also key in confirming demotions and terminations. Here the federal rules and state regulations are robust to ensure that employees are not terminated wrongfully based on any of the protected classes of Title VII of the Civil Rights Act of 1964 (race or color, national origin, sex and religion). Maintaining accurate data while managing employee performance can refute the claim that an employee was terminated for any other reason than poor performance.

What example can you share regarding using data to help make a decision?

I will examine my role in Human Resources and the myriad of employee issues and concerns that I have been privy to over the many years that I have served in the profession. The topic that I will choose a case study from is the area of time and attendance and the responsibility of accurately managing employee time and paying accordingly.

The issue

The Fair Labor Standards Act (FLSA) provides the following: Covered, nonexempt employees must receive overtime pay for hours worked over 40 per work week (any fixed and regularly recurring period of 168 hours – seven consecutive 24-hour periods) at a rate not less than one and one-half times the regular rate of pay. There is no limit on the number of hours employees 16 years or older may work in any workweek. The FLSA does not require overtime pay for work on weekends, holidays, or regular days of rest, unless overtime is worked on such days (www.dol.gov/whd/flsa/).

The Federal Government takes the accurate documentation of time worked and compensation related to the amount of work completed by employees very seriously. Some recent legal cases that exemplify the gravity of altering time otherwise not compensating employees for work completed include:

- In Personette v. UPS approximately 1,100 Washington State package car drivers won $12 million in a case involving unpaid work off the clock, mostly during their one-hour lunch.

- Four thousand Illinois UPS package car drivers won $7.25 million in back pay (and would have won much more but old-guard Teamsters joined the trucking industry in obtaining the repeal of state law overtime rights of truck drivers!).
- Local 556 production workers at IBP won a $3.1 million FLSA and state law judgment, which both sides have appealed to the Ninth Circuit Court of Appeals. Many workers will recover $3,000 to $11,000 if the trial court's judgment is affirmed on appeal.
- New Jersey Pepsi Teamsters won big last year when the New Jersey Supreme Court affirmed a lower court ruling that route drivers were not sales personnel and therefore not exempt from overtime provisions. Over 400 Local 125 members will be awarded a multi-million dollar settlement.
- Non-union workers are also using the FLSA and state law to take on major corporations. Two thousand Taco Bell workers recovered $3 million in Washington State for off-the-clock work following a jury verdict that the company cheated workers.
- Wal-Mart faces 39 class action lawsuits involving hundreds of thousands of workers seeking tens of millions of dollars. The company reportedly paid $50 million two years ago to settle an off-the-clock lawsuit covering 69,000 workers in Colorado, and it recently settled for $500,000 in a case involving 120 workers in Gallup, N. M. (www.tdu.org/resources/workers-win-millions-wage-and-hour-lawsuits).

Each of these legal cases and all others brought forward have one similar underlying aspect: the employee bears the burden of proof to show that the employer did not accurately compensate the employee for all work performed. The employer, however, has the responsibility of maintaining employee data to include time worked and wages. With this responsibility, the opportunity for the employer to practice "time-shaving" or altering employee time worked in order to avoid paying overtime can easily be performed.

The analysis

In my experience in my roles in Human Resources, I have had the opportunity of having to deal with the issue of managers altering time, whether intentional or not, to meet budgetary payroll concerns. One incident in particular involved a manager who, in order to meet payroll projections, would allegedly deduct hours the employees worked that would constitute overtime. The issue I had to address was whether or not the deductions were intentional or was there another reason for the modifications.

The law cited (p. 86) clearly indicates that an employee is to be compensated for all time they have performed work and the case law mentioned above exemplifies the ramifications for not following the laws outlined by the FLSA. In order to make a determination as to the validity of the alleged time infractions and the intent of the manager, it was imperative to review several different data points.

Of these data points, the following were vital:

- employee approved time adjustments;
- electronic time cards of all employees especially those who worked overtime;

- number of times and when the manager made adjustments;
- signed policies and training regarding time keeping.

Once all of the data was gathered, it was then necessary to lay out each piece of data and match each piece by each employee in order to ascertain the magnitude of the problem to see who was impacted and how much. The process of aligning each employee with their respective data was a time-consuming, laborious process as the work required detail and accuracy.

The good thing about the data, however, was that it was very "clean" data in that it was all extracted from the time and attendance electronic source so the data did not contain any other information other than the time punches and the adjustments made by the manager that either contained employee approval of the adjustments or not.

The end result

After reviewing all of the information it was determined that the manager had actually manipulated time in order to prevent the employee from receiving overtime. It was discovered that this practice had not only occurred to the employee who initially brought the issue forward, but to several employees who had not realized the deceit that was occurring.

It was clear that it was necessary to review the data and endure the process as what seemed to be an impact to one employee was actually a much larger issue that included employees that had subsequently left the organization.

What lesson did you learn from the process?

The lesson learned from the process was the fact that data in any form can be vast and overwhelming, but with a well-structured process the data can be broken down to just the relevant information needed to solve the problem presented.

What suggestions do you have for students about data in your discipline?

Human Resources data encompasses a wide variety of topics from payroll, retention, turnover, benefits and more. There are times in a Human Resource Professional's career that these areas all coincide in a situation requiring an immeasurable amount of data to be gathered. My suggestion for students regarding data in Human Resources is to take a moment to outline processes to handle large amounts of data and make sure to stay focused on the area that has brought the problem forward so that you are not caught floundering in erroneous data.

Implications of STMA for the twenty-first-century organization

Now that we recognize the critical importance of STMA in shaping the destiny of organizations, what can we do to build analytics capabilities and develop analytical talent?

The McKinsey Global Institute (2015) estimates that by 2018, the US economy will have a shortage of 140,000 to 190,000 people with analytical expertise and a shortfall of another 1.5 million managers and analysts with the skills to understand and make decisions.

In line with this finding, Ransbotham, Kiron, and Prentice (2015, p.3) quote Mathew Chacko, an IT executive at Coca-Cola, who describes his company's need to transform a gap in data skills into an organizational capability:

> We need people who are interested in data discovery – really willing to work with messy data and different sets of data – to find insights and create recommendation engines or predictor models that can have a life of their own. I would love to have that capability within the organization.

Equally, most executives are aware of the need for Analysts and Data Scientists. More importantly, nine in ten CEOs expect human resources leaders to be proficient in workforce analytics. More than half (57 percent) said providing actionable human capital data was a key to developing broader HR influence within the organization (Ferguson, 2015). Therefore, embracing a talent management approach to HR/Talent Analysts, Data Scientists and similar profiles becomes necessary. Moreover, universities and educational institutions need to contribute to the development of talents with core competencies in HR analytics and data science.

References

Davenport, T. H., Harris, J., & Shapiro. J. (2010, October). Competing on talent analytics. *Harvard Business Review,* 1–6.

Farndale, E., Scullion, H., & Sparrow, P. (2010). The role of the corporate human resource function in global talent management. *Journal of World Business, 45*(2), 161–68.

Ferguson, M. (2015). The argument: Recruiting by numbers. *Workforce, 94*(9), 36–39.

Galagan, P. (2014). HR gets analytical. *T+D, 68*(3), 22–25.

Gallardo-Gallardo, E., & Thunnissen, M. (2016). Standing on the shoulders of giants? A critical review of empirical talent management research. *Employee Relations, 38*(1), 31–56.

Gartner. (2009, February 18). *Business intelligence ranked top technology priority by CIOs for fourth year in a row.* Retrieved from www.gartner.com/newsroom/id/888412

Global human capital trends 2015: Leading in the new world of work. (2015). Deloitte University Press.

Grillo, M., & Hackett, A. (2015). *What types of predictive analytics are being used in talent management organizations?* Retrieved from http://digitalcommons.ilr.cornell.edu/student/74

Harris, J., & Mehrotra, V. (2014). Getting value from your data scientists. *MIT Sloan Management Review, 56*(1), 14–18.

Harris, J., Craig, E., & Egan, H. (2010). How successful organizations strategically manage their analytic talent. *Strategy & Leadership, 38*(3), 15–22.

Kapoor, B. (2010). Business intelligence and its use for human resource management. *The Journal of Human Resource and Adult Learning, 6*(2), 21–30.

Kim, C. K., & Scullion, H. (2011). Exploring the links between corporate social responsibility and global talent management: A comparative study of the UK and Korea. *European Journal of International Management, 5*(5), 501-523.

Lytle, T. (2016, February). The growing demand for HR analysts, *HR Magazine.* Retrieved from www.shrm.org/publications/hrmagazine/editorialcontent/2016/0216/pages/0216-hr-analysts. aspx#sthash.CVmEI8OR.dpuf

McKinsey Global Institute (n.d.). Deep analytical talent: Where are they now? Retrieved from www. mckinsey.com/features/big_data

Ransbotham, S., Kiron, D., & Prentice, P. K. (2015, April). The talent dividend: Analytics talent is driving competitive advantage at data-oriented companies. *MIT Sloan Management Review.* Retrieved from http://sloanreview.mit.edu/projects/analytics-talent-dividend/

Scullion, H., & Collings, D. G. (2011). *Global Talent Management.* New York: Routledge.

Scullion, H., Vaiman, V., & Collings, D. (2016). Guest editorial. *Employee Relations, 38*(1). doi: 10.1108/er-11-2015-0203.

Shen, K. (2011). The analytics of critical talent management. *People and Strategy, 34,* 50–56.

Silzer, R., & Dowell, B. E. (Eds.). (2010). Strategic talent management matters, in R. Silzer and B. E. Dowell (Eds.), *Strategy – driven talent management: A leadership imperative* (pp. 3–72). San Francisco, CA: Josey Bass.

Talent management: Understanding the dimensions. (2006). Chartered Institute of Personnel and Development. Retrieved from http://www.cipd.co.uk/NR/rdonlyres/6101AA06-F0C7-4073-98DA-758E91C718FC/0/3832Talentmanagement.pdf

Talent management: An overview. (2008). Chartered Institute of Personnel and Development. Retrieved from http://www.cipd.co.uk/hr-resources/factsheets/talent-management-overview.aspx

The digital universe decade – are you ready? [Report] (2010, May). International Data Corporation. Retrieved from https://www.emc.com/collateral/analyst-reports/idc-digital-universe-are-you-ready.pdf

5

ANALYTICS IN SPORT MARKETING

Ceyda Mumcu

The use of analytics has been growing throughout the sport industry. The general population is most familiar with performance analytics due to Michael Lewis' famous book *Moneyball* and media outlets' focus on player statistics and its use in player drafts, game analyses, and fantasy leagues. Similarly, General Managers and executives primarily focus on performance analytics due to the emphasis on winning on the field or court. However, today there are other high-stakes issues on the table for the executives of sport teams. The sport industry has become very saturated, and without an on-going winning streak, customer loyalty, strong attendance and high revenues are not guaranteed. Business analytics has become an important tool in managing sport teams and leagues more effectively. Within this category, marketing applications receive the most attention. Ticket sales, ticket pricing, fan experience, fan loyalty, campaign management and sponsorship sales are the areas that benefited from analytics the most (Davenport, 2014; King, 2015). With this chapter, we will take a closer look into using analytics in managing fan relationship, evaluation of promotional campaigns, ticket pricing, and finally sponsorship sales. The chapter will begin with a brief history of market research in the sport marketing field to demonstrate where we came from and continue with the current use of analytics in the field.

Development of market research in sport

Sport teams, leagues and events have conducted market research for decades for a variety of reasons. Historically, market research was conducted by a third-party vendor as an occasional project when sport organizations needed answers. For example, during the 1997–98 season, the NBA wanted to understand who their fans were, and with the help of a third-party vendor in-arena surveys were administered to develop a fan profile. Based on the results, the NBA had a clear picture of what their fans looked like in terms of gender (68 percent male), age (average age of 38), marital status (65 percent married), education level (64 percent college graduate) and household income (average of $72,400) ("Warriors Demographics," 1998). As the sport industry grew, sport organizations started to hire market researchers in-house. In addition to the demographic profile of fans, sport teams evaluated different facets of events and facilities with the goal of improving fan experience. For example, the New England Patriots administered surveys to evaluate concessions, parking, personnel, bathroom cleanliness and other factors at every home game to improve fan experience (Davenport & Harris, 2007). Other major league teams also conduct market research in-house. However, not all teams have access to the same resources. Therefore, league offices also provides support to its teams in market research. One of the greatest examples is the NBA's Team Marketing and Business Operations (TMBO) division, which was launched in 2000 (Lombardo, 2013b). The market researchers within TMBO assist NBA, WNBA and D-League teams with research on various areas including but not limited to ticketing research, sponsorship research, and PR impression measurement research (Mullin, Hardy, & Sutton, 2014). In recent years, the sport industry has been utilizing market research more frequently to drive business decisions. Technological developments have improved the data collection capabilities of sport organizations and resulted in an increase in volume and variety of data available. Today, sport organizations with an analytical mindset have customer relationship management (CRM) systems and a data-warehouse. They use advanced analyses to gain insights about their customers and the market, to make informed decisions, and to maximize the performance and efficiency of their marketing activities.

Customer analytics in sport

The goal of marketing in spectator sports is to attract individuals to games and events. A general misconception is confusing fandom with guaranteed repeat consumption. It is undeniable that there are many individuals who identify themselves as sport fans today whether they are fans of a specific team, a specific sport or an athlete. In fact, a recent online survey revealed that 65 percent of adults in the US and 38 percent globally are NFL fans (Mander, 2015). Similarly, European football, especially the English Premier League, Spanish La Liga and German Bundesliga, have a large global following. In 2011, Manchester United Football Club had 354 million fans, worldwide, according to German SPORT+MRKT (O'Connor, 2011). However, being a fan does not convert these individuals into loyal attendees. Today, there are many more ways to consume your beloved sport team's games or any sporting event than ever before. Each unsold ticket to a sport event and an empty seat at a sport facility are lost revenues. The ultimate challenge of sport marketers is converting fans into long-term loyal customers. In this process, sport marketers compete for fans' limited discretionary income as one of many entertainment options, and fans' loyalty to their team should not be taken for granted. Sport fans will attend games and/or events only if attending benefits them, and fulfills their wants and needs. In order to convert fans into long-term repeat customers, sport organizations need to have a deeper understanding of their fans' wants and needs, and present a willingness to fulfill those needs, consistently (Jobber & Fahy, 2012).

Successful sport organizations understand the importance of fans and practice customer relationship management (CRM) as a business philosophy. This can be defined as "a company's goals can be best achieved through identification and satisfaction of the customers' stated and unstated needs and wants" (Customer Relationship Management, n.d.). In 2014, more than 75 percent of all NBA teams had a CRM system, and every major league sport team in the US was expected to have a CRM system within a couple years (Zeppenfeld, 2014). CRM systems provide a comprehensive view of an organization's customer base via information technology systems (Zikmund, McLeod, & Gilbert, 2003), and allow organizations to engage with their customers effectively by sending the right message, to the right person, at the right time via the right platform (Green, 2015).

In sport industry, CRM systems gather information on customers at every possible touch point, and data is used to direct a sport team's relationship with its customers, building a loyal fan base, and increasing sales, and therefore revenues (Sutton, 2013). The English Premier League's Manchester City Football Club (MCFC) performs customer-based, data driven marketing successfully. The club provides its supporters with member cards called "Clever Cards" to be used to enter the stadium, buy tickets, make purchases at the stadium, and so on. Furthermore, their stadium has a system with RFID tag readers, which interacts with the Clever Cards and gathers fan data throughout their visit to the stadium. The data is stored in their CRM system simultaneously and allows MCFC to understand their fans in great detail. The club uses the insights derived from data analyses to engage with their fans, build deeper long-term relationships and add value (Skalli, 2012). The benefits one can gain from customer analytics are dependent on what data is available. It is important to invest in CRM systems, gathering data on fans at every opportunity, and building a data-warehouse. However, not all sport organizations have the resources to invest or conditions to implement a system. For instance, a team might be renting a municipal sport arena for its games, and WiFi and tracking systems might not be available. Similarly, promotion-led sports are less suitable to have a CRM system as they deal with organizing events at different locations for first time customers. Today, sport organizations might have access to big data or niche data, or might not have a tool to collect systematic data at all. Regardless of having or not having a CRM and information system, traditional market research methods, such as questionnaires, focus groups and interviews, continue to provide data and support marketing efforts of sport organizations. No matter what the source is, data creates value and analytics provide insights to the sport organizations.

Sport organizations can perform an array of customer analytics based on the marketing objectives set by the organization. Think about a case where a sport team's marketing objective is to increase fan base by 5 percent at the end of the upcoming season. How could you achieve this objective? One can possibly acquire new customers or focus on retaining more customers. If you choose to acquire new customers, you will need to identify potential customers and their needs, design your marketing campaigns and promotions in a relevant way and deliver your message via the right channel. If you choose to retain more customers, you will need to identify the value of your current customers, and retain the valuable customers and upsell or cross-sell the less valuable customers to increase their value to your organization. Normally sport organizations will target both current and prospective customers at the same time, though with different campaigns and approaches. Sport organizations with an analytical mindset and a working CRM system could reach all of this information via customer analytics and design their marketing activities accordingly.

Customer value estimation

Professional sport teams often interact with thousands of customers on and off season. However, not all fans are equally profitable to the teams. Usually, a small portion of existing customers generate more revenue than most other customers. In the industry this is known as the 80–20 rule which indicates that 80 percent of consumption/revenue comes from

20 percent of the consumers. Obviously, some customers are more valuable to an organization than others, and it is important to retain these customers. For that reason, customer value estimation (CVE) is one of the most important customer analytics in sport industry. The CVE is especially useful to sport organizations, if one or more of the following conditions are present (Laursen, 2011):

1. The average earnings per customer are declining for the organization.
2. The organization is not aware of which customers or segments are profitable.
3. The organization wants to focus on retaining the most valuable customers.
4. The organization wants to acquire new customers who will be valuable.

Customer value is estimated as the difference between earnings per customer and cost of acquisition per customer. Customer earnings are calculated based on the average earnings per period and the length of relationship between the customer and the sport team, which is known as customer lifetime.

CVE = Total Earnings per Customer − Acquisition Cost per Customer

Total Earnings per Customer = Average earnings per period × number of periods

Essentially, marketing strategies rely on this valuation. Sport organizations should focus their attention on retaining the most valuable customers, and targeting less valuable fans with upselling and cross-selling to grow their value to the organization. This idea is closely linked to the fan escalator concept which is a graphical representation of consumers based on their involvement with a sport organization. The most involved fans are at the top steps, medium involved fans are in the middle section, and the least involved (or completely uninvolved fans) are at the base or just getting on the escalator. The fan escalator suggests retaining avid fans high on the escalator and moving casual fans up on the escalator to higher involvement levels, and then allocating resources to acquiring new customers (Mullin *et al.*, 2014). The reason behind this strategy is explained by the "propensity of loyal customers to spend more with the organization and the decreased cost of serving such customers" (Jobber & Fahy, 2012, p.185).

As an outcome of customer value estimations, some sport organizations have developed membership programs to reward their valuable fans. The New York Mets created the Amazin' Mets Perks program that provides a variety of benefits to their season ticket holders. The goal of the membership programs is to demonstrate the value of being a season ticket holder via exclusive benefits that are not available to others. According to Mark Bradley, founder of the Fan Experience Company, making season ticket holders feel valued is extremely important in retaining them as loyal fans and increasing their lifetime as customers (MacGregor, 2015). In addition to membership programs, sport organizations invest in customer loyalty programs as a way of increasing customer value and rewarding loyalty. Loyalty programs aim to grow and retain the best customers. The more a customer uses their loyalty card, the more points he or she collects, and as a result more perks become available. While the loyalty programs encourage less valuable fans to increase their frequency of purchase, they also benefit sport organizations by tracking buying habits of the card users. Knowing what is important to sport fans allows sport organizations to be relevant and meet the customer expectations.

Propensity models

At this point, the importance of retaining profitable fans and increasing the value of less profitable fans is obvious. Based on the customer value estimation formula, three ways of increasing customer value are reducing the acquisition cost, increasing sales to the customer and increasing the customer's lifetime. It is known that servicing existing customers is less costly than acquiring new customers. As stated in Mullin *et al.* (2014), "replacing a customer costs up to five times more than servicing an existing customer" (p. 220). In addition, an increase in sales is more likely to be achieved by increasing the frequency of sales to existing customers rather than acquiring new customers. Both of these marketing principles emphasize the importance of current customers and retaining them. However, even if an organization is very successful in providing relevant promotions and creating value to its fans, some of the fans will discontinue their relationship with the sport organization. Knowing whether your current fans are likely to renew or discontinue their season ticket holder status or knowing that they are undecided is very helpful in communicating with them in a timely fashion and possibly convincing them to continue their purchase.

Sport organizations use propensity models to predict their fans' future behavior. A propensity model is a statistical analysis of customers, and it relies on extensive information about the customers such as who they are, what they buy and how they buy (Pardes, 2014). An algorithm compares a customer to many other former customers, and predicts the customer's likelihood to perform different behaviors that are being researched. For example, Major League Baseball's San Diego Padres utilize a retention model to predict the season ticket holders' likelihood of renewing their tickets for the next season. Their model is built based on the activities of current season ticket holders such as number of tickets, usage rate, and number of years purchasing tickets (i.e. lifetime). The algorithm calculates a propensity score for each season ticket holder ranging from 1 to 10; 1 being least likely to renew and 10 being most likely to renew. As season ticket holders with high and low propensity scores are likely to have made their decision, Padres' sales team focuses their attention to fence-sitters who are season ticket holders with mid-range propensity scores. Contacting these individuals with relevant offers increases their likelihood to stay with the organization and extends their lifetime as season ticket holders. With this model, the Padres increase the efficiency of their sales team, prioritize leads, and increase their retention rate (National Sports Forum, 2013). Similar models were implemented by many teams in the NBA, NFL, and MLS, and proved to be valuable. The New England Patriots' retention model resulted in 97 percent renewal of season tickets in the 2010 season (Davenport, 2014). Of course, having a winning team can significantly increase renewal rates.

Segmentation

Throughout this chapter, the importance of understanding customers and targeting them with relevant marketing tactics were emphasized repeatedly. Considering the large number of sport consumers, it should be obvious that not every individual consumes sports, whether as a spectator or a participant, for the same reason. In order to fulfill customers' wants and needs, sport organizations segment the market. The goal is to not treat all fans as if they are alike, and to develop targeted marketing tactics for each segment (Davenport, 2014).

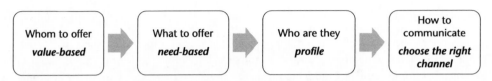

FIGURE 5.1 Sequence of analytics

Segmentation is "a process of dividing a large, heterogeneous market into more homo-genous groups of people, who have similar wants, needs, or demographic profiles, to whom a product may be targeted" (Mullin *et al.*, 2014, p.114). The two most common ways to segment a market are value-based segmentation and need-based segmentation. The value-based segmentation divides current customers into segments based on the value they create for an organization (Laursen, 2011). The customer value estimation section discussed how to estimate customers' value for a sport organization and presented examples of how sport organizations target their profitable and less profitable fans accordingly. This is an example of value-based segmentation. Retaining and increasing the lifetime of the most valuable fans, and growing the value of less profitable fans are strategies relying on value-based seg-mentation and the tactics associated with each are the examples of how value-based segmentation was utilized by marketing departments.

The need-based segmentation is "a categorization of customers with similar buying criteria which could be based on price or product features" (Laursen, 2011, p.15). This type of segmentation requires data on customers' transactions. With almost two thirds of ticket sales occurring online (Guilfoyle, 2015), and with the integration of ticket cards, loyalty cards, and RFID chips, today's sport organizations can track sport fans' purchase habits in great detail. The availability of data allows sport organizations to conduct a cluster analysis, which groups customers with similar consumption patterns into subgroups and identifies the number of these homogenous subgroups within data (Laursen, 2011). As the segments are identified, analysts examine the consumption pattern to understand the underlying customer needs for the specific consumption pattern. Once the buying pattern and the need behind the behavior are understood, marketing activities are tailored accordingly to emphasize the feature that will fulfill the need behind the behavior.

Manchester City Football Club implements need-based segmentation successfully. As mentioned earlier in this chapter, MCFC has a rigorous data tracking and a CRM system. With the extensive amount of data collected on fans and their transactions over time, the club identified 33 segments and developed accurate descriptions of each segment (Skalli, 2012). This allows the club to understand the needs of their fan segments. However, targeting all 33 segments would be too expensive. The goal is not only to understand the fans and grow fan segments, but also to grow the profitable fan segments. Sport organizations incorporate customer value estimations into need-based segmentation. In other words, they identify the return on investment (ROI) of each segment to the organization, and target the valuable fan segments with marketing activities tailored to fulfill their needs. The success of these marketing activities is evaluated periodically to examine if the valuable fan segments are satisfied and expanding.

Major League Soccer's (MLS) segmentation method and the marketing efforts built upon it are great examples to demonstrate. The MLS divides its fans into groups based on their past consumption habits and its value, and their interest in the MLS and its teams.

The fans are grouped based on their usage rate and the value generated by it. In addition, fans' interest in the MLS and its teams are incorporated into the segments to have a clear understanding of fans' needs. Based on this understanding, the MLS provides the fan segments different promotions and different loyalty programs with various benefits based on the segments' needs and the level of involvement (Shin, 2014).

Customer profiling

After identifying the value of segments and describing the buying patterns, the next step is profiling the segments. Customer profiling is creating a portrait/persona for your existing customers by adding demographic, geographic, psychographic and behavioral variables ("What is customer profiling," n.d.). Upon completion of customer profiling, a 360-view of existing customers by segments becomes available including who the customers are, their lifestyle preferences, what they care about, why they consume your product, how they consume, and how much they consume.

Sport organizations can benefit from customer profiling in two ways: 1) by increasing sales to and value of the existing customer, and 2) by generating leads and acquiring new customers, which will be discussed in next section. As stated earlier in the chapter, an increase in sales is more likely to come from existing customers. Knowing what each fan segment looks like and why they attend and/or view sporting events provides advantages to marketers in targeting existing customers. Due to the in-depth understanding of existing fans, marketers can develop specific offers, tailored promotions and marketing campaigns that will fulfill fans' needs and expectations and will increase the volume and frequency of sales. For example, a sport team might identify a long-term, mid-value casual fan segment that is made up of young professionals who are attending several games per season to socialize with friends and have a good time. Due to being long-term frequent attendees, this segment might have potential to upsell. This segment could be targeted with a campaign introducing a new lounge providing opportunities to socialize at the games which comes with a membership to a loyalty program provided by the best fitting sponsor. With the campaign, the sport organization could communicate the added value to the experience and encourage them to attend more frequently.

Customer acquisition

As discussed previously, acquiring new customers is more costly than marketing to existing customers. However, some of the existing customers will churn (not renew) regardless of the success of the sport organization on and off the field. Therefore, sport organizations are always tasked with acquiring new customers. The organization's understanding of existing customers in terms of what they look like, what their needs are, and the value they provide to the organization are of great value to the sales and marketing department. In this section, some of the best ways of acquiring new customers, how to improve the acquisition process and how to track the quality of new customers per campaign will be discussed.

One of the tools utilized in customer acquisition is look-alike modeling. These models are used to build a larger customer base from smaller segments to create reach for marketers (Kaye, 2013). Analysts identify what their most valuable customer segment looks like, and the sales and marketing team target their acquisition efforts to the prospects that resemble the existing valuable customers based on benchmark characteristics. The MLS develops look-alike models to portray a persona of its fans to use in lead generation. Data of prospects that resemble MLS' current fans are purchased from a third party and then these prospects are targeted for first-time sales.

Another tool used in customer acquisition is lead scoring models. Lead scoring models calculate the potential of leads in converting them into customers. Calculations are done based on criteria determined by evaluating the characteristics of the current customer-base; ranging from demographics to buyer behavior to user activity ("Measure the quality," n.d.). The purpose of lead scoring is to identify prospects who are more likely to become paying customers; therefore to utilize sales force and other resources effectively in new customer acquisition. The San Diego Padres have a lead scoring model based on existing fans' demographics. They profile their current fans and target prospects that look like their current fans. Other sport organizations might input more than demographics in their lead scoring models based on the availability of data and the model they choose to build in lead scoring.

While look-alike and lead scoring models allow sport organizations to identify leads with higher propensity, conversion of leads into fans is not guaranteed. In addition, growing a new fan base that doesn't turn into repeat customers doesn't hold a great value to sport organizations. By evaluating previous marketing campaigns, sport organizations can identify the campaigns with higher conversion rates, and also the campaigns that acquired customers who have become loyal fans. By calculating customer value estimates and customer lifetime per campaign, analysts identify which campaigns acquired long-term customers with higher value to the organization. As prospects do not only look like current fans, but are also expected to consume like current fans, repeating the campaigns with higher customer lifetime and value estimates will reach prospects who are more likely to become valuable fans.

For example, assume that a sport team rolled out two marketing campaigns. The first campaign gave a discount to first-time attendees both on tickets and concession items. As a result of this campaign, the team had 1,000 new attendees at its game. However, only 1 percent of these first-time attendees returned to any games the following weeks. The second campaign provided a one-hour training session to an individual, whether an adult or a child, with a coach and a player at the team's facilities, and resulted in 600 new attendees at its game with an 80 percent return rate. As a result, the second campaign reached to the first-time customers who are more valuable to your organization when compared with the first campaign. Knowing the outcome of a campaign from a value-segmentation perspective allows the organization to repeat similar campaigns. Profiling these first-time attendees, and also your most valuable segment, would give a profile for the ideal customers to go after with the advertising campaigns.

Sport organizations task their sales staff with acquiring new fans on a daily basis. At some of the MLS teams, for example, sales personnel are only responsible for first time sales, and their fan relationship department handles the renewals. For MLS teams and other organizations with similar structure, customer acquisition is very important. And in this process customer profiling for existing segments, look-alike models and propensity models would be of great value. By looking at what the prospect looks like, a sales person would know which fan segment the person might belong to and approach the prospect accordingly. Understanding how to acquire new customers effectively is invaluable for sport organizations and of utmost importance to sales personnel.

Campaign evaluations

Marketing campaigns are vehicles, which might include promotions, advertisements and a variety of digital marketing components, designed to communicate with a market and position a brand in a certain way, and to generate leads and increase sales. In sport industry marketing campaigns, promotions have often relied on traditions. In MLB, as an example, bats, miniature helmets, and bobble-head dolls have been used for many years without measuring their outcome. Due to limited marketing budgets and increasing competition in the market place, sport organizations started to examine effectiveness of marketing campaigns. Analysts can identify which games should give away bobble-heads and which should provide different types of promotions. Furthermore, effectiveness of campaigns is examined to find out which campaign works for which group of customers. Finally, the outcome of marketing activities is measured. The Cleveland Indians collected data on public relations impressions, traditional and digital media spending and game day promotions, and compared the outcome of these activities for sales and revenue generation (Davenport, 2014).

Today, sport organizations optimize marketing spending by analyzing their current campaigns for their return on investment (ROI), and discontinuing unprofitable campaigns and repeating the campaigns with higher ROI. The return on investment for a marketing campaign is the revenue generated due to a campaign compared with the cost of the campaign (Laursen, 2011). Measuring the cost of a campaign is easier than measuring the revenue generated through the campaign. Oftentimes a variety of marketing campaigns are run simultaneously and it is hard to know what "call to action" convinced prospects to become paying consumers. Therefore, assigning revenue to one specific marketing campaign could be challenging. Some of the most commonly used key metrics in evaluating marketing campaigns are:

1. the number of leads and cost per lead;
2. the number of wins (new customer) and cost of customer acquisition;
3. customer lifetime value; and
4. incremental sales.

The cost per lead (CPL) metric measures how cost effective your campaign is. It compares the cost of a marketing campaign with the number of leads generated through that specific campaign (DeMers, 2014). For example, if you spent $2,400 for a campaign including the invisible cost, and reached 800 prospects, your CPL would be $3. Obviously, the success of a campaign would be a low cost per lead, and marketers can easily compare the CPL of different campaigns and identify which campaign is more successful. To continue with our example, let's take a look at another campaign and compare the two to identify the more successful campaign. If the second campaign cost you a total of $5,000 and generated 10,000 prospects, the CPL for the second campaign would be 50¢. For this hypothetical case, the second campaign not only has a lower cost per lead, but also has a higher volume of leads, which makes it a more successful marketing campaign. However, generating a high volume of leads is not sufficient. Acquiring a high volume of high quality leads, who are more likely to convert to paying customers, is important for the success of marketers.

Another metric to investigate is the number of wins per campaign. The ultimate goal is to have new customers, and generating leads is just a step in the process. While successful marketing departments aim to attract quality leads via campaigns, sales departments work on converting the leads into paying customers, which is also known as wins. The number of wins per campaign allows marketers to measure the outcome of a marketing campaign more effectively by calculating the cost of customer acquisition (CoCA). To continue with the example from the CPL section, let's incorporate conversion rates, which reports the percentage of leads converted into customers, into the example and assume that campaign 1 and campaign 2 have a conversion rate of 15 percent and 5 percent, respectively. These conversion rates would result in 120 wins for the first campaign (800 leads × 15 percent) and 500 wins for the second campaign (10,000 leads × 5 percent). Now, we have a better understanding of the campaigns' effectiveness due to the ability to calculate cost of customer acquisition for each campaign. The cost of acquiring a new customer would be $20 ($2,400 cost/120 wins) for campaign 1, and $10 for campaign 2 ($5,000 cost/ 500 wins). Based on the number of wins and the CoCA, campaign 2 is still a more successful marketing campaign than campaign 1. Although number of wins and cost of customer acquisition provide invaluable insights, they still do not present the full picture in campaign evaluation.

Until now, all the metrics discussed are the tools of evaluating a campaign based on its cost and how to minimize the cost. Customer lifetime value (CLV) is the next metric which requires marketers' attention in campaign evaluation. The CLV approaches campaign evaluation from a different perspective and measures the value a customer will bring to an organization. The CLV is "the expected profit that you will realize from sales to a particular customer in the future" (Hughes, 2016). The CLV calculations rely on past customer history and are based on expected average value of sales, retention time and number of transactions in a set period (Sugar, 2012).

CLV = Average value of a sale × # of transactions × Average retention time (in years or months)

In order to continue with our example and see an application of CLV, let's incorporate average value of sales in dollars, number of transactions, and average retention time in years into our example. For the campaigns, our numbers are as follows:

Campaign 1: Average sales value is $90 for 5 transactions with 2 years of retention.
Campaign 2: Average sales value is $60 for 7 transactions with 3 years of retention.

The CLV of a customer acquired via campaign 1 would be $900 ($90 × 5 × 2), and the total value generated by the campaign in two years would be $108,000 (120 customers × $900). On the other hand, the CLV of a customer acquired through campaign 2 would be $1260 ($60 × 7 × 3), and the total value generated by the campaign in three years would be $630,000 (500 customers × $1260). As a result of this example, we see that both campaigns generate profits for the organization, while campaign 2 is more successful in bringing in valuable customers.

The last key metric to discuss in campaign evaluation is incremental sales. An incremental sale is "a sale in which a customer buys a product because of a campaign when he/she was not going to, and/or a sale in which a customer buys more than he/she intended to due to the campaign" (Lewis, n.d.). The key idea to understand about this metric is that the increase in sales is attributed to a specific campaign. If a campaign is not generating sales or if customers and prospects were going to make a purchase with or without the campaign, then that specific campaign is not effective and does not provide a positive ROI to the organization. A successful result would report incremental sales exceeding the initial cost of the campaign. To sum, CPL, CoCA, CLV and incremental sales provide various insights about effectiveness of marketing campaigns and utilizing them together provides a comprehensive view of the campaigns.

Analytics in ticket pricing

Ticket sales are one of the big revenue sources for sport teams along with broadcasting and sponsorship fees. According to *Forbes* (Badenhausen, 2015), MLB generated an impressive $9 billion gross revenue in 2014 and 41 percent of their revenue came from ticket sales and ancillary revenue due to attendance (7 percent concessions and parking). However, teams did not sell-out all of their games which means they lost inventory, therefore revenue. Considering the big impact ticket sales have on revenue generation, maximizing seating capacity use and pricing tickets right are essential, yet challenging tasks.

Traditionally, sport teams set ticket prices eight to nine months prior to the season's opening day, and prices stayed the same for the entire season. The only differences in prices were due to the level of seating. Fans have been well aware of the difference in experience based on where you sit in the arena or the stadium, and they have been willing to pay higher prices for a better experience like the court side seats in the NBA provide. Other than the seating level, there was no difference in prices, and sport teams priced their tickets lower than optimal for several reasons (Fort & Winfree, 2013). First and foremost, teams understand the importance of fans for their business and do not want to upset their fans with high ticket prices. Second, lower ticket prices show teams' goodwill by making it available to all fans from different income levels. Third, sell-outs due to lower ticket prices result in higher ancillary revenue (concession and parking) at game-days, and maximize the revenue for the team. Finally, sold-out games show fans' interest to the team and bring higher revenue through sponsorship and broadcasting fees.

With the development of the secondary ticket market in early 2000s, sport teams saw that fans are willing to pay more for the tickets, at least for certain games. Within the secondary ticket market, ticket resales take place mostly online with a larger inventory than a scalper can hold, and bring a large number of sellers and buyers together. Sellers set a price for their ticket, which could be higher or lower than the face value of the ticket, based on the market demand. With the fluctuation of prices in the secondary ticket market, sport organizations realized that they were not optimizing their prices and had been missing the opportunity to generate higher revenues through pricing their tickets correctly.

> We are talking about a pile of revenue. This shouldn't be done on a whim or gut feeling anymore.
>
> *Chad Estis, Legends Sales and Marketing (King, 2012)*

Sport teams have started to use different pricing strategies by utilizing analytics. The first move away from the set ticket prices for an entire season was variable ticket pricing, which refers to "setting the price of a sporting event ticket based on the expected demand for that event" (Rascher, McEvoy, Nagel, & Brown, 2007, p.407). By following the prices in the secondary ticket market, sport organizations have seen that some games are more valuable than others, and fans are willing to pay more for those games. The variable ticket pricing is based on two factors: the quality of the opponents and the timing of the games. If a game is played against a rival or one of the top teams in the league or a team with a star player, then the game becomes more appealing and fans are willing to pay more for these games. In addition, day of the week, time of the game, holidays, and time in the season impact the demand for games and the ticket prices. For example, a weekend game has a higher demand than a weekday game. Similarly, a play-off game has a higher demand than a regular season game. By having an understanding of the value of each game, sport teams set up different prices for their games, but the variation in pricing is set ahead of time and stays static throughout the season.

There are many examples of variable ticket pricing in the industry. This pricing strategy has been especially valuable for MLB due to the large number of home games and larger seat inventory to sell when compared with the NBA and the NHL. The Colorado Rockies were the first adopter of this pricing strategy, and all MLB teams followed their lead in early 2000s. The VTP strategy has been used by NBA teams as well. In 2012, all of the NBA teams were using variable ticket pricing (King, 2012). The WNBA also utilized variable pricing in 2013 to capitalize on the appeal of their three new rookies – Brittney Griner, Elena Della Done, Skyler Diggins – and the interest they drove to the league (Lombardo, 2013a). The NFL is the late adopter of the VTP strategy. The league started to implement variable ticket pricing in 2014 much later than other sport leagues due to limited number of home games and having a high percentage of season tickets. However, in 2015, half of the all NFL teams were using variable pricing (Smith, 2015).

Another pricing method that utilizes analytics is dynamic pricing. Dynamic pricing refers to "adjusting ticket prices upward or downward based on real-time market conditions such as fan demand and ticket scarcity" (Solomon, 2014, para 4). This strategy relies on the sport event's characteristics and customer demand, and estimates prices based on these factors with a mathematical algorithm. Some of the event characteristics could be the current success of the team, success of the opponent, weather, and so on. Prices can change on a daily basis even several times a day as conditions and supply and demand change. Some dynamic ticketing models use over 140 variables in helping to set ticket prices.

Dynamic ticket pricing has become a common pricing method in the industry from MLB to NBA, NHL to college athletics to NFL. The first example of dynamic ticket pricing in college athletics was seen in 2013. The Northwestern Athletic Department utilized dynamic pricing for their football game against the Ohio State, and generated 162 percent more revenue by selling tickets at almost triple their face value. Just one year later, in 2014, 15 percent of Football Subdivision Schools were using dynamic ticket pricing for football games (Solomon, 2014). The first MLB team utilizing dynamic ticket pricing was San Francisco Giants in the 2009 season, and they were followed by 16 other MLB teams in 2012 (King, 2012). By applying dynamic pricing, the league was able to increase full-price attendance by 15 percent and total ticket revenue by 30 percent (R. D., 2012). In 2013, the number of MLB teams utilizing dynamic ticket pricing reached 26 (Sachdev, 2013). Similar to the adoption of the variable ticket pricing method, the NFL was reserved in implementing dynamic ticket pricing, too. The St. Louis Rams set ticket prices dynamically for their game on November 15th against Chicago Bears in 2015. Initial price for the lower-level 20-yard-line seats was $134, which was increased three times to reach the final price of $222 on October 12th. Some other NFL teams also tested dynamic ticket pricing with a small percentage of their individual tickets in 2015 (Kaplan, 2015).

The main goal of variable and dynamic ticket pricing strategies is to set optimal prices to maximize revenues. In some cases, prices are lowered to increase the number of tickets sold which results in larger revenue than empty seats with higher prices. In other cases, market demand indicates that the market will bear higher prices due to the characteristics of the game, and fans' demand and willingness to pay. In this process, teams forecast the demand for their games, estimate price elasticity, and identify the predictors of ticket prices and the value of these variables. Once the value of the predictors is known, a model is built to predict the value of future games which provides insight to the teams' management in setting prices for each game accordingly (Brustein, 2010).

Analytics in sport sponsorship

Sponsorship is one of the most valuable marketing elements in the sport industry. In 2015, global sport sponsorship spending in fees was estimated to be $57.5 billion ("Global Sponsorship," n.d.), and non-alcoholic beverages and automotive brands were the most active sponsors of global sports ("2015 Recap," 2015). This number was $14 billion for the US market (Hartley, 2015), and the NFL's sponsorship revenue totaled a little over $1 billion in 2014 ("NFL Sponsorship," 2015). Sponsorships are not only large revenue sources for sport properties for the time being, but are expected to continue to be large revenue sources based on the comparison of the spending of corporations on sponsorships and other promotion alternatives. In 2014, corporations' sponsorship spending increased 4.2 percent, while their spending on advertising and public relations/promotions/direct marketing increased 3.1 percent and 2.8 percent, respectively (Hartley, 2015).

Although the size of the sport sponsorship market is undeniably large, its outcome and effectiveness is still not measured as frequently as other promotional tools. According to the Association of National Advertisers, only 35 percent of marketers examine the impact of their sponsorship activities, and only 50 percent of which implement a valid process isolating the impact of sponsorship from other marketing activities (Nanji, 2013). Measuring the outcome of a sponsorship would benefit sponsors in several ways: identifying effective sponsorships and renewing those, value justification of sponsorship and pricing renegotiations, modifying activation methods, and justifying the sponsorship budget. A well-known example in which measurement of a sponsorship outcome resulted in a meaningful decision is the National Guard's NASCAR sponsorship. The National Guard spent $88 million for its NASCAR sponsorship between 2011 and 2013 (Brook, 2014) with the goal of building awareness of the National Guard as a career option among NASCAR's fan base (Bruce, 2014). Unfortunately, the National Guard could not sign a single recruit in 2012 through the NASCAR sponsorship and in 2013 the number of prospects associated with NASCAR dropped to a level that did not warrant pursuing the sponsorship again (Brook, 2014). The ineffectiveness of this campaign generated significant backlash through the US Federal Government, and the next year it was discovered that many professional teams who were hosting events to celebrate military veterans were actually being paid to host such events and the negative backlash associated with that caused government officials to critically examine all sport spending.

The National Guard example presents the importance of understanding the performance of a sponsorship. The challenge marketers are up against is how to measure the performance and that discussion starts with the objectives of a sponsorship. Each organization signs a sponsorship deal with a sport property for a different reason such as increasing public awareness, enhancing brand image, increasing sales/market share, and generating media benefits such as impressions, web traffic, social media buzz, and so on. Based on the sponsorship objectives, IEG suggests a variety of methods in measuring sponsorship outcomes: surveys, web analytics, earned media tracking, broadcast exposure analysis and business metrics ("Sponsorship measurement," n.d.).

In order to see how some of these measures are utilized in measuring sponsorship outcomes, let's take a look at an example. Turnkey Intelligence performs sponsorship evaluation for many sport properties in the US, and publishes its results in the *Sport Business Journal*. As part of the sponsorship evaluation, fans are asked if they could recognize the sponsors of the sport property under investigation, and how likely they are to consume products and services of the sponsors due to their support of the sport property. In 2015, Turnkey Intelligence evaluated NHL fans' recognition of the league's sponsors from ten business sectors: insurance, soft-drinks, energy drinks, fast-food restaurants, wireless services, credit card, beer, automobile, tire, and hotel. Except the soft drink category, fans identified the official sponsors of the league in each category correctly. In addition, results showed that fans were more inclined to purchase products and services of the official sponsors when they were aware of the sponsor. Among the fans who correctly identified the sponsor, likelihood of purchasing the sponsors' product and services ranged from 40 percent for the credit card category to 77 percent for the hotel (Missal, 2015). The case study below entitled "Sponsorship Evaluation" provides an example on sponsorship evaluation.

CASE STUDY: SPONSORSHIP EVALUATION

Name: Jeff Meeson and Kevin Wittner
Title: Vice President and Director, Insights and Strategy
Current employer: Octagon, Inc.
Brief work history: Jeff and Kevin lead Octagon's Insights and Strategy team, which advises the company's roster of blue chip corporate clients on their partnership planning process. Jeff joined Octagon in 2008 after three years at Joyce Julius and Associates. He holds an M.Ed. from Bowling Green State University. Kevin joined Octagon in 2011 following a stint with the Arizona Diamondbacks. He holds an MBA from the University of Arizona.

PHOTO 5.1 Jeff Meeson

How do you think data helps influence your industry segment?

Data serves as the bookends to virtually every project and assignment at Octagon. From target consumer identification to program measurement, our Insights and Strategy group is dedicated to using data and insights to enable better, more objective decision making and create smarter, more engaging activations. One specific area that data has helped to influence is partnership selection. In the earliest days of sponsorship, the decision of which properties a brand should sponsor was dictated by the inherent biases and personal preferences of decision-makers. This phenomenon went by many names, including "execu-whim" or "chairman's choice."

PHOTO 5.2 Kevin Wittner

As sponsorship has evolved as a marketing discipline, so too has the importance of ensuring that the investment delivers a positive return upon the brand's stated objectives. One of the ways that we help our clients produce strong returns is by using data and analytics to be more selective when it comes to where they choose to invest their sponsorship dollars.

We look to increase the probability of success by grounding our recommendations in data-driven insights. This is accomplished by leveraging data to gain a superior understanding of what consumers care about, as well as what marketing objectives a brand hopes to achieve.

What example can you share regarding using data to help make a decision?

The issue

ClearChoice is one of the country's top wireless carriers. Based out of Chicago and holding 20 percent national market share, ClearChoice is one of the most well-established players in the space. While its revenues have seen ups and downs following the recession, business leaders have made big bets on a few major US markets that have paid off and placed the company in a position to succeed. However, ClearChoice's subscribers are disproportionately 40 years or older, as newer wireless carriers have appealed to millennial consumers.

With a $40 million annual sponsorship budget, ClearChoice's portfolio is reflective of its stately, conservative heritage. The carrier has long-term, national partnership deals with the PGA TOUR, Major League Baseball and Academy Awards, among others. In addition, it has over 80 corporate partnerships with teams and entertainment properties across 25 of the largest markets in the country.

The analysis

When the company went through restructuring during the recession, analysts projected that over the next ten years, 25 percent of the company's revenue would come from the San Francisco Bay Area, followed closely by 15 percent in Dallas-Fort Worth, 10 percent in Boston and 10 percent in Chicago, with the remaining 40 percent coming from other markets across the country. In addition, it was determined that consumers living in Top 10 Designated Marketing Areas (DMAs) are willing to pay 25 percent more for their wireless service than people living in smaller markets.

An audit of ClearChoice's sponsorship investments revealed that only 20 percent of the portfolio was invested in the top four revenue-generating markets. Additionally, more than half the portfolio was invested in markets that did not crack the top 10 as revenue generators, and long-time ClearChoice employees noted that many of those partnerships were not leveraged, limiting the impact of those investments to tickets and arena signage. The contracts for many of those properties were set to expire over the course of the next 18 months, meaning ClearChoice needed to begin the decision-making process of which properties to divest of and where it should make its next big bets.

ClearChoice began a two-pronged decision-making process. First, it needed to construct a framework to determine what percentage of its sponsorship budget should be allocated to each market. Second, the carrier had to figure out which properties it should set out to acquire.

In looking to answer the question of how to allocate the budget, ClearChoice turned to a number of data sources. Some of them existed through syndicated research, which showed how many millennials who paid for a wireless carrier lived in each market. Other sources included its own research, indicating the average monthly bill for consumers in each market. Next, the company turned to its own data to gauge the power of its infrastructure within each market. Markets also received scores based upon historic market share and competitive activity. For example, while Chicago was the home market, the company's dominance had led to 90 percent market share in the Windy City, rendering sponsorship assets a proud banner to wave but not something that would make a material difference on the balance sheet.

The resulting analysis provided not only a clear ranking, but also a data-driven rationale for a specific budgetary range each market should receive, given the size of the opportunity, ClearChoice's infrastructure investment and the competitive activity.

The message was clear: the company needed to divest out of its national partnerships, and cut spending in markets that did not significantly deliver to the bottom line.

With the markets prioritized, the next step was to determine which properties to acquire. To do this, marketing leaders developed criteria and thresholds that sponsorship investments should achieve. Some of these were consumer-based data points, such as what percentage of ClearChoice's target consumers cared about the property, or how much more likely were the target consumers to engage with the property compared to the general population. Given the company's aspirational brand positioning of being perceived as cutting-edge, having reliable service and fast download speeds, ClearChoice wanted to ensure that any potential partnership reinforced that imagery. Other criteria the brand considered was whether or not the property provided hospitality opportunities, if ClearChoice could carve out an ownable territory, and whether or not consumers believed the property represented their community.

To score and rank the properties, ClearChoice used several data sources, including syndicated research databases, primary research studies within key markets, and secondary desk research. The results provided a data-driven recommendation for which opportunities to pursue and which to move away from.

The end results

In the two years after having implemented this process, ClearChoice was fully divested out of all sponsorship activities that took place outside of its key markets, and its budget aligned with the data-led allocation recommendation. Today, regular measurement is conducted to ensure that all partnerships and activations deliver the desired return on investment and return on objectives.

Of course, even with an objectives-driven framework in place to vet prospective sponsorship activities, there are some instances in which company leaders require the sponsorship team to pursue opportunities that do not fit the prescribed framework. When this happens, there is a procedure in place to ensure that there is a business case for how this type of partnership will deliver results for ClearChoice.

One final topic that carries ultimate importance in today's sponsorship setting is activation. Sponsors pay additional dollars to engage with fans and spectators at sporting events as putting up a sign is simply not enough in today's highly cluttered sponsorship landscape. Each sponsor looks for ways to communicate and interact with fans and spectators at events and develop a relationship. Any opportunity which allows sponsors to interact with spectators and fans is activation, and performance and effectiveness of these activities should also be measured. The case study titled "Concessions project planning: soft drinks versus beer provisions" is focused on activation of a sponsorship and how numbers are used to provide better service to fans at the events.

CASE STUDY: CONCESSIONS PROJECT PLANNING: SOFT DRINKS VS. BEER PROVISIONS

Name: Lindsay Salt
Title: Account Manager, Sports Property Management and Consulting
Current employer: Octagon, Inc.
Brief work history: As a University of New Haven class of 2010 graduate, I jumped right into the sport world while I was at school and beyond. During my four years, I was a member of the Women's Basketball team while earning my degree in Management of Sports Industries with two minors, one in Communications and one in Marketing. My

desire to work in the sport industry was solidified
following my internship at the New York Mets in
between my junior and senior years working in
their sponsorship division at the new CitiField.
Upon graduation, I was fortunate enough to get
a job at Octagon, Inc., a global sports marketing
and consulting firm out of Connecticut. I have
been able to work on various accounts bringing
me all over to the world working with clients in
NASCAR, global FIFA tournaments, the Super
Bowl, World Surf League events and even with
the UFC.

PHOTO 5.3 Lindsay Salt

- Two years working in the NASCAR industry
  for two official sponsors working in VIP experiences, hospitality, at track activations
  and consumer promotions.
- Three years on a client team for a FIFA World Cup sponsor, including activation at the
  2013 FIFA Confederations Cup, 2014 FIFA World Cup™, FIFA Women's World Cup
  2015™ and currently planning for the 2017/18 tournaments in Russia.
- Other property work includes Major League Baseball, World Surf League, National
  Football League and the UFC.

How do you think data helps influence your industry segment?

Analytics hold a very important role in all parts of the sport business world. Some of the
most important uses of analytics for us at the sports marketing agency are evaluating
sponsorships to recommend to our clients, property health evaluation when looking at
how our current relationships are working, creating ROI and recap materials, and internal
audits for how the client is preforming, and so on. There is not one decision that is made
in our role that does not include research and measurement of some kind and is essential
to the way we do business.

Concessions project planning: soft drinks vs. beer provisions

In all stadium events, there are multiple variables that must be taken into consideration
before the gates open and the consumers flood their seats. Everything from the number
of cups you have for beverages to amount of product you are selling in a retail space needs
to be planned well in advance to ensure that you are creating a positive experience for
the ticket holders, sponsors, teams/entertainers, and so on. This hypothetical case study
will take you through some key practices, terminology and best practices that are typically
implemented into concessions project planning around the world.

One of the most important planning processes is that of a concessions program, i.e.
the food and beverages that are provided to consumers within each venue. Happy
consumers can normally be achieved by three very important considerations:

1. *A wide product offering:* With the rise of the millennial fan, the standard hot dog and beer supply are no longer going to cut it. Properties need to look at what they have the capacity to provide and make sure that they are giving people something that is worth their money.

> Example: One of the first examples I saw of this very practice was with the opening of the New York Mets CitiField Stadium. When I did my internship there during the inaugural season, I was extremely impressed (as were a number of my friends who came to visit) by their product offering. Take just the beer selection into consideration. Due to US Legislation where no beer provider is able to have a monopoly over sales product offering in stadiums, the NY Mets showcased the Official Beer partner, Budweiser, in most point of sale units in the stadium, while allowing for others to be extremely customized with a local flavor, especially in the outfield. An area called "Big Apple Brews" not only offered regional brands such as Brooklyn Lager, but they also took into consideration the rise of gluten allergies and provided a Gluten Free beer and Cider option, which was definitely a first for me and it was highly appreciated that any consumer could now enjoy a cold one at the game.

2. *Competitive pricing:* While the goal of every venue is to make a profit, when taking all overhead costs into consideration they need to ensure that the sales prices of these products are not unrealistically higher than a fair market price. For the most part, fans know that they are going to have to pay more of a premium for these products that they purchase in stadiums, but it cannot be so high as to deter them from that purchase.

3. *Efficiencies:* Another millennial passion point is the speed of the world around us. With the evolution of stadium operations, we are now seeing the rise of in-venue apps that allow products to be ordered from a seat and picked up at the nearest concession stand. While the technology aspect is not mandatory, planning effectively for the number of seats versus the number of concession units is.

So where to get started? Let's first explore some key terminology.

Concessionaire

Every venue/property around the world will have a concessionaire that they do business with. Take the University of New Haven for example; while I was in school we had Sodexo as our concessionaire so to speak. Sodexo was in charge of the food and beverage supply to our University. Everything from organizing the food delivery, to hiring staff members to ordering uniforms, it was up to Sodexo to organize the different vendor contracts to create a great consumer experience, in this case feeding a multitude of hungry college students!

Tender agreement

The tender agreement is the agreement between the concessionaire, the venue and its sponsors/vendors. For example, you have a professional sport venue that has a sponsor/provider for a beer brand as well as a soft drink. It is the job of the property and the concessionaire to ensure that both sponsors are represented with equal opportunities. This would include equal branding, equal sales, etc. This document will put all these processes in place such as the following:

- number of staff members working;
- branding opportunities;
- equipment providers;
- product pricing;
- number of selling points;
- alcohol restrictions based on local legislations.

Point of Sale (POS) unit

A POS unit is exactly as it states, where consumers can purchase products. Every tender agreement will specify the number of POS units that need to be in each stadium/venue, which is normally calculated by the attendance (i.e. for every number of seats, there is a certain number of POS units that need to be set up). There are two areas in which a POS unit can be set up:

- Concourse level: main areas where the fans go to their seats/get into the stadium.
- The bowl: The general seating area that covers everything from the floor seats to the nosebleeds.

Three of the most commonly used POS units are the following:

- Permanent stands: These are the units that are actually built into the stadium infrastructure on different concourse levels. They generally have ample amounts of storage as well as roll down bay doors that can be shut at the end of the game/ concert. Each permanent POS unit will have multiple lines and cashiers to assist customers.
- Mobile units: The most common mobile units are those on wheels that can be freely moved around a concourse level. While they may have fridges or kegs, one of the more widely used is the carts that have coolers.
- Hawkers: If you have ever been to a baseball game, then you should be very familiar with hawkers. The "Beer Here!" or Cracker Jack peanut men are considered hawkers, most likely called that because they hover around the crowds. These salesmen are allowed inside the fan seating areas and have free reign to try to sell during games and concerts providing they aren't disruptive to the main event.

Product offering

As already mentioned, a product offering is partially determined by the different sponsors that are associated with the property or team that utilizes the venue. There are a couple of considerations that a concessionaire should take into account when determining their product offering with different sponsor teams:

- Soft drinks: It is common practice to not only provide a soda beverage, but also water, diet soda and even sport drinks depending on the event. Given the wide variety of products that a soft drink provider may provide within their sponsor product category, they may also have a stipulation as to how these items are arranged within their cooling instruments. For example, as part of the tender agreement they may mandate that the concessionaire restock fridges in a certain way based on case studies showcasing the optimal visual representation of the brand hierarchy. This could be insuring that the soft drink is allocated a certain number of shelves versus the water and diet products depending on which brand is most important to sell in-venue to consumers.
- Beer: One thing to note is that having beer available for purchase at sporting events in the United States is definitely a privilege. In many countries around the world, the common influences of hooliganism at sporting events have caused local legislations to prevent the sale of alcohol during these types of events. That, plus our strict government laws on fair consumption, allow us interesting discussion points:
    - Exclusivity: For the United States and Canada, one brand (or family of brands) cannot have a monopoly over the beer product offerings on site. This is consistent with US Antitrust laws where a beer company cannot have too high of a certain market share within the home country, thus forcing beer companies like AB InBev to sell off some of their brand portfolio when they merge with other organizations. For instance, when ABI acquired Corona on a global scale, it was under the stipulation that they could not hold rights to the sales in the US. So while all the beer is brewed in Mexico, the sales and distribution of the Corona brand are not owned by ABI in the US like they are for the rest of the world. With this understanding, it is no wonder that a tender agreement would have competitive brands selling in the same arena. The team and venue sponsor may hold the majority percentage of the distribution and exclusive branding in the stadium, but the actual products offered must also include an outside presence.
    - Limitations: In an attempt to promote responsible drinking, local legislations generally enforce purchase limitations on the number of beers one consumer can buy and for how long. It is a common practice to only allow a maximum of two or three beers per purchase per fan, as well as cut off beer sales around the seventh inning of a baseball game or the beginning of the fourth quarter at a football game. The goal is to make best efforts to keep intoxication levels lower and try to get fans home safe from all events.
- Special edition products: A common practice for both soft drink and beer providers is to provide fans with the opportunity to purchase special edition products. Generally provided in a souvenir cup, the purchase is meant to be a keepsake for the fan and higher profit margin for the concessionaire as they will charge more and sell more products in a larger cup.

Hit rate

Referring to sales, a hit rate is a metric used by concessionaires to compare how many drinks were sold versus how many people were in the seats that day. For example:

- your stadium capacity is 48,000;
- for Saturday's game, there were 46,357 potential consumers in attendance;
- your reported sales are:
    - ○ $142,670 for soft drinks;
    - ○ $334,127.88 for beer sales.

- In order to get your hit rate, you divide the sales by the number of people in the stands:

- $142,670 soft drinks product revenue/46,357 potential consumers = $3.08;
- $334,127.88 beer product revenue/46,357 potential consumers = $7.21.

- What did we learn from this? There were more beers sold throughout this game versus soft drinks. In this case, there were 46,342 beers sold, which is a great sales metric meaning that almost every consumer in your venue purchased a beer. The caveat is that obviously there are consumers who are non-LDA (aka Legal Drinking Age) from which we can assume that there were instances where some fans had multiple beers while enjoying the game.

Conclusion

In today's saturated market place, it has become more and more challenging to attract consumers' attention, communicate with them efficiently, gain their loyalty, and continuously generate desired levels of revenue. In this effort, use of analytics has grown tremendously. Sport marketers take advantage of the availability of data and perform a variety of analyses to assess the outcome of their current marketing strategies, find the best communication channels, become relevant to sport fans, use their budget efficiently, and achieve desirable outcomes for the sport organizations. Marketing has become data oriented due to fact-based decision-making employed by most marketing managers and the need to prove success.

References

2015 Recap: The most active sponsors of global sports. (2015, December 21). IEG. Retrieved from www.sponsorship.com/iegsr/2015/12/21/2015-Recap--The-Most-Active-Sponsors-Of-Global-Spo.aspx

Badenhausen, K. (2015, April 6). *Opening day graphic: MLB revenue today vs 2010.* Retrieved from www.forbes.com/sites/kurtbadenhausen/2015/04/06/opening-day-graphic-mlb-revenue-today-vs-2010/#2715e4857a0b7ffba54a77aa

Brook, T. V. (2014, May 8). *National Guard's NASCAR sponsorship deal leads to virtually no recruits.* Retrieved from www.usatoday.com/story/news/nation/2014/05/07/national-guard-recruiting-scandal/8813891/

Bruce, K. (2014, August 7). *National Guard ending Hendrik sponsorship*. Retrieved from www.nascar. com/en_us/news-media/articles/2014/8/7/national-guard-sponsor-dale-earnhardt-jr-hendrick-motorsports.html

Brustein, J. (2010, June 27). *Star pitchers in a duel? Tickets will cost more*. Retrieved from www.nytimes. com/2010/06/28/technology/28tickets.html

Customer relationship management [Dictionary definition]. (n.d.). Retrieved from wwwbusiness dictionary.com/definition/customer-relationship-management-CRM.html#ixzz3wPCZbSzI

Davenport, T. H. (2014). *Analytics in Sports: The new science of winning* [International Institute for Analytics research report]. Retrieved from www.sas.com/en_us/whitepapers/iia-analytics-in-sports-106993.html

Davenport, T. H., & Harris, J. G. (2007). *Competing on analytics: The new science of winning*. Boston, MA: Harvard Business Review Press.

DeMers, J. (2014, August 15). *10 online marketing metrics you need to be measuring*. Retrieved from www. forbes.com/sites/jaysondemers/2014/08/15/10-online-marketing-metrics-you-need-to-be-measuring/#2715e4857a0b622f3d83355f

Fort, R., & Winfree, J. (2013) *Two sports myths and why they are wrong*. Palo Alto, CA: Stanford University Press.

Global sponsorship spending from 2007 to 2016 [Statistics report]. (n.d.). Retrieved from www.statista. com/statistics/196864/global-sponsorship-spending-since-2007/

Green, F. (2015, November). Social CRM: Debunking the myth. Fan engagement 2015: Data-Driven Marketing Best Practices. Paper presented at Sport Analytics Europe Conference in November 2015. Retrieved from www.sportsanalyticseurope.com/presentations-fan-engagement/

Guilfoyle, E. (2015, February). Selling out: Understanding the path to purchase for sports tickets. Paper presented at the 9th MIT Sloane Sports Analytics Conference in Boston, MA, USA. Retrieved from www.sloansportsconference.com/?p=16049

Hartley, P. (2015, March 24). *Measuring the value of sponsorships*. Retrieved from www.market strategies.com/blog/2015/03/measuring-the-value-of-sponsorships/

Hughes, A. M. (2016, January 18). *How to compute your customer lifetime value?* Retrieved from www. dbmarketing.com/articles/Art251a.htm

Jobber, D., & Fahy, J. (2012). *Foundations of marketing* (4th ed.). London: McGraw-Hill Education.

Kaplan, D. (2015). Dynamic ticket pricing makes successful debut in NFL. *Sports Business Journal*, *18*(28). Retrieved from www.sportsbusinessdaily.com/Journal/Issues/2015/10/26/Leagues-and-Governing-Bodies/NFL-dynamic.aspx

Kaye, K. (2013, February 5). *What are look-alike models?* Retrieved from http://adage.com/article/dataworks/alike-models/239590/

King, B. (2012). Ticket challenge: Getting the right price. *Sports Business Journal*, *14*(46). Retrieved from www.sportsbusinessdaily.com/journal/issues/2012/03/19/In-Depth/Ticket-pricing.aspx

King, B. (2015). Analyze this. *Sports Business Journal*, *18*(26)*,* 21–30.

Laursen, G. H. (2011). *Business analytics for sales and marketing managers: How to compete in the information age*. Hoboken, NJ: John Wiley & Sons, Inc.

Lewis, J. (n.d.). *Incremental sales ideas*. Retrieved from http://smallbusiness.chron.com/incremental-sales-ideas-37457.html

Lombardo, J. (2013a). For the WNBA, time for a clutch 3. *Sports Business Journal*, *16*(6). Retrieved from www.sportsbusinessdaily.com/Journal/Issues/2013/05/20/Leagues-and-Governing-Bodies/WNBA.aspx

Lombardo, J. (2013b). NBA's TMBO a launchpad for high-level executives. *Sports Business Journal*, *16*(13). Retrieved from www.sportsbusinessdaily.com/Journal/Issues/2013/07/15/Leagues-and-Governing-Bodies/TMBO.aspx

MacGregor, C. (2015, November 23). *Fan engagement 2015: It is all about data!* Retrieved from http://winnersfdd.com/fan_engagement-2015-its-all-about-data/

Mander, J. (2015, January 30). *65% in the US and 38% globally are NFL fans* [Blog]. Retrieved from www.globalwebindex.net/blog/65-in-the-us-and-38-globally-are-nfl-fans

Measure the quality of marketing and sales leads with the average lead score KPI (n.d.). Retrieved from www.klipfolio.com/resources/kpi-examples/marketing/average-lead-score

Missal, J. (2015). Geico rises to top in fallback year for sponsors. *Sports Business Journal, 18*(11), 16–17.

Mullin, B. J., Hardy, S., & Sutton, W. A. (2014). *Sport marketing* (4th ed.). Campaign, IL: Human Kinetics.

Nanji, A. (2013, November 20). *How marketers measure the effectiveness of sponsorship and event initiatives.* Retrieved from www.marketingprofs.com/charts/2013/12106/how-marketers-measure-the-effectiveness-of-sponsorship-and-event-initiatives

National Sports Forum. (2013). Master class: Analytics, marketing automation, and social media best practice. Webinar published by National Sports Forum on December 4, 2013.

NFL sponsorship revenue total up $1.15billion in 2014 season. (2015, April 6). Retrieved from www.sponsorship.com/IEGSR/2015/04/06/NFL-Sponsorship-Revenue-Totals-$1-15-Billion-In-20.aspx

O'Connor, A. (2011, October 13). *Liverpool lag in fight for global fan supremacy as TV row grows.* Retrieved from www.thetimes.co.uk/tto/sport/football/premierleague/article3192868.ece

Pardes, A. (2014, September 11). *What you should know about propensity models and predictive modeling.* Retrieved from www.leadid.com/blog/whatyoushouldknowaboutpropensitymodels andpredictivemodeling

Rascher, D. A., McEvoy, C. D., Nagel, M. A., & Brown, M. T. (2007). Variable ticket pricing in MLB. *Journal of Sport Management, 21,* 407–37.

R. D. (2012, January 9). *The price is right.* Retrieved from www.economist.com/blogs/gametheory/2012/01/sports-ticketing

Sachdev, A. (2013, May 12). *Baseball teams get dynamic with ticket pricing.* Retrieved from http://articles.chicagotribune.com/2013-05-12/business/ct-biz-0512-stub-hub--20130512_1_stubhub-bleacher-ticket-ticket-reselling

Shin, C. (2014). Major league soccer scores with analytics. Presented at Integrated Marketing Week in New York City, NY.

Skalli, I. (2012, April 14). *CRM in football: The case of Manchester City FC.* Retrieved from http://wearedevelopment.net/2012/04/14/crminfootballthecaseofmanchestercityfc/

Smith, M. D. (2015, July 11). *Half of NFL teams now using variable ticket pricing.* Retrieved from http://profootballtalk.nbcsports.com/2015/07/11/half-of-nfl-teams-now-using-variable-ticket-pricing/

Solomon, J. (2014, October 1). *Dynamic ticket pricing gains traction in college football.* Retrieved from www.cbssports.com/collegefootball/writer/jon-solomon/24730405/dynamic-ticket-pricing-gains-traction-in-college-football

Sponsorship measurement (n.d.). Retrieved from www.sponsorship.com/Sponsorship-Measurement. aspx

Sugar, B. (2012, August 8). *How to calculate the lifetime value of a customer.* Retrieved from www.entrepreneur.com/article/224153

Sutton, B. (2013). Industry standouts lead sports into new era of decision-making. *Sports Business Journal, 16*(17), 12.

Warriors' demographics (1998). Retrieved from www.nba.com/media/warriors/Demographics.pdf

What is customer profiling? (n.d.). Retrieved from www.experienceux.co.uk/faqs/what-is-customer-profiling/

Zeppenfeld, C. (2014, June 1). *10 things newbies need to know about the sports CRM world.* Retrieved from http://baylors3.com/10-things-newbies-need-to-know-about-the-sports-crm-world/

Zikmund, W. G., McLeod, R. J. R., & Gilbert, F. W. (2003). *Customer relationship management: Integrating marketing strategy and information technique.* Hoboken, NJ: John Wiley & Sons, Inc.

6

ANALYTICS IN DIGITAL MARKETING

Ceyda Mumcu

Introduction

In recent years, sport fans' consumption habits have changed dramatically with the increased availability and use of the internet. These changes are not only about cord-cutting and moving towards over-the-top sources. Today, sport fans rely on the internet for sport content and news, to engage with athletes and sport teams via social media, and for purchases whether it is tickets, merchandise or online access to games. These changes made digital media and services important parts of marketing, and analytics have been integrated in evaluation of digital marketing. This chapter will cover the use of analytics in email and social media marketing, and website analytics, while also providing some examples.

Rise of digital media and its impact on marketing

The explosion of digital media has created many channels for sport organizations to communicate with their customers beyond the traditional outlets. Consumers have access to information anytime anywhere via World Wide Web, social media outlets, mobile devices and apps, and other digital sources. According to Kantar Media, sport fans' go-to source for sport content is the internet. In 2013, 63 percent of fans went online, 35 percent used mobile and 25 percent used social media to access sport content, and among the fans who live-streamed games 84 percent used a PC, 32 percent used smart phones and 24 percent used tablets (Stadd, 2013). In the third quarter of 2014, 70 million people consumed sports via digital sources ("The year in sports report," 2015), and approximately 15 terabytes of data was used on Super Bowl 50 Sunday among the three largest networks – Verizon, AT&T, and T-Mobile – in the US (Preimesberger, 2016).

In addition to increasing the number of communication channels, digital media has also changed the way sport organizations market to their customers. Prior to digital media, sport organizations implemented one-sided marketing where marketers drove the conversation about their product and services, and customers were passive participants who received messages framed by marketers. With the extensive use of digital media in marketing, the communication mechanism between sport organizations and their customers has changed. Customers have access to perspectives of individuals from their reference groups and what the media says about the organization. Furthermore, customers carry a participative role by communicating with other customers, exchanging opinions, providing reviews and making online comments, and finally by communicating with the companies they do business with (Alt-Simmons, n.d.).

One advantage digital media provides to the sport organizations is analyzing marketing campaigns and assessing their effectiveness in real-time. Digital marketers monitor what is being viewed and for how long, what customers engage with, lead generations, sales conversions, and so on. The ultimate purpose is to give an organization the ability to react and adjust marketing activities quickly and make fact-based decisions (Laursen, 2011).

Email marketing

Email marketing is a type of digital marketing which involves communicating a marketing message with a group of people via electronic mail. Organizations use email marketing to enhance relationships with current and former customers, to acquire new customers or increase current consumer consumption. Email marketing provides several advantages to organizations: it is less costly than traditional mailing, emails can be tailored to the customers, and it is easy to measure the performance of email marketing. Recently the United States Olympic Committee (USOC) sent out emails to existing and prospective customers requesting their support of the US Olympic Team for the Rio 2016 Summer Olympics. These emails were personalized for each customer and they were framed as if written by the individual's favorite athlete requesting his/her donation (see a sample USOC email, p.117). In this process, by analyzing the individual's past purchases, the USOC identified their favorite sport and the athlete, and targeted them with a message from a participating athlete they are a fan of or a celebrity athlete performing the sport they are interested in. Sending out personalized relevant emails is much more effective than sending out a generic one-size-fits-all email. A marketing research conducted by Experian revealed that personalized promotional emails resulted in six-times higher transaction rates and revenue, and higher open and click rates (Gesenhues, 2014), and the USOC raised more than $200,000 in one month through the personalized emails (C. Mumcu, personal communication, January 23, 2016).

In addition to personalizing the content and providing relevant messages that will resonate with the customers, sport organizations can evaluate various metrics to assess the effectiveness of each email marketing campaign. The most frequently tracked metrics are open rate, click-through rate, and churn metrics such as unsubscribe rate, hard bounce rate and complaint/spam rate. The open rate reports the percentage of unique opens and the click-through rate presents the percentage of recipients who clicked on a link within an email. Both metrics indicate the level of customer engagement per email marketing campaign ("2015 Email marketing metrics benchmark study," 2015), and they are important metrics in comparing the performance of email marketing campaigns in-house. Examination of these engagement metrics along with the content of each campaign could identify what type of content attracts your fans' attention. For example, do your fans engage with emails communicating discounted prices or special exclusive events? What type of fans engage with what type of email campaigns? In 2014, New York Red Bulls designed a personalized

Date: Mon, 7 Dec 2015 21:14:07 +0000
To:
From: foundation@usoc.org
Subject: Are you with me, Ceyda?

TEAM USA★FUND

Ceyda, I'm not going to tell you that Team USA's matching gift challenge is as awesome as winning a World Cup or a gold medal. But it's pretty awesome. And here's why:

Anything you donate today to help Team USA will be DOUBLED by a pair of generous donors. Doubled!

It meant so much to have so many people watch the World Cup this year, to be called a hero, to go to the White House and hear the President of the United States say that it's "badass" to play like a woman.

But it can't be an every-four-years thing. It just can't. The kids (and adult) who look up to us need to see every day what it looks like to chase your dreams with passion, no matter how crazy they might seem.

So Ceyda, if helping Team USA go for the gold doesn't sway you, I hope this will.

Donate to help athletes like me, our national team members, and all of Team USA's athletes become role models for American kids—and when you do, your gift will be doubled.

I can't wait for Rio, Ceyda. I have an immense amount of pride when I play for the national team, and I get the biggest smile on my face every time I am able to pull that shirt over my head and wear that crest. It's incredibly special to me.

And you make it possible—for me and for every athlete who pours his or her heart into representing the United States at the Games. It takes the whole country. Everyone is a part of it. So thank you.

Take care,

Megan Rapinoe
Women's soccer player, gold medalist, and World Cup champion

P.S. You might have heard that I tore an ACL a few days ago. In case you're wondering: Yeah, it's tough. But I want you to know thst I'll be fine—and I'm super appreciative of all the love. Thanks again, **and if you decide to make a gift today,** thanks for that, tool

DONATE

🅕 🅣 🅞 🅞

©2015 United States Olympic Committee 1 Olympic Plaza, Colorado Springs, CO 80909

Privacy Policy | About Us | Contact Us

You received this email as a valued subscriber. To ensure delivery, please add foundation@usoc.org to your address book. Questions, comments, or if you want more information, please contact Customer Service. If you no longer wish to receive email from Team USA, click here to unsubscribe.

FIGURE 6.1   USOC targeted email

email marketing campaign delivering messages to the individuals based on their team affiliation and favorite player, and the personalized emails had 39 percent higher unique click rate than the static email (Alford, n.d.). Understanding engagement metrics and looking deeper into the content of each campaign provide useful insights to marketers.

TABLE 6.1 email marketing metrics

Open rate	$\dfrac{\text{Number of unique opens} \times 100}{\text{Total number of delivered emails}}$
Click-through rate	$\dfrac{\text{Number of unique clicks} \times 100}{\text{Total number of delivered emails}}$
Unsubscribe rate	$\dfrac{\text{Number of unsubscribe requests} \times 100}{\text{Total number of delivered emails}}$
Complaint rate	$\dfrac{\text{Number of spam complaints} \times 100}{\text{Total number of delivered emails}}$
Hard bounce rate	$\dfrac{\text{Number of bounced messages} \times 100}{\text{Total number of delivered emails}}$

Source: "2015 email marketing," 2015.

Moreover, day and time of opens should be tracked to identify the ideal timing (day of the week and time of the day) for sending email campaigns which could improve the open rates and initiate customer engagement. Lastly, organizations analyze churn metrics to identify customer disengagement, lost contacts and the health of the email list. The high unsubscribe and complaint rates could be an indication of dissatisfaction with email campaigns, and hard bounces could be due to fake email addresses, issues with domain names and servers in your customer email list which requires careful cleaning. Please see Table 6.1 for these metrics and their calculations.

While engagement and churn metrics provide valuable insights, they do not depict a picture of the bottom line. The ultimate goal of email marketing, just like any other type of marketing, is to drive sales and revenue. Conversion and revenue generated per email marketing campaign are the output metrics for email marketing. Conversion measures the number of individuals who performed a desired behavior due to an email marketing campaign. The desired behaviors can take many forms such as ticket purchase, sign-up for a team's newsletter, engage with an athlete on social media or any other behavior depending on the marketer's objective. Finally, the revenue generated due to an email marketing campaign shows the monetary return of the campaign to the organization.

Social media marketing

The sport business is becoming more and more relationship based and the importance of customer engagement is rising. Fan engagement strengthens fans' emotional connection and increases their loyalty to their team, and helps sport teams achieve sustainability (Bradley, 2012). With over two billion active users, social media has become an ultimate avenue to engage with fans (Dobran, 2015), and sport teams and athletes are taking advantage of the opportunity. Soccer players and European football clubs dominate the social media rankings based on the number of followers. Nine of the ten most popular professional sport teams on social media are football clubs from European leagues, and Los Angeles Lakers is the only non-football team in the top ten (Badenhausen, 2015b). The list of top ten most popular athletes on social media has more variety and includes football, basketball, American football, baseball, boxing, tennis, and track and field athletes (Badenhausen, 2015a). Please see Table 6.2 for the list of most popular athletes and teams

TABLE 6.2 Most popular athletes and teams on social media: follower numbers in millions

Ranking	Athlete (Sport)	Number of followers	Team	Number of followers
1	Cristiano Ronaldo (Soccer)	158	Barcelona FC	100.9
2	Lionel Messi (Soccer) Neymar (Soccer)	93	Real Madrid FC	99.8
3	LeBron James (Basketball)	54	Manchester United FC	70.9
4	Carson Palmer (Football)	43	Chelsea FC	48.7
5	Clayton Kershaw (Baseball)	39	Arsenal FC	39
6	Gareth Bale (Soccer)	36	Bayern Munich FC	32.9
7	Kobe Bryant (Basketball) Zlatan Ibrahimovic (Soccer)	30	Liverpool FC	30.3
8	Floyd Mayweather (Boxing) Kevin Durant (Basketball) Radamel Falcao (Soccer)	25	AC Milan FC	27.1
9	Rafael Nadal (Tennis)	23	Los Angeles Lakers	25.6
10	Luis Suarez (Soccer) Usain Bolt (Track and Field)	21	Paris Saint-Germain FC	22.3

Source: Badenhausen, 2015a; 2015b.

on social media. The fifth annual fan engagement study showed that fans looked at social media as the primary source of sport information, and 75 percent of fans used Facebook, which was followed by YouTube (52 percent), Twitter (37 percent), Google+ (33 percent), and Instagram (17 percent). Super Bowl 50, which was played between the Denver Broncos and the Carolina Panthers, reported similar results with Facebook being fans' primary choice of social media to engage (Preimesberger, 2016). In addition to seeking content about their favorite team and athletes, fans use social media to engage in pre-game talk, game debate, banter, and Q&A with coaches and athletes ("Avid sports fan," 2014).

Social media proves to be a great opportunity to engage with sport fans and by using analytics the outcome of social media marketing could be measured and improved. There are many social media metrics one could track; which ones are useful and meaningful to a sport organization changes based on the objective of social media marketing such as increasing brand awareness, customer engagement or sales. Some of the most commonly measured social media concepts are reach, engagement, brand sentiments, and traffic from social media, and Figure 6.2 presents the metrics for these concepts.

Reach is a measure of potential audience size and it shows the total number of unique people who saw your post (Deering Davis, n.d.). By keeping track of the reach of your social media accounts, you can identify which social media outlet delivers your content to more people, and that can help you make future decisions. Two other metrics that rely on reach are impressions and exposure. When one of your followers shares your post, it appears on the follower's feed and becomes visible to his/her followers. These instances are called impression. Combining your reach and impressions reveals your post's exposure (Dunham, 2014). Tracking exposure of your posts would tell you what kind of posts spread

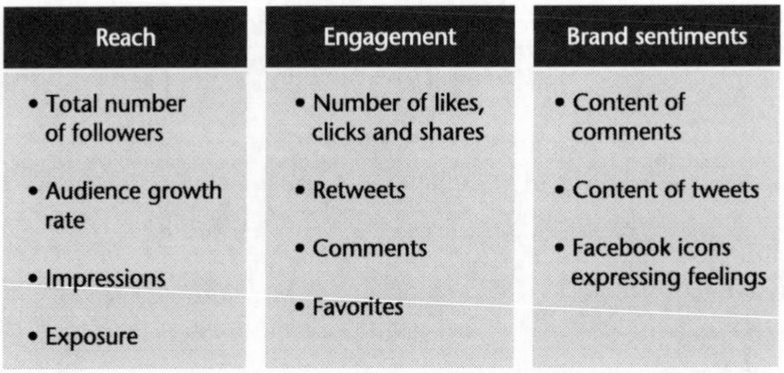

Reach	Engagement	Brand sentiments
• Total number of followers	• Number of likes, clicks and shares	• Content of comments
• Audience growth rate	• Retweets	• Content of tweets
• Impressions	• Comments	• Facebook icons expressing feelings
• Exposure	• Favorites	

FIGURE 6.2   Social media metrics

the most and help you create relevant posts which will expand your potential audience size on social media. Brands that endorse celebrity athletes benefit from the large reach of these athletes in social media. For example, the watch brand Tag Heuer is an endorser of Cristiano Ronaldo who has a total of 158 million followers on Facebook, Twitter, and Instagram. Via Ronaldo's Facebook posts, the watch brand's ad campaign was viewed 35 million times in two days (Badenhausen, 2015a). The final metric that is relevant to the potential audience size is the audience growth rate, which shows the change in number of followers in time. The NBA announced 40 percent growth rate in social media from the end of the 2013–14 regular season through April 2015 ("Record 240 million new fans join NBA on social media," 2015).

Although reach metrics are commonly tracked and used, they only show the potential size of your audience, and do not guarantee that your audience read the post or paid attention to it. Reach metrics should be complimented with engagement metrics such as number of likes, shares, retweets, comments, and favorites. These metrics show whether your followers value your content and find it interesting and relevant, and how successful

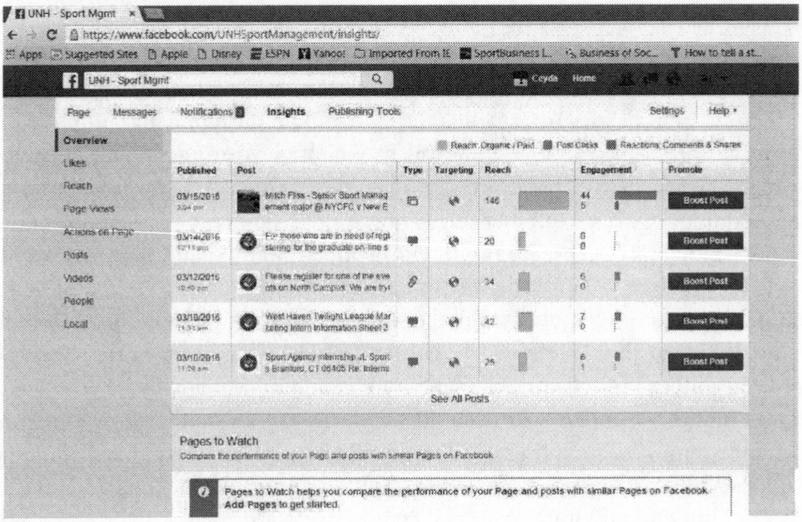

FIGURE 6.3   Analytics around UNH Sport Management Facebook page

you are in having a conversation with them. Careful examination of engagement metrics would identify what type of content and message tone gets the most engagement from your followers and who engages with which network and what type of content. For example, non-Caucasian sport fans tend to use Twitter, Instagram and Vine more than average sports fans, and MLS fans use YouTube (66 percent) more than any other sport fans ("Avid sports fan," 2014). These are great insights on how to communicate with fans and what to provide them. Please see Figure 6.3 for an example taken from UNH Sport Management Facebook page for some 2016 posts.

CASE STUDY: EXAMINATION OF A SOCIAL MEDIA ACCOUNT

Name: Ceyda Mumcu, PhD
Title: Assistant Professor
Current employer: University of New Haven
Brief work history: I have been teaching graduate and undergraduate level sport management courses at the University of New Haven for three years. I hold a PhD in Sport Administration from the University of New Mexico with a minor in Quantitative Research Methods.

How do you think data helps influence your industry segment?

The change in sport fans' consumption habits made social media channels impactful communication outlets for any sport property. Today, sports fans are outspoken and engaged, and want compelling content, and social media provides the perfect recipe. Sport properties can communicate with fans in real-time, publish their own news within seconds, and reach the masses without a geographic boundary. The insights provided by the social media channels themselves and outside companies make substantial information about followers and their behavior available to sport properties instantly. Social media metrics provide valuable information that could be used in creating awareness, audience building, stimulating interest, and generating revenue. Insights derived from social media are used in making smarter decisions, creating engaging content, and so on. In general, the development of technology and availability of data had become opportunities for sport properties, and decision-making moved from the traditional "we have always done it that way" to data-based decision-making in every aspect of the industry.

What example can you share regarding using data to help make a decision?

The issue

With this case study, we are going to take a look at UNH Sport Management Department's Facebook account. The Facebook account for the department was created five years ago. Although an organization can use social media to generate awareness and exposure, build an audience, enhance customer service, drive website traffic, generate leads and improve sales, we have not used Facebook for these purposes. Our main purpose in using Facebook has been sharing internship and employment opportunities with our students. As students often receive a lot of emails every day, and tend to delete quickly or fail to read them closely, it was thought that Facebook could be a communication tool to send students the highly appealing information on internships and job opportunities. Therefore, the Facebook account has been used mostly for this purpose mostly due to the fact that the department does not have a designated staff member to develop content and run social media accounts regularly.

The analysis

As we continue to use the Facebook account to communicate with our students, recently we started to make posts about the upcoming on-campus events, guest speakers, workshops, field trips and also success stories of our own students. In this section, we will take a look at some of the metrics provided by Facebook in analyzing our recent posts and derive insights from it.

Between March 21st and 28th, we made ten posts. Four of these posts were communicating either an internship or a job opportunity, another four posts were about campus events, and two were sharing our students' success stories. In the following table, you will find more detailed information about each of these posts. Although not reported in the table, post times were investigated for all ten posts and there was not a particular trend between reach and engagement numbers and the time posts were made.

The four internship/job opportunity posts reached a limited number of individuals except the job opportunity posted on March 28th. None of these posts had a photo, and

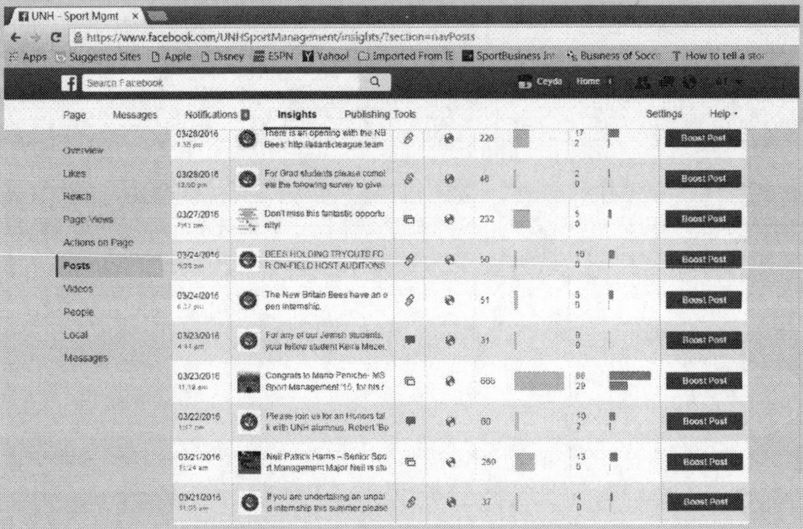

FIGURE 6.4 Sport Management Facebook page analytics

TABLE 6.3 Analytics around UNH Sport Management Facebook page

	Type	Photo	Link	Reach	Engagement	Engagement rate
Post 1 3.21.16	Internship opportunity	No	Yes	37 5 non-followers	4 Clicks 0 Comments/ Shares	11%
Post 2 3.21.16	Student success	Yes	No	269 6 non-followers	13 Clicks 0 Comments/ Shares	5%
Post 3 3.22.16	Campus event	No	No	60 8 non-followers	10 Clicks 2 Comments/ Shares	20%
Post 4 3.23.16	Student success	Yes	No	668 326 non-followers	66 Clicks 29 Comments/ Shares	14%
Post 5 3.23.16	Campus event	No	No	31 4 non-followers	0 Clicks 0 Comments/ Shares	0%
Post 6 3.24.16	Internship opportunity	No	Yes	51 4 non-followers	8 Clicks 0 Comments/ Shares	16%
Post 7 3.24.16	Job opportunity	No	Yes	50 6 non-followers	10 Clicks 0 Comments/ Shares	20%
Post 8 3.27.16	Campus event	Yes	No	232 6 non-followers	5 Clicks 0 Comments/ Shares	2%
Post 9 3.28.16	Student engagement	No	Yes	46 6 non-followers	2 Clicks 0 Comments/ Shares	4%
Post 10 3.28.16	Job opportunity	No	Yes	220 26 non-followers	17 Clicks 2 Comments/ Shares	9%

all of them included a link to the job application site. Although the potential audience size for these posts is rather small, engagement rate is larger than the other type of posts. In other words, the individuals who saw these posts found the content valuable and engaged with it. The one post that reached a relatively large audience has the lowest engagement rate among this type of posts.

When we look at the three posts about campus events and the one single post asking students' action, we saw a similar situation with the job/internship opportunity posts. Three of these four posts reached a very limited audience. The information about an upcoming campus event posted on March 27th reached a larger audience and the post included a photo. However, contrary to the job opportunity posts, these posts received very minimal engagement from the audience except the post about the honors program talk made on March 22nd.

Finally, when we turn our attention to the posts sharing student success, we see that these two posts had the largest audience among all posts discussed in this case study, but their engagement rates vary greatly. The post with the largest audience is about one of our international graduate students and almost half of the audience for this post is not among our followers on Facebook. Therefore, this post had the most impressions and overall exposure among all posts.

The end results

What does all this mean? Although the audience size is small for the posts about job/internship opportunities, individuals who see the post value the content. It is important for us to expand the audience size for posts of this type as they are aimed to support our students, and we would like these posts to reach more students. Information about the upcoming events often has a smaller reach unless the post includes a photo, and students do not engage with these posts. Therefore, photos should be included to test if this really increases the audience size for this type of post. Nevertheless, followers do not engage with these posts and reach numbers do not communicate whether they read the post or not. These posts are made to make students aware of upcoming opportunities on campus and include full information on the events. Therefore, perhaps lack of engagement numbers for these posts is not surprising. Student success stories clearly reach the largest audience among all types of posts. Engagement numbers and rates vary from post to post which could be devoted to the content. Finally, an overall comment should be made in evaluating the Facebook posts and the metrics. The results show that the UNH Sport Management Facebook page has a small audience that is interested in the department's posts and consistently engages with the posts. In order to expand the number of engaged followers, the size of the audience should be expanded with other types of posts and a relationship and interest should be built with relevant content.

While a sport organization can see whether their audience and the engagement received from them are growing or not by tracking the aforementioned metrics, these metrics could be misleading without understanding the sentiment of conversation around their brand on social media. For example, there were more than 60,000 tweets on #DeflateGate within three days of the claim that New England Patriots used deflated footballs against the Colts during an AFC Championship game in 2015 (Earl, 2015). The number of tweets and mentions in other social media outlets skyrocketed, but the sentiment behind them was mainly negative. Around 70 percent of NFL fans supported Brady's suspension and fining of the Patriots (Smith, 2015). Without reviewing the content of the tweets and mentions, higher vanity metrics – size of reach, number of tweets, retweets, favorites, and so on – would appear as a positive outcome. Social listening allows marketers to measure the tone of a conversation, observe customer perspective and understand how the audience is reacting to their brand, whether it is positive, negative or neutral. Careful investigation of the brand sentiments provides invaluable feedback to sport properties and brands that associate with these entities.

Finally, the bottom line of a business – customer acquisition and sales, and how social media marketing contributes to the bottom line and the metrics to track. As discussed previously, social media is a great avenue to interact with your fans and engage them in a conversation with you. However, the bottom line is turning these interactions into revenue for the sport organization, and gaining a return from your investment in social media marketing. Two metrics that are used in this area are number of clicks and traffic from social media which measure the success of social media posts in bringing fans into the organization's website. In order to measure clicks and traffic, marketers include a shortened URL in social media posts to direct their followers to their website. By tracking clicks and traffic, marketers can pin point which social media network works better for them and which posts perform better in calling people into action. High quality content, photos and videos are known to be effective at piquing followers' interest and encouraging them to click (Dawson, 2016).

Another way to generate revenue through a sport property's social media efforts and following is marketing through sports. In other words, knowing who is following you and what is being discussed online can be utilized to attract advertisers and sponsors. The fifth annual fan engagement study conducted by Catalyst showed that 80 percent of sport fans, who were associated with a brand on social media, either discussed the brand or shared their original content or bought a product from them ("Avid sports fan," 2014). In 2013, Phoenix Suns became the first professional team that received Nielsen Twitter TV ratings. The Suns were able to identify the size of their audience, its impact and the key topics discussed. They used this information to attract advertisers and sponsors, and to push promotions and ticket offers to their followers (Lombardo, 2013). In January 2016, Nielsen announced that in addition to Twitter, they will start tracking TV ratings on Facebook and Instagram. According to Sean Casey who is the president of Nielsen Social, sport programming made up only 3 percent of all TV programming in 2015, yet 50 percent of the conversation about TV shows on Twitter. This data suggests that sport programs have added value to advertisers and sponsors beyond who watches them live (Deggans, 2016).

Web analytics

As mentioned at the beginning of this chapter, sport fans' main source for sport content is the internet. According to Nielsen's sports media report, as cited in Ourand (2014), over 87 million individuals consumed sport content by visiting sports sites on a computer, and approximately 62 million by using their smartphones. The average time spent during these visits was 105 minutes and 92 minutes for computer and smartphone use, respectively, and the time spent on sports sites further increased in 2015 by 22 percent ("The year in sports media report," 2016). These statistics clearly communicate the importance of well-functioning, appealing websites for sport organizations. If you visit the NBA's official website at nba.com, you will see that the website fulfills a variety of functions for the league such as ticket sales, merchandise sales, registration for NBA TV, delivering content about games, athletes, teams and the league, brand management and many more. The league has a very comprehensive website which requires careful analyses to understand what their users are interested in, if the pages function with ease, and how to improve the content, format and functionality.

Web analytics are used to assess the impact of a website on its users, and most often the number of visitors and how many of them are unique visitors and how many are repeat visitors, how they came to the site, how long they stayed and their behavior on the site during their visit, and when they left the site are investigated. Some of the basic metrics tracked to understand these concepts are defined (Burby, Brown, & WAA Standards Committee, 2007) and explained below.

- Number of page views is a simple count of times a page is viewed (Burby *et al.*, 2007). By reviewing the number of page views within a website, one can learn which pages are viewed more than the others, and looking into the content of these pages closely identifies the top content your audience is looking for. The most viewed pages are often the pages with the top content.

- Number of unique visitors reports the number of individuals (distinct cookies) who visited a page during a time period (Burby *et al.*, 2007). This is a good metric to measure the size of the audience of a page. While a page could have been visited millions of times, some of these visits could have been made by repeat visitors. The number of repeat visitors shows the size of your loyal audience and deeper investigation of their behavior on the website identifies whether your content is engaging and relevant or not.

- Entry page is the first page for a visit while the exit page is the last page accessed during a visit (Burby *et al.*, 2007). By viewing this information, one can identify where a visitor started their journey on your website and where they left. If we go back to the NBA's official website, a visitor's entry page could be one of many pages depending on the keywords used in a search engine. If one used 'nba store' in a search engine, it would send them to store.nba.com and it would be recorded as the entry page for that particular visit, and the last page the individual viewed would be the exit page for their visit.

- Landing page is similar to an entry page in the sense that it is the first page an individual visits. However, it is due to a marketing effort and the page is designed as the beginning of the user experience (Burby *et al.*, 2007). For instance, the NBA might have a promotion on its league pass for a specific game and could distribute information on this special promotion via their social media accounts and include a URL in these posts. The individuals, who click on this URL on social media, would view the landing page for the special promotion. Therefore, they would begin their experience via the specific landing page which would allow the marketers to identify the marketing tactic responsible for the lead. This allows a company to try multiple marketing approaches and then have real facts to show which campaign produced the best results.

- It is important to understand how people come to your website. As mentioned in previous bullets, people can reach your website through search engines and URLs placed in your marketing campaigns. In addition, direct traffic and URL clicks from referring sites send traffic to websites. Direct traffic is people reaching a website by typing the URL or using a bookmark. In other words, existing customers who know your web address reach the site directly. Lastly, other websites send traffic to your website through the links you placed into banner ads, product campaigns, and so on.

Therefore, the four traffic sources are search engines, URL clicks from referring sites, direct traffic, and campaigns. All sport organizations should strive to have a balanced portfolio of these traffic sources.

- Visit duration is the length of a session and is usually reported in hours and minutes. Site administrators are interested in knowing how long their audience spends time on their website, and whether they leave the website after viewing one page or click on other content. Sport properties use websites as tools in communicating with sports fans and want them to search through their website and get exposed to their own content and also the advertisers' content as much as possible. For instance, if you visit ESPN.com, you will see stories about daily sport news, game scores, pictures and videos, and also advertisers' banners. Visit duration is an important metric, and a longer duration increases the audience's likelihood of being exposed to these advertisements. That is one reason why a website needs interesting content, videos, photos, and other highlights that keep a person glued to their screen.
- Click-through is the number of times a link is clicked which simply is a count. When measured as a rate, the click-through rate is the number of times the link is clicked divided by the number of times the link is viewed (Burby *et al.*, 2007). The click-through metric is often used for advertising activities and measured for links internal and external to the website. If we continue with the NBA's official website as an example and review the site, we come across several promotional messages calling individuals to action such as "Get started now!" or "Buy now!" Measuring the click-through rate for these internal links would determine whether individuals take action or not, and which links bring business to the website.
- Conversion rate is the percentage of site visitors completing a targeted action (Kaushik, 2006), which could be signing up for a newsletter, clicking on an advertisement banner, purchasing a merchandise, ticket or service, and so on, and these targeted actions are dependent on the objectives of the company who owns the website.

By monitoring these metrics and others, website administrators can determine if the pages are working properly, which pages receive more traffic, what contributes to the company bottom line. While these metrics present the current state of the website, online testing, specifically A/B testing, can identify how to create a better user experience. The A/B testing compares two versions of a page by tracking a variety of metrics including but not limited to conversion rates, visit duration, and number of page views (Grover, 2015), and identifies which version produces better results. The ultimate goal is to optimize the website or mobile application, provide the content in the most effective way possible, and improve the communication with your audience.

Conclusion

In summary, today, digital media channels – web, social media, mobile applications, and email marketing – are used as marketing tools and complement the sport organizations' traditional marketing efforts. Successful sport organizations are aware of the value of well-designed, functional websites, engaging social media presence, relevant email marketing, and endless content provided via mobile applications. By utilizing all these sources and the insights derived from these efforts, sport marketers create a consistent, engaging and relevant customer experience, connect with the fans at a deeper level, and encourage increased levels of consumption.

References

2015 Email marketing metrics benchmark study [IBM white paper]. (2015). Retrieved from www.silverpop.com/marketing-resources/white-papers/all/2015/email-metrics-benchmark-study-2015/

Alford, J. (n.d.). *What major league soccer knows about predictive analytics marketing?* [SAS White Paper]. Retrieved from www.sas.com/en_us/insights/articles/marketing/what-pro-soccer-knows-about-predictive-analytics-marketing.html

Alt-Simmons, R. (n.d.). *Digital marketing: are you ready to go agile?* [SAS white paper]. Retrieved from www.sas.com/en_us/whitepapers/digital-marketing-107609.html

Avid sports fan: 2014 digital media habits (2014, October 14). [Graph Illustration 5th Annual Catalyst Fan Engagement Study]. Retrieved from www.catalystimg.com/fan-engagement-study/

Badenhausen, K. (2015a, June 10). *Cristiano Ronaldo heads the most popular athletes on social media.* Retrieved from www.forbes.com/sites/kurtbadenhausen/2015/06/10/cristiano-ronaldo-heads-the-most-popular-athletes-on-social-media/#67863bc854cb

Badenhausen, K. (2015b, July 15). *Barcelona and Real Madrid head the most popular sports teams on social media.* Retrieved from www.forbes.com/sites/kurtbadenhausen/2015/07/15/barcelona-and-real-madrid-head-the-most-popular-sports-teams-on-social-media/#7977199a5e5e

Bradley, M. (2012, December 7). *Supporter liaison officer: An opportunity for a different perspective.* Retrieved from http://bradleyprojects.com/blog.php?id=6

Burby, J., Brown, A., & WAA Standards Committee. (2007). *Web analytics definitions.* Retrieved from www.digitalanalyticsassociation.org/Files/PDF_standards/WebAnalyticsDefinitionsVol1.pdf

Dawson, J. (2016, February 12). *Three ways content can covert social media fans into customers.* Retrieved from www.entrepreneur.com/article/270478?utm_source=Latest&utm_medium=site&utm_campaign=iScroll

Deering Davis, J. (n.d.). *5 essential & easy social media metrics you should be measuring right now.* Retrieved from https://blog.kissmetrics.com/essential-social-media-metrics/

Deggans, E. (2016, January 22). *Nielsen to use Facebook and Twitter in new social TV ratings.* Retrieved from www.npr.org/2016/01/20/463740422/nielsen-to-use-facebook-and-twitter-in-new-social-tv-ratings

Dobran, B. (2015, July 9). *From engagement to leads: The psychology behind converting social media fans.* Retrieved from www.marketingprofs.com/articles/2015/28029/from-engagement-to-leads-the-psychology-behind-converting-social-media-fans

Dunham, K. (2014, May 19). *The Beginner's guide to social media metrics: Reach and exposure.* Retrieved from http://blog.hootsuite.com/beginners-guide-to-social-media-metrics-reach-exposure/

Earl, J. (2015, January 21). *Twitter trolls New England Patriots with #DeflateGate tweets.* Retrieved from www.cbsnews.com/news/twitter-trolls-deflatriots-with-deflategate-tweets/

Gesenhues, A. (2014, February 6). *Study: personalized emails deliver 6x higher transaction rates, but 70% of brands fail to use them.* Retrieved from http://marketingland.com/study-70-brands-personalizing-emails-missing-higher-transaction-rates-revenue-73241

Grover, S. (2015, November 3). *Digital marketing, predictive analytics, and making personalization delicious* [SAS blog]. Retrieved from http://blogs.sas.com/content/customeranalytics/2015/11/03/digital-marketing-predictive-analytics-making-personalization-delicious/

Kaushik, A. (2006, July 23). *Stop obsessing about conversion rate.* Retrieved from www.kaushik.net/avinash/stop-obsessing-about-conversion-rate/

Laursen, G. H. (2011). *Business analytics for sales and marketing managers: how to compete in the Information Age.* Hoboken, NJ: John Wiley & Sons, Inc.

Lombardo, J. (2013). Twitter TV ratings to track Suns traffic. *Sports Business Journal, 16*(30). Retrieved from www.sportsbusinessdaily.com/Journal/Issues/2013/11/11/Franchises/Suns.aspx

Preimesberger, C. (2016, February 8). *No surprise: Super Bowl 50 obliterates data usage records.* Retrieved from www.eweek.com/mobile/no-surprise-super-bowl-50-obliterates-data-usage-records.html

Ourand, J. (2014). Sports media. *Sports Business Journal, 17*(4), 16–19.

Record 240 million new fans join NBA on social media. (2015, April 16). Retrieved from www.nba.com/2015/news/04/16/record-number-of-fans-join-nba-on-social-media/

Smith, M. D. (2015, May 14). *Poll finds most fans support NFL suspending Brady.* Retrieved from http://profootballtalk.nbcsports.com/2015/05/14/poll-finds-most-fans-support-nfl-suspending-brady/

Stadd, A. (2013, August 5). *More sports fans turning to digital media over TV.* Retrieved from www.adweek.com/socialtimes/sports-digital-media-tv/488442

The year in sports report: Digital steps up to the plate [Nielsen report]. (2015, February 5). Retrieved from www.nielsen.com/us/en/insights/news/2015/the-year-in-sports-digital-steps-up-to-the-plate.html

The year in sports media report [Nielsen report]. (2016, February 3). Retrieved from www.nielsen.com/content/dam/corporate/us/en/reports-downloads/2016-reports/nielsen-year-in-sports-report-feb-2016.pdf

7

SPORT FINANCE BY THE NUMBERS

Peggy Keiper and Dylan Williams

Introduction

At some point in time, it is fair to assume that every student, scholar, or professional within the sport industry has had a question posed to them about the scope and size of the sport industry. The size and the scope of the sport industry, though often financially measured by annual sales, revenue generated, or estimated value, is not as clear as one would think. For example, *Forbes Magazine* reported that, as researched by PricewaterhouseCoopers (PwC), the sport market possesses a worth of $60.5 billion (Heitner, 2015). On the other hand, Plunkett Research, Ltd. estimated the size of the US sport industry to be $498.4 billion and the global sport industry to be $1.5 trillion ("Sports, teams and leisure industry statistics." n.d.).

The variance in market estimations or value does not exploit any issues in calculation or estimation but instead illuminates the considerable fluctuation in defining what the sport industry includes. A prime example is whether or not to include eSports in the sport industry. eSports are personal computer games such as *Dota 2, League of Legends* and *StarCraft II* played in professional competitions and watched by fans through the internet (Gaudiosi, 2016). Although ESPN covers eSports and some college athletic departments such as Robert Morris University in Illinois have added eSports as a varsity sport, there could still be a valid argument that eSports are indeed not part of the sport industry based on the minimal or lack of physicality (Jenny, Manning, Keiper, & Olrich, 2016). This distinction is important to consider because the eSport industry is valued, in 2015, as nearly a billion dollar global industry ("eSports market brief," 2015). Moreover, valuation and worth can vary based on what factors are being included.

The point here is to not estimate the size of the sport industry or decipher what organizations are part of the industry. The purpose is to demonstrate the sport industry is very complex and composed of blurred edges and areas of overlap. For example, a general manager at a stadium who has a single professional sports tenant will spend a considerable amount of their time working with the arena staff to book other outside, non-sporting entertainment events to fill the nights the team does not play. Also, consider many major companies who have a separate sport marketing arm which concentrates it's efforts to marketing their company's product *through* sport. Coca-Cola's senior vice president for connections, investment, and assets spends a considerable amount of time with the marketing of the Coke product through sports, but Coke is not a sport company (Smith, 2015). Thus, areas of overlap are prevalent in the sport industry.

Conclusively, the sport industry varies from profit to non-profit entities. There are sport organizations for both professional and amateur sports. There are entities operating on a local level and others dealing with sport for the global good. There are non-sport organizations that possess a division solely for marketing their good or service through sport while others produce the core sport product. Even with the vast nature of the sport industry, it is not obligatory to have an understanding of each entity making up the industry in order to understand how financial analytics are used. Many of the basic financial principles, means of financial analysis, and use of financial data remain the same regardless of the entity at hand. This chapter focuses on how data analytics are used for financial decision-making in sport. First, let us consider traditional financial analysis as the foundation to more modern and advanced financial analytics being used within the industry.

Traditional financial analysis

Managers of any sport organization must understand how to analyze financial statements and develop skills in financial planning. Financial statements are similar to box scores or statistical sheets from prior contests, which allow managers to assess their organization's health in financial terms (Brown *et al.*, 2010). While all financial statements are important, the two statements most commonly analyzed are an organization's balance sheet and income statement (Jablonsky & Barsky, 2001; Ōstring, 2003). These statements are compiled from a firm's accounting records and typically follow a standard set of guidelines for financial reporting. For organizations within the United States, nongovernmental firms are required to follow the established standards known as Generally Accepted Accounting Principles (GAAP), which are created by the Financial Accounting Standards Board (FASB) and recognized as authoritative by the Securities and Exchange Commission (SEC) and the American Institute of Certified Public Accountants (AICPA) ("Facts about FASB," n.d.).

GAAP allows organizations to maintain their financial statements with two different bases of accounting. Smaller organizations often use a cash basis accounting system where all transactions (i.e. sales or purchases) are recorded as money is received or paid out. In comparison, larger sport organizations often use the accrual method, which accounts for transactions when they occur as opposed to when money is received. Specifically, the accrual method of accounting records transactions when orders are made, items are delivered, or when services occur, regardless of when the money for these items is actually received or paid. Sport organizations can anticipate millions from a broadcast contract or luxury box leases but may not have yet received that money (or they might owe players under the terms of the contract). While money may not have exchanged hands, the amounts are real and the money either will come or will have to be paid. Whichever basis of accounting an organization utilizes, the numbers generated from this accounting practice form the basis for numbers found in the financial statements.

Balance sheet

The balance sheet provides a picture or snapshot of the financial condition of an organization at a specific point in time, as if the firm were standing still (Jablonsky & Barsky, 2001). It offers information regarding a company's assets, liabilities, and owner's equity. Assets are the items a company owns such as cash, inventory, equipment, and facilities. Liabilities are the organization's financial obligations or debts it owes to others. For example, a sporting good manufacturer's assets would include the apparel and equipment being produced and their liabilities would include facility rent and staff salaries. Owner's equity is an estimated measure of the ownership value of a company and is equal to the company's assets minus its liabilities. Stated differently, a company's assets must be balanced by the sum of a company's liabilities and owner's equity (Fried, DeSchriver, & Mondello, 2013). In order to ensure an organization's balance sheet is balanced, transactions are recorded through double-entry bookkeeping. This GAAP procedure requires an entity's transactions to be entered and recorded twice as a financial journal entry, once on the debit side of accounting records and once on the credit side. These journal entries ensure balance is maintained as debits must equal credits in order to be recorded. Figure 7.1 displays the balance sheet for Nike (2015) at the end of its last two fiscal years (May 31, 2015 and May 31, 2014 respectively). For each year, Nike's assets are equal to the total of its liabilities and owner's equity.

Assets listed on the balance sheet are provided in order of liquidity, or how quickly an asset can be converted into cash, with the most liquid assets listed first (Jablonsky & Barsky, 2001). The entries listed under current assets are the most liquid because they are expected

	May 31, 2015	May 31, 2014
ASSETS		
Current assets		
Cash and cash equivalents	$ 5,924	$ 5,142
Accounts receivable and other current assets	5,715	4,607
Inventory	4,337	3,947
Total current assets	$15,976	$13,696
Property, equipment, and other long-term assets	5,624	4,898
TOTAL ASSETS	$ 21,600	$ 18,594
LIABILITIES AND OWNER'S EQUITY		
Current liabilities		
Accounts payable	$ 2,131	$ 1,930
Other current liabilities	4,203	3,097
Total current liabilities	$ 6,334	$ 5,027
Long-term liabilities	2,559	2,743
Total liabilities	$ 8,893	$ 7,770
Owner's equity		
Common stock and other equity	8,022	5,953
Retained earnings	4,685	4,871
Total owner's equity	$ 12,707	$ 10,824
TOTAL LIABILITIES AND OWNER'S EQUITY	$ 21,600	$ 18,594
Total common shares outstanding	1,536	1,532

FIGURE 7.1   Modified Nike balance sheet

to be converted to cash within one year or less. Examples of current assets include cash, accounts receivable, and inventory. In comparison, machinery, equipment, and buildings are considered long-term assets as they possess the least liquidity. Liabilities are similarly listed according to their maturity, or when the liability or debt is due to be paid by the organization. Liabilities due within one year are classified as current liabilities while those due after one year are labeled long-term liabilities. Common examples of current liabilities include accounts payable and employee salaries while loans for facility construction and employee pension obligations are considered long-term liabilities. Finally, owner's equity represents an estimate of the value or ownership stake of the company and reflects decisions about the sources of financing for the business (Brown *et al.*, 2010).

Income statement

The income statement measures a business's profitability over a specific period such as a year (Jablonsky & Barsky, 2001). The income statement can also be referred to as the statement of earnings or the profit and loss statement. Over the specified time period, the income statement lists the organization's revenues, or money generated from business activities (i.e. sale of goods and services), and expenses, or the costs of doing business. Figure 7.2 provides the annual income statements for Nike's most recent fiscal years (May 31, 2015, 2014, and 2013 respectively). Each income statement covers a 12-month period ending on May 31st each year.

	For the year ended May 31		
	2015	2014	2013
Total revenue	$ 30,601	$ 27,799	$ 25,313
Cost of goods sold	16,534	15,353	14,279
Gross profit	$ 14,067	$12,446	$ 11,034
Operating expenses	9,892	8,766	7,780
Operating income	$ 4,175	$ 3,680	$ 3,254
Interest income (expense), net	(28)	(33)	3
Other income (expense)	58	(103)	15
Income before income taxes	$ 4,205	$ 3,544	$ 3,272
Provision for income taxes	932	851	787
Net Income	$ 3,273	$ 2,693	$ 2,485

FIGURE 7.2 Modified Nike income statement

Under US GAAP, revenue is recorded when an exchange of goods or services occurs. Furthermore, revenue and expenses are reported when they occur, even if the transfer of cash does not occur. For example, when goods and services are sold for credit, associated sales and profits are reported even if payment has not been received. This system is known as accrual basis accounting. When expenses are deducted from revenues, the resulting figure is the organization's net income (or net loss if expenses exceed revenue). Net income can also be referred to as net earnings or net profit (Fried *et al.*, 2013).

Financial ratios

The information found on these financial statements can be used to compute financial ratios, which provide additional insight into the health of the organization. Additionally, financial ratios allow for comparisons among competitors within a particular industry, firms of similar size and scope, and an organization's own past history.

Keep in mind just because an organization is part of the sport industry does not mean that it makes sense to compare two organizations or that meaningful comparisons can be made between two organizations solely because they operate within the sport industry. For example, the financial ratios from a billion dollar, for-profit venture, such as Nike, will look significantly different from a small, non-profit sport commission such as the West Michigan Sports Commission. Moreover, comparing the financial ratios of the two organizations would not result in any significant conclusions because the two organizations operate within significantly different sectors of the sport industry. Thus, to draw meaningful conclusions when utilizing financial ratios to compare against competitors, the size and similar scope must be considered.

Nearly every company or organization, regardless of scope or size, utilizes financial ratios. Some of the commonly utilized financial ratios focus on five key areas. These areas include liquidity, asset management, leverage, profitability, and market value.

Liquidity

The liquidity ratios measure the ability of a business to meet short-term financial obligations with its short-term assets. A company lacking sufficient short-term assets to pay off their current obligations may be forced to refinance its debts or borrow additional money to meet its financial liabilities. An example of a sector within the sport industry which has seen significant financial issues related to liquidity is the extreme racing industry. Companies such as Red Frog Events and Tough Mudder, have seen much financial success and thrive in the extreme racing/event production sector within the sport industry. However, many other organizations have not been able to see similar success and have failed to be significant movers in the market. The outcome of lacking sufficient short-term assets when putting on extreme racing events comes in the form of cancelled races/events, which is due to the inability to cover debts such as venue cost. The cancellation of extreme racing events by unestablished racing companies has been quite common within this subsector of the sport industry.

A. Current ratio

One way an events company, or any company, would analyze its liquidity is through the current ratio. The current ratio measures an organization's ability to meet its current short-term liabilities with its current assets. It is calculated with the following formula:

Current ratio = Current assets/Current liabilities

Using data from Figure 7.1, Nike's current ratio for May 31, 2015 is calculated as follows (Note: The figures from Figure 7.1 were abbreviated and rounded to the nearest million. For the current ratio and other ratio examples, we add six zeros to each of the values reported on Figures 7.1 and 7.2, except for stock share information):

$$\text{Current ratio} = \frac{\$15,976,000,000}{\$6,334,000,000} = 2.52$$

The current ratio suggests Nike has the ability to cover its short-term liabilities 2.5 times over with its current assets. In general, a current ratio of 2.0 is preferred as it represents a healthy ability to cover current debts with cash and accounts receivable. Further, a company with a high current ratio is less likely to need to convert long-term assets into cash or borrow money to cover its debts. However, a current ratio can be too high. According to Helfert (2002) and Shapiro and Balbirer (2000), a current ratio above 2.0 could signal that a company is not maximizing its use of its cash or is carrying excessive inventory. Nonetheless, the current ratio, as well as most other financial ratios, should always be evaluated in context when used as a comparative tool. In other words, before determining whether a company's current ratio is too large, it should be compared with its competitors in its industry as well as the company's own history. These ratios should be examined relative to values in previous time periods in order to evaluate trends in financial position (Brown *et al.*, 2010).

B. Quick/acid-test ratio

A second measure of liquidity is the quick, or acid-test, ratio. This ratio is similar to the current ratio as it provides information regarding whether a company can cover its current liabilities with its current assets. According to Fried *et al.* (2013), inventory is the least liquid of any of the current assets due to its difficulty to convert into cash. Companies may take months to sell their inventory at full value or substantially discount inventory to sell it rapidly. Higgins (2009) noted sellers may receive 40 percent or less of an inventory's book value through a liquidation sale. Due to the volatility of inventory, the quick ratio is viewed as the more conservative liquidity ratio (Brown *et al.*, 2010). However, the quick ratio deducts inventory from current assets as shown below:

Quick ratio = (Current assets − Inventory)/Current liabilities

Nike's quick ratio for May 31, 2015 is calculated as follows:

$$\text{Quick ratio} = \frac{\$15,976,000,000 - \$4,337,000,000}{\$6,334,000,000} = 1.84$$

Nike can cover its short-term liabilities 1.84 times over with its current assets excluding inventory. For an apparel company with a large quantity of inventory, Nike possesses sufficient assets to cover its short-term debt if necessary.

Asset management

Asset management ratios measure how effectively a company manages its assets to generate sales. All companies have a limited amount of resources, and those that are most efficient in using their resources to generate sales are likely to be successful. There are several ratios measuring asset management, but the two most common are the asset turnover ratio and the inventory turnover ratio.

A. Asset turnover ratio

The asset turnover ratio gives an indication of how efficiently a firm utilizes its assets to generate sales. It is calculated by dividing total revenues for a particular period by the average total assets for that period.

Asset turnover ratio = Revenues/average total assets

As discussed earlier, revenues are found on the income statement while total assets (both current and long-term) are found on the balance sheet. To find average total assets, one must calculate a company's total assets at the beginning and end of a period of interest, which is often the fiscal year. For Nike, these asset values are given in Figure 7.1. Total assets at the end of 2015 were $21,600,000,000 while the beginning year assets are assumed to be equal to the totals from the prior year. As such, total assets at the end of 2014 were $18,594,000,000. These figures are averaged together in order to determine the average total assets. The entire calculation proceeds as follows:

$$\text{Asset turnover ratio} = \frac{\$30,601,000,000}{(21,600,000,000 + \$18,594,000,000)/2}$$
$$= \frac{\$30,601,000,000}{\$20,097,000,000} = 1.52$$

During the FY 2015, Nike's revenues exceeded assets by a considerable amount, which suggests the company is using its assets effectively in the generation of sales. If an asset turnover ratio is relatively high, the firm is efficiently using its assets to generate sales. However, if the ratio is relatively low, the firm may need to consider selling off assets in order to improve its sales figures.

B. Inventory turnover ratio

The inventory turnover ratio measures how often a company sells and replaces its inventory over a specified period of time (often a fiscal year). For organizations in manufacturing and retail, such as Adidas or Spalding, this ratio is an important one as inventory is typically a large asset for these companies. It is calculated with the following formula:

Inventory turnover ratio = Cost of goods sold/average inventory

Cost of goods sold (COGS) includes all costs directly related to the production of goods or products to be sold such as raw materials and labor costs. COGS, which can also be called cost of sales or cost of revenues, typically precede net sales near the top of the income statement. In comparison, inventory is found on the balance sheet. Similar to the asset turnover ratio, average inventory is the average of a company's beginning and ending inventory for a period of interest. A relatively high turnover ratio is usually preferable as it signals inventory is replenished several times throughout the period of interest.

Using data from figures 7.1 and 7.2, we calculate Nike's inventory turnover ratio for 2015 as follows:

$$\text{Inventory turnover ratio} = \frac{\$16,534,000,000}{(\$4,337,000,000 + \$3,947,000,000)/2}$$

$$= \frac{\$16,534,000,000}{\$4,142,000,000} = 3.99$$

To interpret this figure, we say Nike turned over, or sold and replenished, its inventory almost four times during the 2015 fiscal year. However, one must also keep the industry analyzed in mind. For example, industries selling low-cost items, such as a grocery store, will turn over inventory much more rapidly than industries selling luxury items such as jewelry. Furthermore, this ratio may not be an important indicator for certain industries. For example, while Nike uses this ratio as a vital metric, most professional sport franchises do not consider it an important indicator since they do not create goods in the same way as a manufacturer or retailer.

Leverage

Financial leverage refers to how an organization chooses to finance its operations with debt versus equity. Companies relying extensively on borrowing money in order to conduct their operations are considered to be heavily leveraged (Brown et al., 2010). As such, firms with high financial leverage relative to their peers in their industry have a greater likelihood of financial distress and bankruptcy.

A. Debt ratio

One measure of financial leverage is the debt ratio, which is calculated as follows:

Debt ratio = Total liabilities/total assets

Both total liabilities and total assets can be found on the balance sheet. A lower debt ratio is generally preferable as a higher value indicates a firm has increased financial risk due to higher borrowing. From data from Figure 7.1, we calculate Nike's debt ratio for May 31, 2015 as:

$$\text{Debt ratio} = \frac{\$8,893,000,000}{\$21,600,000,000} = 0.41$$

This ratio is typically reported as a percentage. Thus, Nike possesses debt that is valued as 41 percent of its assets. In other words, money borrowed from creditors comprises 41 percent of the assets owned by Nike.

B. Interest coverage ratio

An additional financial leverage measurement is the interest coverage ratio, or the times interest earned ratio. This calculation measures a company's ability to pay its interest on the debt it incurs. According to Brown et al. (2010), some companies with debt may not be able to pay their liabilities in full, but should be able to pay the interest owed on the debt. If not, the company may be at risk of significant financial problems. The interest coverage ratio is calculated with the following formula:

Interest coverage ratio = Earnings before interest and taxes (EBIT)/interest expense

EBIT is found on the income statement and is defined as operating revenue minus operating expenses plus any non-operating income. When a company does not report any non-operating income, EBIT may be called operating income or operating profit. Using data from Nike's income statement (Figure 7.2), the interest coverage ratio for the 2015 fiscal year is:

$$\text{Interest coverage ratio} = \frac{\$4,175,000,000}{\$28,000,000} = 149.11$$

According to this calculation, Nike can cover its interest expenses over 149 times with its EBIT or operating income.

Profitability

One of the most critical figures for examining a company's success is its corporate earnings (Fried *et al.*, 2013). The primary purpose for any for-profit business is to generate sufficient earnings in order to continue their growth and reward stakeholders. Several measures of profitability are used, but the most common ratios are net profit margin, return on assets, and return on equity.

A. Net profit margin

The net profit margin is the percentage of total revenues (or sales) that was net profit (or income). This margin measures the effectiveness and efficiency of an organization's operations. It is calculated with the following formula:

Net profit margin = Net income/total revenue

A higher percentage indicates a company is efficient in its production and operations while a lower percentage reflects inefficient operations and poor management. A lower ratio also indicates a company may be at risk financially if sales were to decline. During the 2015 fiscal year, Nike's net profit margin is calculated as:

$$\text{Net profit margin} = \frac{\$3,273,000,000}{\$30,601,000,000} = 0.11$$

Nike's net profit margin was approximately 11 percent. Stated differently, Nike spent 89 percent of the money it generated in sales on its various selling, general, and administrative expenses while 11 percent was returned to the company and its shareholders as profit.

B. Return on assets

The return on assets (ROA) ratio is a key indicator of profitability for a company as it shows whether management has generated a reasonable return on the assets utilized in operations (Ōstring, 2003). It is calculated as a percentage as follows:

Return on assets = Net income/total assets

ROA can also be referred to as return on investment (ROI) since it reflects the amount of profit earned on the investment of all assets of the firm (Fried *et al.*, 2013). In other words, ROA measures the amount of profit made by a company for every dollar invested in assets, showcasing its ability to generate profits before utilizing any type of debt or leverage. Thus, if a company opts to purchase a new asset, it should be able to generate increased returns in terms of net income in comparison to a risky financial investment. Nike's return on assets for its FY 2015 is calculated as:

$$\text{Return on assets} = \frac{\$3,273,000,000}{\$21,600,000,000} = 0.15$$

Like the net profit margin, ROA is reported in percentage form since it represents the percentage earned on the company's assets. Thus, Nike generated a 15 percent return on its assets for the 2015 fiscal year.

C. Return on equity

Similar to ROA, the return on equity (ROE) ratio measures the profitability of a firm. However, ROE measures financial success of an organization based on the investment by stakeholders (Östring, 2003). In comparison, ROA measures profitability earned through a firm's investments through its assets, which may include lenders, creditors, and other stakeholders (Fried *et al.*, 2013). ROE is calculated as:

Return on equity = Net income/total owner's equity

ROE is considered the basic accounting ratio for investors as all profit earned by a company is ultimately for the benefit of stakeholders (Leach, 2010). In general, a higher ROE will please all stockholders (Östring, 2003). Nike's ROE for FY 2015 is calculated as:

$$\text{Return on equity} = \frac{\$3,273,000,000}{\$12,707,000,000} = 0.26$$

ROE is also presented as a percentage, representing the percentage of owner's equity that the company's ownership realized as profit during the reported period. Nike's ROE for the 2015 fiscal year was 26 percent, which is a very high return for stakeholders.

Market value

The final set of financial ratios provides the overall value of the firm in the market-place. Market value is based on the amount investors are willing to contribute in order to invest in a company or the amount they feel is fair when considering a sale (Fried *et al.*, 2013).

A. Market value ratio

For publicly traded companies, the market value can be readily determined by the number of shares the company currently has outstanding and the current price on the stock market for each share. Remember, many organizations operating within the sport industry are not publically traded and this ratio would thus not apply. The market value ratio can be calculated with the following:

Market value = Price per share of common stock × Number of outstanding shares

While this method of estimating a company's value is easy, Brown *et al.* (2010) caution users of financial statements that this methodology is not the most precise. This is due to the change in stock prices due to investor speculation about the future potential of a company opposed to its current performance.

To estimate Nike's market value, we can refer to stock information found on Nike's balance sheet (Figure 7.1). Nike had 1,536,000,000 shares of outstanding stock at the end of its 2015 fiscal year. Stock price, on the other hand, does not appear on Nike's financial statements. Instead, stock prices for publicly traded companies can be found on various websites such as Google Finance, Yahoo! Finance, Morning Star, and a company's own website. Nike's stock closed at $50.84 at the end of trading on May 29, 2015.[1]

As of 2015, Nike's market value can be calculated as follows:

Market value = 1,536,000,000 × $50.84 = $78,090,240,000

Based on the closing stock price, Nike is valued at $78 billion at the end of the 2015 fiscal year.

B. Earnings per share ratio

Similar to ROE, the earnings per share (EPS) ratio indicates the profitability of a company from the stakeholders' perspective and is widely used in financial analysis (Leach, 2010). The EPS formula is:

Earnings per Share = Net income/number of outstanding shares

Because the calculation of net income assumes that all expenses have been paid, investors view net income as belonging to them based upon their investment in the company (Bull, 2008). As such, companies may choose to reward their investors by offering dividend payments. However, management may also decide to retain earnings in order to fund future business activities. Nonetheless, investors will utilize EPS to indicate a return on investment, indicate a company's retained profit, and calculate the price-to-earnings ratio (Leach, 2010). Nike's earnings per share for the 2015 fiscal year is calculated as follows:

$$\text{Earnings per Share} = \frac{\$3,273,000,000}{1,536,000,000} = 2.13$$

This ratio shows that for every share of Nike stock outstanding, a shareholder will earn $2.13 for every stock the shareholder owns.

C. Price-to-earnings ratio

The price-to-earnings ratio, or P/E ratio, is the most common measure of corporate performance and value among investors (Brown *et al.*, 2010). According to Harrington (2003), the P/E ratio estimates how much investors will pay for each dollar of a company's earnings. Further, the P/E ratio represents the number of years it will take for a company to generate a profit equaling the share price (Leach, 2010). The ratio is calculated as:

Price-to-earnings ratio = Price per share of common stock / Earnings per share

Using the earnings per share ratio calculated earlier and Nike's stock price on May 29, 2015 ("Nike Inc. Historical Prices," 2016), we determine Nike's P/E ratio as:

$$\text{Price-to-earnings ratio} = \frac{\$50.84}{\$2.13} = 23.87$$

Nike's stock price at the end of the 2015 fiscal year was nearly 24 times the company's earnings. Generally, a high P/E ratio is preferred as it can indicate how much confidence the market has in a particular company. However, a high P/E ratio could also mask subpar earnings or net income and simply increase due to a company's potential for growth since the value of outstanding shares is a component of the formula (Brown *et al.*, 2010). Thus, a P/E ratio signals to investors about the potential future of the company as much as it does about the company's current performance (Higgins, 2009).

Beyond traditional financial analytics

Financial statement analysis and the interpretation of financial ratios are standard means of financial standing for any business. However, traditional financial statement analysis is not the only way financial information and other data are used in the sport industry. Like many other analytical methods, financial analytics are continually evolving and being applied to the sport industry. Three common areas of applied financial analysis for data-based decision-making within the sport industry include profit maximization, utilization of the balanced scorecard, and sport valuation.

Profit maximization

Generally speaking, most professional sports teams are profit maximizing firms. The basic concept of profit maximization surrounds the idea of firms adjusting the quantity or price of a good or service they produce in order to increase, or maximize, the gap between revenue and cost. Brunkhorst and Fenn (2010) point out the vital fact that just because a team makes a profit does not mean that team maximizes its profits. Thus, commonly used profitability ratios do not tell the entire story in reference to maximizing profitability.

In order to maximize profits, owners need to pay close attention to both revenue and costs incurred during each season (Brunkhorst & Fenn, 2010). Consider the five major sports leagues in the United States: the NBA, NFL, MLB, MLS and NHL. It is clear that media is the king when it comes to revenue generation. However, most teams have very little control over profit maximization for media due to league-wide media restraints that require owners to share revenue. Even though owners, generally speaking, cannot control the revenue brought in from media, they can control the revenue brought in through tickets. Thus, the opportunity to maximize profit presents itself in ticket pricing which is discussed in Chapter 5.

Forecasting is fundamentally predicting how a business will perform financially in the future. Namely, revenues and expenses are often looked at into the future as many business decisions rely heavily upon future events. Sport organizations, like any other business, need to plan for an uncertain future especially in the ever-changing global economy. For example, sport has long been considered recession or economy proof because of fan devotion.

However, the Great Recession spanning from 2007 to 2009 in the US exposed the lack of economic uniqueness of professional sport. Nearly every professional sport and professional sport franchise saw dips in advertisements, attendance, and sponsorship sales (Holmes, 2009).

Forecasting is linked to virtually every decision an executive needs to make in a business Historically, when sports were considered to be recession proof, forecasting was looked at as more of a luxury option to consider changes in demand. Now, forecasting is a necessity for sport managers to understand. The key to effective forecasting is that the forecaster must make the best use of available data (Chambers, Mullick, & Smith, 1971). Financial forecasts can be linked to sales, expenses, cost of goods sold, cash flows, or even start-up costs.

Financial modeling and forecasting start with a goal and a time frame for the forecast. The forecaster or financial manager also needs to have an established plan or goal for the financial model as well as an understanding of what the use of the data is going to be. Let us take into consideration an already existing minor league team. The team wants to forecast future operational costs. The minor league team would pull the data from previous years of operation. Such sources of data could be rent, insurance costs, vehicles, advertising, and employee wages. The data for this forecast would come from the organization's financial statements. Additional information to be considered in the forecast would include demographic trends such as population changes, competitors in the market place, and potential law changes in the future.

The information derived from the above forecast could be used in a multitude of ways for decision making. The forecaster could have set out with the goal of trying to understand if a stadium renovation was affordable. They also could have set out with the goal of setting up a 12-month budget for the season. In either of the above cases, the team forecaster would forecast the revenues during the same time period. Forecasting and financial modeling are also used for contracting, expanding, valuation, financing, and many other financial-based decisions.

Budgeting is a key component of financial forecasting. A sport organization cannot operate without a road map (or GPS) and the budget serves as the financial road map. Forecasting can estimate future projected revenue and expenses, and these numbers are plugged into a budget. A budget has very little value if it is not followed, which is why data is needed in real-time for a sport organization to know instantly how much revenue has been received, what expenses have been incurred, and what future expenses will occur. If the organization is spending more than they are receiving, they need to realize that before the difference gets out of hand and the organization goes bankrupt. The key to tracking the difference between expected budgetary revenue and expenses and actual numbers is called a variance analysis. Data can be obtained from accounting software to help track revenue and expenses and then action can be taken to increase revenue or decrease expenses. One example is revenue collection. For example, a team could have $100,000 in tickets sold on credit and can be waiting for customers to pay. If there is no way to track the delinquency of those accounts, the team could be helping finance late accounts. In other words, the team would be losing money or possibly never be able to recover some of that owed amount.

CASE STUDY: BUILDING AN EFFECTIVE PROGRAM BUDGET

Name: Lindsay Salt
Title: Account Manager
Current employer: Octagon, Inc.
Brief work history: As a University of New Haven class of 2010 graduate, I jumped right into the sports world while I was at school and beyond. During my four years, I was a member of the Women's Basketball team while earning my degree in Management of Sports Industries with two minors, one in Communications and one in Marketing. My desire to work in the sport industry was solidified following my internship at the New York Mets in between my junior and senior years working in their sponsorship division

PHOTO 7.1   Lindsay Salt

at the new CitiField. Upon graduation, I was fortunate enough to get a job at Octagon, Inc., a global sports marketing and consulting firm out of Connecticut. I have been able to work on various accounts bringing me all over to the world working with clients in NASCAR, global FIFA tournaments, the Super Bowl, World Surf League events and even with the UFC.

Analytics hold a very important role in all parts of the sport business world. Some of the most important uses of analytics at the sports marketing agency are evaluating sponsorships to recommend to our clients, property health evaluation when looking at how our current relationships are working, creating ROI and recap materials, internal audits for how the client is preforming, and so on. There is not a single decision made in our role that does not include research and measurement of some kind and it is essential to the way we do business.

While not the more glorious end of the sport and event industry, the ability to build an effective budget speaks volumes about how you look at the overall task at hand. No matter what kind of agency or client team you work on, at the end of the day the decision to move forward with a potential execution is being able to answer the following questions:

- What is a realistic number that it will take to make this a successful event?
- Where can we trim costs vs. what are necessary to the program?
- Are there any items that we are not considering?

It must be stressed how crucial the above questions are to an activation plan. The quickest way to lose business and the trust of your coworkers is at the end of a program having to go back to ask for more money in order to cover your overages (i.e. excess expenditures).

A key term to be aware of throughout this case study is Scope of Work (SOW). A SOW is a written legal explanation of what event you are proposing to your boss or client. It acts as a binding document that, once agreed upon, is signed by both parties whereas the client/boss is obligated to pay for the services that are being put in front of them. At no point should there be any additional costs that are both not in the budget and not in the SOW. Data is required throughout this process as real-time knowledge of expenses is critical to address over-spending. A client might understand a 10 percent increase in the SOW if presented early in the process, but would normally not accept that 10 percent increase at the end. That is because earlier in the process the client might be able to modify the SOW, but would not be able to do anything at the end, and at that point they will probably become an ex-client.

With that in mind, I have outlined the baseline costs that every budget should reflect no matter what the project is. Even if the amount applied to the item is zero, at least it shows that you have taken it into consideration.

Staffing/Fees

In the agency world, staff planning is a crucial part to any SOW and budget. Without adequate manpower, the project cannot be executed up to its full potential. Depending on the level of the work, different titles (Vice President, Account Director, Manager, Intern, etc.) are proposed to outline exactly what the duties of that person will be.

While the client's goals, such as Nike or Heineken, are driven by how much product they can sell or the buying behavior of consumers in order to show a positive return on investment (ROI), the agency world runs on the fees that they charge to their clients. As I mentioned above, the staffing plan is crucial when determining the type of work that you are going to produce not only for the receiver of these services, but also for the agency itself. The way that an agency turns a profit is to charge fees based on the salary of the position that they are agreeing to in their staffing plans. Depending on the level of involvement in a project, there are multiple variations to consider when charging an adequate fee that will not be too expensive for a client, yet still allow the agency to make money off the project:

- Time Rate Card: This practice is utilized when you have a high-level executive team member billable to your client. This executive, let's say a Vice President, may have multiple clients and a portion of their time is divided up amongst those individual organizations. So, for example, take an arbitrary salary approximation of $100,000 for a VP at a fictional company called The Sports Agency. For 2016, Company X would like to enlist 10 percent of the VP's time throughout the year in order to provide valuable strategy work for a property that they are looking to sponsor. If you think of their $100K salary as a pie graph, 10 percent of their time would equate into 10 percent of their salary. In the Scope of Work, The Sports Agency would take that 10 percent of time required (i.e. 10 percent of their salary) and add a premium of say an additional 15 percent as an agency fee that the client would be required to pay. The idea would be that Company X is paying for 10 percent of the VP's salary and the additional 15 percent would be applied to the bottom line of The Sports Agency. This 15 percent is then applied to different departments that do not work off of client billing such as Administrators, New Business Development, office supplies, company outings, etc.

- Let's take an example of a staffing plan with a team of eight people, all at different levels and different billable time, including our Vice President example above:

	Base Salary	Billable to Company X	The Sports Agency Fees	Total Charged to Company X
Vice President	$ 100,000.00	10%	15%	$ 25,000.00
Account Director	$ 80,000.00	50%	15%	$ 52,000.00
Account Manager	$ 60,000.00	100%	15%	$ 69,000.00
Account Manager	$ 60,000.00	100%	15%	$ 69,000.00
Account Executive	$ 40,000.00	100%	15%	$ 46,000.00
Account Executive	$ 40,000.00	100%	15%	$ 46,000.00
Account Executive	$ 40,000.00	100%	15%	$ 46,000.00
Account Executive	$ 40,000.00	100%	15%	$ 46,000.00
			TOTAL SOW COST	$ 399,000.00

FIGURE 7.3 Staffing fees breakdown

Staff travel costs

Staff travel costs are a huge, yet sometimes overlooked, part of every budget that should be accounted for throughout each calendar year. A team may have the activation plan for a world class event, but without anyone there running the actual program, it will never come to fruition. There are a few factors that should always be taken into consideration:

- Hotel Costs: Hotels tend to be the bulk of every staff travel budget due to the sheer cost of them alone. Depending on the event location, every company will normally have an internal database that each employee must choose from in order to stay within company policy of what is appropriate at that location. This is to prevent extravagant spending and potential pitfalls later on when you have to explain the business reason for staying at a hotel outside the company's policy limitations. With that being said, there are times when you may be forced to go above company policy to book more expensive accommodations during an event that is in high demand. When this happens, it should be outlined ahead of time so that there are no surprises when doing budget reconciliation after the event is over.

  The following is an example for how to build an effective hotel budget for the 2014 FIFA World Cup Brazil™. You have been given a staff of eight people in order to cover all 64 matches. There should always be one person at each match in order to run all programs on the ground and team members will rotate from Host Cities while always having one hotel room in Rio de Janeiro as a home base to fly back to in order to pick up tickets, do recap reports, attend meetings, etc. You also must take into consideration

Host City	# of Hotel Rooms	# Nights	Cost per Night Local Cost (BRL)	Total Local Cost (BRL)	Global Cost (USD)
Belo Horizonte	1	15	R$ 800.00	R$ 12,000.00	$6,000.00
Brasilia	1	15	R$ 780.00	R$ 11,700.00	$5,850.00
Curitiba	1	8	R$ 700.00	R$ 5,600.00	$2,800.00
Cuiaba	1	10	R$ 750.00	R$ 7,500.00	$3,750.00
Fortaleza	1	16	R$ 950.00	R$ 15,200.00	$7,600.00
Natal	1	9	R$ 745.00	R$ 6,705.00	$3,352.50
Porto Alegre	1	11	R$ 740.00	R$ 8,140.00	$4,070.00
Recife	1	11	R$ 980.00	R$ 10,780.00	$5,390.00
Salvador	1	13	R$ 760.00	R$ 9,880.00	$4,940.00
Manaus	1	12	R$ 800.00	R$ 9,600.00	$4,800.00
Sao Paulo	1	14	R$ 650.00	R$ 9,100.00	$4,550.00
Rio de Janeiro	8	34	R$ 1,600.00	R$ 435,200.00	$217,600.00
				TOTAL HOTEL COSTS	**$270,702.50**

FIGURE 7.4   Staff travel costs breakdown

that all billing will be done in local currency. Due to the fact that in 2014, the Brazilian Real (BRL) was weak compared to the US Dollar (USD), you must factor in local currency costs associated with building out potential budget items. In this case, we take an average of the BRL being 50 percent higher than the USD. So with our first example in Belo Horizonte, if the local currency is quoted at R$12,000 to cover all matches, then you would budget for $6,000 in your planning.

- Flight Costs: Also taking into consideration the 2014 FIFA World Cup™ activation, you must also plan for a staff of eight people and there will be a lot of flights associated with covering this very large country. The best way to plan effectively is to take an average of flight costs across the whole month based on a low flight cost versus a high flight cost.

For example, you know that each team member will be starting from Rio de Janeiro for travel purposes as that is base camp for all activations. The closest Host City to Rio is São Paulo, with a high frequency of flights leaving throughout the day

Team Members	# of Flights	Average Flight Cost	Total Per Team Member
Team Member 1	9	$ 400.00	$ 3,600.00
Team Member 2	11	$ 400.00	$ 4,400.00
Team Member 3	15	$ 400.00	$ 6,000.00
Team Member 4	13	$ 400.00	$ 5,200.00
Team Member 5	9	$ 400.00	$ 3,600.00
Team Member 6	18	$ 400.00	$ 7,200.00
Team Member 7	12	$ 400.00	$ 4,800.00
Team Member 8	10	$ 400.00	$ 4,000.00
		TOTAL FLIGHTS $	**38,800.00**

FIGURE 7.5   Staff airfare costs breakdown

to travel back and forth between the two. On the other end of the spectrum, Manaus is the furthest away from Rio de Janeiro and will be most expensive due to a low frequency of flights and the distance needed to travel.

- Transportation: In order to effectively plan a transportation budget you must combine a few of the items that we have already outlined. There are multiple types of transportation options that can be utilized in effective operations planning, but for the purpose of this exercise, we will explore airport transfers and daily rentals.

  - Airport transfers: Based on the aforementioned schedule, you know how many flights your team members will be taking. Thus it will be easy to determine how many airport transfers you will need. The best way to work this out is to assume that you will need two airport transfers for each flight: one to pick each team member up at the airport upon arrival and the second to return them on their travel day to the airport from the hotel.

  - Daily rentals: While many transport companies will differ in costs, the types of services that are provided are typically very consistent. With a daily rental, you will typically receive a quote for a driver for a 12-hour time period where the mileage is not tracked and you may utilize them throughout the day around your activations. So this could include stadium visits, ticket drops, errands for a production team, etc. You should always stress to your individual team members that they should not go over this 12-hour time period. Otherwise the company will charge a premium for the additional services of the driver. An easy way to equate this for our purposes is to take the above flight numbers and subtract them from our 34-day activation. The idea behind this is that each flight would represent one day throughout the 34-day time period where a car would not be utilized since they are in transport, but rather the two airport transfers as we outlined previously.

- *Per Diem*: One item that should definitely not be overlooked is what is referred to as "*per diem*" or meal allowance, so food that your employees can purchase throughout the day that will be covered. It is best to set a realistic allowance that should cover the costs of food that your team members could potentially incur without being extravagant.

Team Members	# of Flights	# of Airport Transfers	# of Daily Rentals	Cost Per Airport Transfer	Cost Per Daily Rentals	Total Per Team Member
Team Member 1	9	13	25	$ 150.00	$ 500.00	$ 15,200.00
Team Member 2	11	22	23	$ 150.00	$ 500.00	$ 14,800.00
Team Member 3	15	30	19	$ 150.00	$ 500.00	$ 14,000.00
Team Member 4	13	26	21	$ 150.00	$ 500.00	$ 14,400.00
Team Member 5	9	18	25	$ 150.00	$ 500.00	$ 15,200.00
Team Member 6	18	36	16	$ 150.00	$ 500.00	$ 13,400.00
Team Member 7	12	24	22	$ 150.00	$ 500.00	$ 14,600.00
Team Member 8	10	20	24	$ 150.00	$ 500.00	$ 15,000.00
					TOTAL TRANSPORT	**$ 116,600.00**

FIGURE 7.6 Staff vehicle costs breakdown

Team Members	# Travel Days	Per Diem	Total Per Diem
Team Member 1	34	$ 65.00	$ 2,210.00
Team Member 2	34	$ 65.00	$ 2,210.00
Team Member 3	34	$ 65.00	$ 2,210.00
Team Member 4	34	$ 65.00	$ 2,210.00
Team Member 5	34	$ 65.00	$ 2,210.00
Team Member 6	34	$ 65.00	$ 2,210.00
Team Member 7	34	$ 65.00	$ 2,210.00
Team Member 8	34	$ 65.00	$ 2,210.00
		TOTAL PER DIEM	**$ 17,680.00**

FIGURE 7.7 Staff food costs breakdown

For the purposes of this budgeting example, let's assume that every employee is given an allowance of $65 per day. With employee traveling for our same 34-day time period, you multiply the number of days with $65 per day allowance and number of employees to come out with what should be set aside for food.

So with the above staff costs, you can see how quickly budgets add up and we haven't even taken into consideration any activation costs such as production of a stage for a musical act, signage and space rentals for a 6v6 soccer tournament, t-shirts for a fan giveaway, etc. The list goes on depending on the size of your event which will be customized depending on your needs. For the purposes of pulling all the above information together as a baseline example for activations, if this were an event, your SOW proposal to a client team for Staff Expenses and Agency Fees would look like the following based on our 34-day activation period:

Team Members	Cost to Client
Agency Fees	$ 399,000.00
Staff Hotels	$ 270,702.50
Staff Flights	$ 38,800.00
Transportation	$ 116,600.00
Per Diem	$ 17,680.00
TOTAL OPERATIONS	**$ 842,782.50**

FIGURE 7.8 Compiled expense budget

For any event, analytics come into play when developing the budget to include in the SOW, tracking the costs in real-time so a manager can effectively manage the costs, and then undertaking a variance analysis at the end to see how close the budget matched actual expenses. Of course, every business would like to come in under budget as that would create more profit. If some of those savings are passed back to the client, then the client would be very happy.

A key note on forecasting and trying to predict the future is that forecasting and prediction are very difficult to do and often inaccurate. Some of the reasons for inaccurate forecasting lie in the horizon or time the forecaster tries to predict into the future (Metcalf, n.d.). Another common pitfall with inaccurate forecasting lies with bad or insufficient data. For example, say a retail giant such as Nike was trying to forecast sales into the future. If Nike was to only consider one year of sales data to predict five years into the future, the forecast would likely turn up as inaccurate. As easy as that sounds, it is a very common mistake in forecasting. Other areas of difficulty in forecasting lie in biases and changing economic patterns.

The question is, how can you, as a future sport manager, best prepare to understand financial analysis and analytics in the sport industry? In a series of research papers, a renowned forecasting researcher named Philip Tetlock identified a set of factors leading to more accurate forecasts. Tetlock identified intelligence, expertise in the domain, practice with forecasting, teams of forecasters, and training in probability as common characteristics of accurate forecasting predictions. The key finding in Tetlock's research however was that algorithms, not humans, made worse predictions while the most accurate forecasting models came from people who could use and understand statistical models (Frick, 2015). The key take away when discussing forecasting is that in order to accurately forecast, the sport manager must not only understand finance but also have a significant grasp of the sport organization and statistical methods.

The balanced scorecard

The Balanced Scorecard (BSC) is a commonly used strategic planning and management system which was developed in 1992 by Harvard Business Professors Robert Kaplan and David Norton (Kaplan & Norton, 1993). The BSC takes into account both financial and non-financial metrics as a means to measure overall company success and form long term vision and strategy.

The BSC essentially breaks down an organization's strategic perspectives into a series of strategic objectives. In the BSC approach, company success is still measured by common financial metrics such as revenue, budget, and target profit. However, the BSC takes into consideration the perspective of the internal business processes, learning and growth, and customer perspectives (Kaplan & Norton, 1993). Many of the non-financial data used in the BSC method comes from customer satisfaction surveys or requires compilation of existing data such as standards and compliance. Ultimately, the BSC looks to "balance" the four perspectives (e.g., financial, internal business process, learning and growth, and customer satisfaction) to drive long-term financial success for organizations. The BSC process is an applied business method driven by the analysis of various sources of data.

With an emphasis placed on financial success, one could easily assume the BSC strategy would only be appropriate for profit seeking ventures. However, this is not the case. The BSC can be applied to any competitive environment, market situation, or organization (Kaplan & Norton, 1993). The beauty of the BSC is that it is meant to be customized to the business at hand. Let us revisit the notion that though the sport industry is vast and complex, many financial analytical tools are universally used regardless of the organization. The BSC is a prime example of a commonly used financial analytical tool. The BSC method can be used for a non-profit sport organization, such as an NCAA Division I university's athletic department, or a for-profit organization, such as a minor league baseball organization.

For example, in 2008, Daniel Delaney applied the BSC method to evaluate the performance of the University of Connecticut's (UCONN) Athletic Department. Delaney utilized various financial and non-financial metrics for the four quadrants of the balanced scorecard for the athletic department. He considered metrics such as media revenue and academic retention rate for the customer's quadrant as both fans and student-athletes are considered customers. For the financial quadrant, Delaney gave attention to ticket revenues, donations, and NCAA/Conference Distributions. Next, learning and growth metrics included such things as athletic facilities and academic support. The last quadrant of the BSC is internal business processes. For UCONN's Athletic Department, Delaney addressed fundraising trends and recruiting metrics. All of these metrics combined were then evaluated against the overall mission of the athletic department. Delaney was able to make suggestions on how to "balance" the scorecard for the UCONN athletic department.

Utilizing the balanced scorecard incorporates a variety of existing data for analysis such as revenues. The BSC also involves collecting data through surveys such as an employee satisfaction survey. Not only does the balanced scorecard method utilize financial analytics but the method can also be used to identify where and how big data can be applied to the business at hand.

For example, say a minor league sport team recognizes they have an area of weakness in the financial quadrant. Specifically, assume the team identified a strategic objective to annually exceed sales revenues of the previous season. The strategic objective, or key performance indicator, for the minor league team could be to achieve $100,000 in new business sales. One of the performance indicators to reach that strategic objective is to increase their prospective sponsors and season ticket holder pipeline. Some good sources of readily available data for the minor league team to increase their pipeline could be through LinkedIn, Twitter, or Reference USA.

A concept similar to BSC is Key Performance Indicators (KPI). While BSC examines several keys areas, KPI can refer to any measurable value that demonstrates how effectively an organization is achieving key objectives. Every sport organization will have KPIs. The KPIs will focus on every facet of the organization. They could examine HR and the efficiency of hiring, to how effective a marketing campaign is, to profit projections. Whatever a sport organization sets as a goal or objective, there needs to be a way to measure it and make progress to achieve the KPI. The KPI is the score and the way a sport organization can track their success. There is no one correct KPI. It all depends on the individual sport organization. The key is to identify the goal/objective, find a way to measure it, measure it, and then take action as appropriate.

CASE STUDY: USING DATA TO MAKE INTERCOLLEGIATE ATHLETIC DECISIONS

Name: Lisa Miller, PhD
Title: Professor of Health Sciences and Sport Management
Current employer: American Military University
Brief work history: I focused on teaching sport and health courses in higher education for over ten years covering topics such as sport leadership, sport and exercise psychology, sport and exercise management, and sport and exercise research methods. My education includes a Bachelor of Science in Psychology and a Master of Labor and Human Resources from The Fisher College of Business at The Ohio State University. I then earned a PhD in Sport and Exercise Management with a specialization in Counseling and Sport Psychology in

PHOTO 7.2 Lisa Miller

addition to a concentration in Research on Human Development. I later added a Graduate Concentration in Education and Religious Studies from Harvard University. Currently, I provide service as the Editor for the Global Sport Management News and as a consultant to the Harvard Leadership Conference.

How do you think data helps influence your industry segment?

Data analytics play an important and growing role in higher education. Analytics could be used for various decisions on recruiting student athletes, retaining players, budgeting in the athletic department, and strategizing for future changes. New approaches to the use of analytics are rising as a new foundation for decision making in several aspects of university leadership. These approaches could be used for coaches' salary negotiations, athletic department performance reviews, and athletic budgeting. The possibilities are endless for various types of reports and forecasting for the future of higher education and athletics.

What example can you share regarding using data to help make a decision?

The issue

For university leadership, accreditation standards and governing requirements are important to meet. This requires accountability of classroom design and student performance along with athletic department oversight. Data analytics help to organize information and provide feedback about how students are doing in the classroom and on the athletic field.

Athletic governing bodies also require data analytics from athletic departments on various forms to create a way to compare programs and ensure meeting regulatory requirements set by the National Collegiate Athletic Association (NCAA) and conferences. University leadership would be wise to develop an extensive and comprehensive data analytics strategy for compelling decision-making in all aspects of university life, including athletics. Budgeting in athletics often links closely with the university budget. Budgeting must be done at the more comprehensive level of the university and at the more micro level of team budgeting. For example, a tennis team must budget for matches and tournaments. Data analytics help calculate reasonable analysis of the past and helpful prognoses of the future for the team.

The analysis

Analytics could be applied to the athletic department for estimating revenue and expenses for team management, compensation plans, or tournament hosting. Budgets are helpful not only for the current year, but an analysis of the budget from past years could help to estimate and make decisions for the future. Upon review of past analytics, a university team could then estimate reasonable predictions with likely changes in expenses and revenue. This analysis helps with strategizing for marketing, communications, and staffing.

It would be useful for athletic departments and even individual units, such as individual teams, athletic trainers, sport information, and other units, to undertake a Balanced Score Card or Key Performance Indicator (KPI) view of their operation to make sure that the money spent is used wisely and helps meet required goals and objectives. For example, instead of just looking at how much athletic tape was used and if it meets the budgetary guidelines, the athletic trainer's department can be evaluated based on service quality, innovative treatment, and reduced injuries as a result of preventive medicine. All these variables might not appear on any financial statement, but represent whether quality service is being provided.

The key for any such analysis will be to have data collection throughout the department to monitor financial performance as well as service quality. Besides doing stock inventory before a fiscal year and at the end to see how many rolls of athletic tape were used, an athletic department can monitor athlete injury rates, quality surveys, and other data points to determine if the athletic trainer's department is operating effectively. The data will expand the analysis beyond just fiscal operations and determine if the various units are operating effectively, meeting institutional goals, and operating in an ethical manner. A unit that meets its budget but provides horrible service or violates rules becomes a major burden for any sport organization.

The end results: Overall, data analytics provides a more valid and reliable source of accountability for athletic teams and departments. The increase in data analytics will also require coaches being trained on data analytic systems.

What lesson did you learn from the process?

From data analytics, I learned that decisions improve with a systematic accountability process. Ethical use of the data would be helpful to discuss with an athletic advisory committee when initiating a new data analytics system. Ethical and legal approaches will require extensive training and a checks and balance system. Data analytics will benefit athletic departments by providing communication standards to explain why decisions align with the strategy of the athletic department and the university.

What suggestions do you have for students about data in your discipline?

My suggestion would be to develop skills in data analytics and look for places where new data analytics systems would benefit the organization. An analytical approach will communicate the valuable skills of students with data analytics knowledge. Students may be able to detect areas in organizations where data analytics could be applied that would provide a more stable and valid way to make important decisions. Data analytics in sport provide numbers to facilitate decisions rather than using unfounded opinions. This will help avoid suggestions that could lead an athletic organization to ineffective methods.

Valuation

Value represents the monetary worth of an item and can be expressed as what you could obtain on the open market if you had to sell an item (Fried *et al.*, 2013; Siegel, Shim, & Hartman, 1992). The value one can place on a particular item can vary significantly from individual to individual. All industries, including sport, must understand the context of a valuation. Valuation is the process of determining the value of a business, requiring a clear description of the entity's industry as well as the entity's future expectations (Brown *et al.*, 2010). However, valuation is uncertain as both the asset being valued and the methodology utilized to determine value possess uncertainty.

The most common standard of valuation is fair market value. Fair market value is the net price for an asset that would result in a transaction between a willing buyer and a willing seller. Both the buyer and the seller are under no compulsion to engage in a transaction, have reasonable knowledge of the relevant facts, and both parties being at arm's length. Arm's length refers to the relationship between the buyer and seller as neither party is related in any capacity. Once these conditions are met, a baseline valuation can be determined.

There are many methodologies to assist firms with the valuation of assets such as the market transactions approach and the discounted cash flow analysis. The market transactions approach determines the value of a particular asset by referencing the value of comparable assets that have been sold within a reasonable period of time. Professional sport franchises utilize this approach often when negotiating the fair market value for some of their highly regarded players. For example, a general manager of a Major League Baseball (MLB) team wishing to resign his star shortstop can determine the fair value of a contract based on recent activity for the shortstop position within the MLB free agency market.

The discounted cash flow analysis determines an asset's fair market value by determining the present value of its expected future cash flows (Humphreys & Mondello, 2008). As discussed earlier, businesses make projections on the amount of cash they expect to generate in future years for both their overall business and individual assets. We can then project the present value of these future cash flows using a suitable discount rate (Kaplan & Ruback, 1995). These discounted figures are then added together to provide an estimate on the value of a business or an asset.

Forbes Magazine utilizes the discounted cash flow methodology to determine the values of all professional sport franchises. As of 2016, the most valuable sport entity is Real Madrid, which is valued at $3.26 billion. According to Badenhausen (2015), Real Madrid generated the highest revenue in all sports worldwide in 2014 at $746 million and earned a profit of $171 million. Part of this annual revenue includes Real's $277 million broadcasting deal and $155 million sponsorship deal with Adidas (Badenhausen, 2015; Navarrete, 2016).

Taking these cash sources in mind, *Forbes* calculates the present value of these expected cash flows for Real as well as other professional franchises to determine their value annually. As such, valuations can change rapidly as franchises explore new sources of revenue generation. For example, when the Dallas Cowboys secured AT&T as a sponsor of their stadium (AT&T Stadium), the value of the Cowboys franchise increased by $100 million because of the increase in revenue the franchise received from the sponsorship (Ozanian, 2013). Thus, business managers should analyze all potential revenue sources that could potentially increase the value of their business.

Conclusion

Many readers would assume finance and data are basically the same. In some respects they significantly overlap, as there is no way to financially manage a sport organization without data. However, there are various significant differences that need to be examined. The raw data in other disciplines might tell a story by themselves, but the financial numbers need to be analyzed to help determine if financial objectives are being met. Through examining various ratios, a sport organization can benchmark its performance compared to past performances and those of competitors. Other financial tools such as forecasting, budgeting, balanced score card, key performance indicators, and appropriate valuation all help tell a story through data as to how well a sport organization is doing.

Note

1 Nike's normal year-end closing date, May 31st, was a Sunday in 2015. The markets are traditionally closed on Sundays. Thus, the closing price on May 29th, 2015 is utilized to determine the market value ("Nike, Inc. Historical Prices," 2016).

References

Badenhausen, K. (2015, July 15). *The world's 50 most valuable sports teams*. Retrieved from www. forbes.com/sites/kurtbadenhausen/2015/07/15/the-worlds-50-most-valuable-sports-teams-2015/#647762e57fd0

Brown, M., Rascher, D., Nagel, M., & McEvoy. (2010). *Financial management in the sport industry*. Scottsdale, AZ: Holcomb Hathaway.

Brunkhorst, J. P., & Fenn, A. J. (2010). Profit maximization in the National Football League. *Journal of Applied Business Research, 26*(1), 45.

Bull, R. (2008). *Financial ratios: how to use financial ratios to maximize value and success for your business*. Burlington, MA: CIMA Publishing.

Chambers, J. C., Mullick, S. K., & Smith, D. D. (1971) How to choose the right forecasting technique. *Harvard Business Review, 49*(4), 45.

ESports Market Brief 2015/2016 Update. (n.d.). Retrieved from http://superdata-research.myshopify.com/products/esports-market-brief-2015

Facts about FASB. (n.d.). Financial Accounting Standards Board. Retrieved from www.fasb.org/jsp/FASB/Page/SectionPage&cid=1176154526495

Frick, W. (2015, February 2). What research tells us about making accurate predictions. *Harvard Business Review.* Retrieved from https://hbr.org/2015/02/what-research-tells-us-about-making-accurate-predictions

Fried, G., DeSchriver, T., & Mondello, M. (2013). *Sport finance* (3rd ed.). Champaign, IL: Human Kinetics.

Gaudiosi, J. (2016, January 22). *Why ESPN is investing in eSports coverage.* Retrieved from http://fortune.com/2016/01/22/espn-invests-in-esports-coverage/

Harrington, D. R. (2003). *Corporate financial analysis in a global environment* (7th ed.). Cincinnati, OH: South-Western College Publishing.

Heitner, D. (2015). *Sports industry to reach $73.5 billion by 2019.* Retrieved from www.forbes.com/forbes/welcome/

Helfert, E. (2002). *Techniques of financial analysis: A guide to value creation* (11th ed.). New York, NY: McGraw-Hill/Irwin.

Higgins, R. (2009). *Analysis for financial management* (9th ed.). New York, NY: McGraw-Hill/Irwin.

Holmes, B. (2009, December 30). *This time around, sports aren't recession-proof.* Retrieved from http://articles.latimes.com/2009/dec/30/sports/la-sp-economy30-2009dec30

Humphreys, B., & Mondello, M. (2008). Determinants of franchise values in North American professional sports leagues: Evidence from a hedonic price model. *International Journal of Sports Finance, 3,* 98–105.

Jablonsky, S., & Barsky, N. (2001). *The manager's guide to financial statement analysis* (2nd ed.). Hoboken, NJ: John Wiley & Sons, Inc.

Jenny, S. E., Manning, R. D., Keiper, M. C., & Olrich, T. W. (2016). Virtual(ly) athletes: Where eSports fit within the definition of "Sport." *Quest, 1–18.*

Kaplan, R. S., & Norton, D. P. (1993). *Putting the balanced scorecard to work.* Retrieved from https://hbr.org/1993/09/putting-the-balanced-scorecard-to-work

Kaplan, S., & Ruback, R. (1995). The valuation of cash flow forecasts: An empirical analysis. *The Journal of Finance, 50,* 1059–93.

Leach, R. (2010). *Ratios made simple: A beginner's guide to the key financial ratios.* Hampshire, UK: Harriman House.

Metcalf, T. (n.d.). What are the dangers of inaccurate financial reporting? *Houston Chronicle.* Retrieved from http://smallbusiness.chron.com/dangers-inaccurate-financial-reporting-79357.html

Navarrete, L. (2016, January 29). *Adidas to sign new sponsorship deal with Real Madrid worth €140 million per year.* Retrieved from www.managingmadrid.com/ 2016/1/29/10867794/adidas-real-madrid-new-deal-2016

Nike, Inc. (2015). *2015 annual report on form 10-k and notice of annual meeting.* Retrieved from http://s1.q4cdn.com/806093406/files/doc_financials/2015/ar/docs/nike-2015-form-10K.pdf

Nike, Inc. historical prices. (2016). Retrieved from www.google.com/finance/historical?q=NYSE%3ANKE&ei=Af_yVvjILoW0e8qekRA.

Östring, P. (2003). Investigating what is behind financial figures. In P. Östring (Ed.) *Profit-focused supplier management: How to identify risks and recognize opportunities* (pp. 44–112). New York, NY: American Management Association International.

Ozanian, M. (2013, July 26). *Value of Cowboys up $100 Million from stadium naming rights deal.* Retrieved from www.forbes.com/sites/mikeozanian/2013/07/26/ value-of-cowboys-up-100-million-from-stadium-naming-rights-deal/#17a8a5016937

Shapiro, A., & Balbirer, S. (2000). *Modern corporate finance: A multidisciplinary approach to value creation.* Upper Saddle River, NJ: Prentice-Hall.

Siegel, J., Shim, J., & Hartman, S. (1992). *The McGraw-Hill pocket guide to business finance – 201 decision-making tools for managers.* New York, NY: McGraw-Hill.

Smith, M. (2015). *Coke's new sports chief: "I'm looking at things afresh."* Retrieved from www.sportsbusinessdaily.com/Journal/Issues/2015/04/13/Marketing-and-Sponsorship/Ivan-Pollard-Coke.aspx

Sports, Teams and Leisure Industry Statistics. (n.d.). Retrieved from www.plunkettresearch.com/statistics/sports-industry

8

SPORT LAW BY THE NUMBERS

Gil Fried

Imagine you are the general manager of a semi-professional baseball team. You want to minimize the amount of liability you have from fans being hit by foul balls and broken bats. That represents the problem to be researched. The data to help answer that problem could be gathered from incident reports from fans previously hit by foul balls, feedback from ushers, information from other teams, facility executives, information from the league offices, insurance companies, newspaper/internet stories about fan experiences, and numerous other sources of information. At that point you have to decide what the real risks are, if any, and then what strategies can be utilized to minimize the risks. Strategies could include, what is often called, the layering technique: screening the most dangerous part of the ballpark, putting a warning notice on the back of a game ticket, announcing a warning on the public address system, posting a warning on the scoreboard, having signs prominently displayed, and having ushers personally warn fans as they initially sit and throughout the game (Fried, 2015). These strategies might have worked in the past or show promise for the future. Data can be leveraged to see what really works rather than just throwing numerous strategies at a problem to see if something works. The team would not need to follow each strategy, but the more appropriate strategies they implement (i.e. the right strategies derived from data) the greater is the likelihood that people will be effectively warned, protected, and will hopefully not be injured and/or sue for any injuries. This is just one example of sport law/risk management as well as representing an overlap with facility and event management. Sport law is not an isolated area, but there are numerous points where data can impact sport law.

Many people think sport law deals with contract law for professional athletes or antitrust law and player unions. However, as future or current sport managers the legal issues that are actually faced and need to be addressed are significantly broader. One issue that generated significant legal attention in 2015 was who owned the data generated by wearable technology such as Fitbit devices. While an athlete generated the data and might upload the data to track their progress, the company could actually analyze the data and possibly even sell it. Should that data be owned by the athlete or by the company (Socolow, 2015)? Another interesting legal issue arose in 2015 when a former St. Louis Cardinals employee broke into the Houston Astros' computer system and took sensitive recruiting and scouting information. This led to the former employee pleading guilty to five counts of unauthorized access of a protected computer, i.e. hacking ("Pleads guilty to hacking," 2016). These are just two examples with the intersection of the law and data.

Sport organizations often have to determine whether or not to pursue legal claims/ defenses when they are presented. Sport executives need to focus on tort law basics (such as negligence, product liability, nuisance, and defamation), contract law, employment law, constitutional law, property law, tax law, intellectually property issues, and antitrust concerns to name a few concerns that could arise on a regular basis. These legal areas can all raise potential data intensive issues such as whether a law was violated (the proof might be in the data) or what legal recourse might be available (how much someone was actually harmed as calculated by data). Individuals with a strong grasp of analytics can determine whether a case is worth pursuing or if a case should be settled.

Legal issues impact the entire sport enterprise and an executive needs to address not just underlying legal claims but also how to manage attorneys (whether in-house or outside counsel) and reduce legal costs since high legal bills normally result in lost profit. One such issue is the expanded use of analytics to break down legal bills from attorneys to make sure the costs are appropriate and inline. Such efforts can save significant sums and can also be used to negotiate different legal rates – such as value based billing versus per hour billings.

Data is impacting more than just the legal cases; it also impacts how sport and technology collide. One example is player/athlete related data. Lawsuits have been filed against fantasy sport companies regarding whether they can use player performance data without compensating the players. Players will want to lobby for owning these rights during collective bargaining efforts with professional leagues. The data also raises issues of privacy and who is liable if the data is not properly secured and a hacker steals the data? Similar ownership issues revolve around GPS and other data collected from amateur and recreational athletes. Such information can be valuable not just to the players and coaches, but also to gamblers, media, marketers, doctors, and broadcasters . . . so who owns the data? Another issue is the cost for insurance associated with prizes (hole in one or shooting a full-court shot) which will be based on statistical probability and the amount offered for the prize. Thus, data can impact what is done on the field/court from athletes to fans and possibly the winning prize.

This chapter will explore legal issues from several perspectives. The primary focus will be on how data are used in the courtroom and legal practices, tort law related issues, risk management, contract law, antitrust law, and government regulations. Special focus will be given to the negligence area as risk management is one of the most proactive steps a sport executive can undertake to help prevent harm to others and which is more likely to lead to possible litigation.

Data in the courtroom

Most attorneys would hate to say that the law is a gamble, but it really is. Think about it from your experience as a driver. Whenever you speed on the freeway you are taking a gamble that you will not be pulled over by a police officer. If you drive five miles an hour over the speed limit what is the likelihood you will be pulled over? What if it was 20 miles an hour over the speed limit? What other variables might impact the chance of getting pulled over? Even if you are pulled over, can you fight the ticket? What is the likelihood that the officer would give you a warning or that the judge might throw out the ticket? These are all part of the legal gamble.

The same kind of gamble occurs with every sport law matter. Will a team be able to use a parody of a well-known product without running afoul of the law? Can an athlete take performance enhancing drugs and not get caught? Can a stadium be built and meet its entire loan covenants? Will a jury believe a given witness in a sport injury case? Should a university take a case to trial and risk a major victory or a possible significant loss – or should they settle the case? These are all parts of the gamble associated with sport law matters and executives are often trying to find ways to protect themselves – it is similar to how a gambler might try to strengthen their odds through counting cards.

Numbers are broken down in numerous ways around a case. For example, who is the judge? Data is available on their past decisions. How have they ruled on certain motions? Do they have a proclivity to support a certain type of argument? What percentage of their cases settle and through what means? If the judge has been around for a number of years there might be significant information available, but if the judge is a relatively new judge then there might not be as much information available.

The same type of analyses can be undertaken on both the opposing counsel and their employer. How experienced is the attorney? How have they fared with a given judge or jurisdiction? What do attorneys who have gone up against them say about their skills/ ability? Who are the attorney's other clients and how much do they bill them on an annual basis? Is the attorney the best attorney money can buy? All this data can help attorneys know the other legal team similar to how professional scouts know another sport team.

If a case is pursued, besides knowing about the court, judge, opposing sides and related information, it is imperative to have as much information about the case as possible. This can include interviewing people working for the athletic department, as an example. Who did what, who said what, how the incident arose, and numerous other questions might be asked. If we are talking about an injury case, there might be a form completed by an employee indicating some of the key facts (who, what, where, when, and why?). These forms might be pieces of paper or could be in electronic form. Some organizations document to such an extent that they might have video statements from witnesses. Normally the more data the better, but that is not always the case.

Hopefully the data is the right data. When examining legal issues it is more important to have factual or objective data rather than subjective opinion. It is more important to document that a person slipped and fell at a given location than to try to blame someone for not doing their job. This is a skill that all employees need to be taught to ensure both accurate and helpful information. A picture of where the person fell can be wonderful, but the data in the picture needs to be analyzed. Were they wearing appropriate footwear, what clothing were they wearing, was the floor wet near where they slipped, etc.?

Besides internal data, the discovery process allows a party to find information from an opposing side. This process can include questions (interrogatories), request for admissions (to admit or deny certain facts), request for production of documents, independent medical examination, and deposition (sworn testimony before a court reporter). This process allows both sides to obtain relevant and necessary information. However, it is critical to ask for the right information. The other side will not just willingly give all access to their information. They will often be very specific and look at every word of the request to try to minimize exactly what material will be produced. The minutia often examined in many cases helps highlight how critical the discovery process is in identifying relevant and necessary data that can help an attorney win–lose a case.

Besides the discovery process, data can be used throughout a possible trial. Every attorney is scared of possible jurors. A jury is supposed to be composed of peers, but it can just as easily be composed of jurors who hate a given party. Many judges give potential jurors a questionnaire or ask them questions directly to make sure they are not going to be biased. However, everyone is biased. Thus, jury consultants can help attorneys figure out if a potential juror might be a benefit or harm to a case.

Juror bias is seen not just in their opinions about the case, but also the parties and the attorneys. Many cases are not won based on the fact, but if the jurors like a given attorney or their client. If an attorney is attractive and not overbearing then they might have an easier time in front of a jury compared to an old cantankerous attorney that rubs people the wrong way, even though that attorney might have the better case/facts. There has been significant research over the years that a jury is normally willing to award a higher award to a man injured during an accident when it affects their ability to earn an income. In contrast, women received higher awards when their injury impacted their attractiveness and marriageability. These types of biases play into an attorney's decision to go forward with a given case.

All the data available to an attorney and a team can be used to help decide if it is worth pursuing a claim or if it is smarter to litigate. Sometimes it is not just the data that drives a legal decision. It might be a corporate policy to litigate all claims. A company might believe that if they strongly fight all cases, and rarely settle, attorneys might be scared of bringing the weaker cases for fear they would have to spend so much litigating the case they would never get their money out of a case. This strategy is pursued in part by Wal-Mart which rarely settles cases (The Wal-Mart Litigation Project, 2015).

Tort law

After examining data about the attorneys, the court, the judges, the jurors, and the various parties, it is important to examine the potential facts and issues that can give rise to a legal concern. The first topic we will cover is tort law. There are two types of tort law – intentional torts and negligence. Intentional torts include some claims seen in sport, such as defamation and nuisance claims. These two types of claims can raise significant data related issues.

Many people are familiar with defamation claims associated with someone saying something harmful about another person that is not true. There are several data points here. One is whether or not a statement was true or false. Data can help prove someone was telling the truth or lying, but that might take time and effort. Another key data point is what the damages are. If someone was really injured financially they should be compensated, but damages cannot be speculative.

There have been numerous sport related defamation cases. One of the most publicized cases involved disgraced Tour de France winner Lance Armstrong, who sued the English paper *The Sunday Times* in 2004, claiming they defamed him about using drugs. The paper settled with him in 2006 for £300,000. When it was revealed that Armstrong actually used drugs the paper and one of its writers sued Armstrong to get the settlement back. In 2013 the parties reached a confidential settlement (Associated Press, 2013). The entire performance enhancing drug issue spawned defamation lawsuits or threats of lawsuits from stars such as Major League Baseball's Albert Pujols and Roger Clemens.

In defamation cases the issue is not just whether a statement was truthful, but was someone really harmed. Generally, there are three types of damages in a defamation case: 1) actual damages, 2) assumed damages, and 3) punitive damages. Actual damages are designed to compensate someone for their actual injuries. If a defamed player lost a million dollar endorsement deal then the actual damages are one million dollars. Under assumed damages (only in libel [written defamation cases]) courts can assume that the plaintiff has suffered harm to his or her reputation, or experienced shame, mortification, or even hurt feelings and can try to develop a value for such suffering. Lastly, punitive damages are designed to punish a party for their actions if they are considered especially egregious.

Since jurors are not in the best position to determine complex economic harm, expert witnesses are often brought in to help calculate damages. The first thing an expert would do is to project the plaintiff's (injured party's) revenue based upon his or her life expectancy and retirement age. This is done by analyzing the plaintiff's historical earnings. Next, the expert needs to calculate the future revenue and earnings based upon the plaintiff's damaged reputation, and compare that data to the revenues and earnings projections if no damages had occurred. All this information relies on data, such as the plaintiff's income tax returns, W-2s, employment contracts, age, gender, the state of the economy, the state of the industry in which the plaintiff is engaged, as well as the salary of other people in the same industry who have similar backgrounds to that of the plaintiff. Thus, a star athlete would be analyzed compared to another star rather than a weaker player.

Australian sports scientist Stephen Dank was at the center of a controversy concerning his oversight of a supplements program to players at Essendon Football Club (a Melbourne Australian Football League team). In 2013 his solicitors (attorneys) announced his plans to sue for defamation. His defamation claim, which asked for $10 million, was based on perceived false allegations in the media that Mr. Dank (and others) sold illegal drugs to athletes (Hickey, 2013). Damages for hurt feelings are capped in Australia, and the outcome of related proceedings (criminal) were to be taken into account. As of August 2014, most of Dank's defamation claims had been thrown out due to poorly written paperwork or insufficient evidence (he was also trying to sue several team/league executives). The one claim that was allowed to move forward was against the Nine Network (AAP, 2014).

Nuisance claims are the other type of intentional tort claim where data can be used. A nuisance is an interference in use/enjoyment of property. A nuisance is any human activity (playing loud music) or physical condition (bad smell or lighting trespass) on someone's property that is harmful, indecent or offensive, or that interferes with someone else's use and enjoyment of his or her property. To calculate damages it has to be determined if the nuisance is temporary or permanent. It is harder to recover damages for temporary nuisance such as a monthly loud party. A permanent nuisance can occur if a sport facility is built next to a neighborhood and the floodlights, speakers, and fireworks after games continually impact neighbors. Damages in such circumstances are determined by the diminution of property value caused by the nuisance. If a home was worth $300,000 before the stadium was built and now is worth $200,000 then there could possibly be $100,000 in diminished value.

The law used to be that if someone moved near to a nuisance they could not sue. Thus, if someone bought a house near an existing airport runway, they could not sue if the noise impacted their sleep because they knew there would be noise from the airport. In contracts, if the airport was built after the houses the impacted homeowner could sue for the reduced value and enjoyment of their property. In the United Kingdom case of Coventry v. Lawrence ([2014] UKSC 13) a speedway racing track was built in 1975 and modified for offering motocross as well in 1992. In 2002, permanent permission was granted for motocross events, but limited the speedway's use to certain days, prescribed hours, and specified noise levels. A homeowner bought a house next to the track in 2006 and filed a complaint thereafter. The case worked its way to the Supreme Court where the court sided with the homeowners that they could have a claim for nuisance. The court examined the facility's use and if there had been changes in its use the neighbors impacted by the change could then challenge the new nuisance caused by the facility. Whatever the nuisance, the facility or organization will need to measure the light, noise, or other nuisance, develop a baseline, and show that they are reasonable in using their property.

Besides intentional torts where a party intentionally does something to harm another, there are unintentional torts classified as negligence cases. There are four elements to a negligence claim: 1) duty, 2) breach of duty, 3) proximate cause, and 4) injuries (Fried, 2015). If a basketball player chases after a loose ball during a game and runs into a wall, should they be able to recover? Several questions would be raised such as was the athlete paying attention, were they pushed by another player, was the floor in good shape, were the walls protected, and numerous other questions. One of the arguments often raised in these types of cases is whether the facility lived up to its duty to provide a reasonably safe facility.

Neither a basketball gym, nor any other sport facility, needs to be perfectly safe. They just need to be reasonably safe. One aspect of the reasonably safe discussion is how much room existed between the basketball court's end line and the wall. Most people would say that you need room for players to run out of bounds, but how much room is enough? Some might advocate that you need padding on every wall. Some might say you need at least three feet of space, others might suggest six feet, yet others could argue for at least ten feet of space. The question becomes, which is the right measure? If a basketball facility will be examined to determine if they breached a duty, the question is who sets the duty and how is it breached if there is no consensus? The NCAA and the NBA, among others, advocate at least three feet of a buffer zone. FIBA rule 16.3 requires that all spectators must be seated at a distance of at least 5,000 mm (approximately 20 inches) from the outer edge of the boundary line of the playing court. These are rules or guidelines for the highest level of competitive basketball. However, what if the gym is an elementary school gym or a fitness facility? This is where data can come into play. In most negligence cases a facility operator needs to live up to a duty to provide a reasonably safe facility and their actions will be judged based on similar facilities and executives with the same experience and training. Such an industry standard is normally examined through looking at what other facilities do. If there are ten local schools with the average distance between the end line and wall being four feet, then that might be considered the "industry standard," for that type of facility in that location. Besides what others do, it is important to examine what has happened at the gym in the past. If there was only three feet of a buffer zone, but there had never been any incidents in 15–20 years, then it could be assumed the facility was reasonably safe. In contrast, there could be a gym where there might be 20 feet (6 meters) of space between an end line and a wall and there might be 20 injuries. That would tend to show that the second facility was not reasonably safe, even with the extra room. This is where data comes into play. A sport executive should undertake research to determine whether there are any standards or guidelines that should be followed, make sure they are in fact appropriate, and then follow them if they are appropriate. A Google Scholar search of state case laws in the United States produced 1,140 basketball related cases referencing end lines in August, 2015. Such a large number of cases shows that this area of law is far from settled and producing more cases every year. This helps show that there is no set standard for adequate safety zones in the United States.

The key point for data analysis will normally focus on foreseeability. Foreseeability under the law is the connection between the duty, breach of that duty, and the resulting injury. Foreseeability determines if the harm resulting from an action could reasonably have been predicted. This is a numbers game. If something was so unlikely to occur that there was only a one in a million chance of an injury occurring most people would say the incident was then an act of God or some other intervening cause that breaks the chain of causation and ultimately leads to a defense verdict. However, if it is reasonably foreseeable that someone could be injured then it is imperative that the sport organization undertake specific strategies to reduce their exposure and minimize the risk of injuries.

No matter what happens and why someone is injured, the analysis will move at a certain point to the damages and how they can be quantified. Similar to the analysis undertaken with identifying damages in defamation cases, in an injury case the court will look to various data points to determine possible damages. These data points can include life expectancy tables (how long should the person live), loss of income, loss of future income, pain and suffering, past medical bills, future medical bills, and other categories. Such calculations can become intense when there is a serious injury that will impact the injured party for the rest of their life.

CASE STUDY: COMPARING FOUL BALL SAFETY

Name: Takao Ohashi
Title: Attorney-at-law (Partner)
Current employer: Toranomon Kyodo Law Office
Brief work history: From 1991 to 2003 I was an employee of the Tokyo Dome Corporation. I became an attorney-at-law in 2004. In 2011 I joined the Toranomon Kyodo Law Office as a partner. One area I practice in is sport law.

PHOTO 8.1   Takao Ohashi

What example can you share regarding using data to help make a decision?

I would like to undertake a comparison of response to foul ball accidents by MLB (United States) and NPB (Japan).

1 Comparison of Japanese and US professional baseball stadiums

There are 30 teams and stadiums in Major League Baseball (MLB), while there are 12 teams and home stadiums in Japan's professional baseball league (Nippon Professional Baseball Organization; NPB).

Stadiums in Japan and the United States have major differences. Six of the NPB home stadiums are domed stadiums, meaning that the proportion of domed stadiums is larger than in the US. Furthermore, more stadiums in Japan (83 percent) have artificial turf than do MLB stadiums. Moreover, most stadiums in Japan are provided with safety nets to protect spectators in the infield seats from baseballs.

On the other hand, backstop netting is provided only behind the home plate in MLB stadiums while one finds virtually no stadiums in which the infield seats are provided with protective netting. In December 2015, MLB made a recommendation regarding installing protective netting for some infield seats. There will probably be teams that agree with this recommendation and will install protective netting for their home stadium infield seats. However, stadiums in Japan traditionally have protective netting for their infield seats.

Japan has often followed the US in baseball innovation. The first roofed stadium in MLB was the Astrodome which was opened in 1965, followed by The Kingdome in 1976. In Japan, Tokyo Dome, which was modeled on the Metrodome, opened in 1988 followed by the Fukuoka Dome in 1993, the Osaka Dome and the Nagoya Dome in 1997, the Seibu Dome in 1999, and the Sapporo Dome in 2001.

In terms of artificial turf, the first stadium using it in the US was the Astrodome. The first use of artificial turf in Japan was at Korakuen Stadium in 1976 (the precursor to the Tokyo Dome), and after that, most stadiums in Japan converted to artificial turf.

The trend for Japan to follow the lead established by MLB stadiums ends when it comes to protective netting of seats beyond those protected by backstops behind the home plate area. While some MLB teams are considering adding screening to their dugouts, stadiums in Japan have been providing more protection for years. In 2005, the Tokyo Dome protected field seating with netting installed so as to extend in front of infield and outfield seats. Similar netting was used in 2008 at the Seibu Dome, in 2010 at the Osaka Dome, and in 2013 at the Yokohama Stadium. However, in 2005, the protective netting for the infield seats was removed at Yokohama Stadium, and the netting for the infield seats was removed from the Sapporo Dome in 2006.

In Japan, announcements are typically made before and during games at ballparks to protect spectators from being hit by foul balls. Warnings are also displayed on signs and on scoreboards, employees blow whistles when a foul ball is hit, warnings are printed on the backs of the tickets, and fan viewing rules are posted on the team websites, as examples. It has been my experience that these measures may not differ greatly between Japan and the United States. But it is my impression that warnings are more frequently issued over stadium PA systems and scoreboards in Japan.

2 Comparison of foul ball accident litigation

The major question I wanted to explore was the extent of foul balls and litigation differences between the NPB and MLB.

According to recent research (Fried *et al.*, 2012), from 1913 to 2008, there were 82 cases of foul ball accidents that made it to the appellate court level in the United States. In contrast, the first verdict in a foul ball injury case in Japan was handed down in the Kleenex Stadium case in 2011. That same year saw a verdict in the Kamagaya Stadium case, followed by a verdict in the Koshien Stadium Case in 2014, and a verdict in the 2015 Sapporo Dome case (the appeal was finalized in 2016). Thus, the law in Japan is much less developed. Prior to becoming an attorney, I worked for a professional baseball stadium management company and had experience with a foul ball accident lawsuit (this particular case was resolved in an out-of-court settlement).

One might say that the difference in the number of foul ball accident lawsuits between Japan and the United States lies in the fact that, in contrast to the litigious nature of American society, Japan has a history of avoiding disputes that can be traced back to the constitution authored by the great eighth-century leader, Prince Shotoku, one clause of which maintains, "Harmony is to be valued, and the avoidance of wanton opposition to be honored." Most striking is the number of cases since 2011 in which foul ball accident lawsuits have gone to a judgment. There is a tendency to believe that the reasons underlying this have been the sudden increase in the number of attorneys in Japan as a consequence of reforms in the legal system that began in 1999 and the sense that someone needs to take responsibility for sport injuries. However, the Basic Act on Sport that went into effect in 2013 clearly articulates a right to sports (that it is a right of all people to lead happy and rich lives through sport), and I believe that what we are seeing here is the effect of an increasing awareness among the Japanese people of infringements of their rights in places where they can "engage in, see, and support" sport.

Many states in the US use the "limited duty rule" in foul ball accident cases and this rule limits the potential liability ballparks might face when someone is hit by a foul ball or bat when the most dangerous part of the ballpark is protected by netting. This rule though has come under scrutiny by courts such as in New Mexico in 2010 in the Edward, C. v. City of Albuquerque case. Thereafter, decisions were issued in cases in the states of Idaho and Georgia which denied the application of the limited duty rule.

There is a similar trend in Japan, although the number of decisions is small. There is no limited duty rule in Japanese law, and the point at issue in foul ball accident litigation is construction liability (Civil Law, Article 717), which focuses on whether or not the stadium is "as safe as it normally should be." Specifically, these cases focus on the safety of locations where foul ball accidents occur and generally take into consideration the physical situation and measures undertaken to alert people to foul ball accidents. According to this standard of judgment, up until 2013 Japanese case law recognizes that conditions are safe to the extent that there is appropriate balance between three elements: protection of spectators' safety, the obligation for spectators to exercise due caution, and the sense of presence that is an essential element of professional baseball. Further, this standard recognizes that the responsibilities assumed by teams and stadium owners are limited to the extent that spectators having a normal capacity to make decisions would obviously be aware of foul balls when they watch a professional baseball game at a stadium. All three of the cases up to 2013 were lost by the injured plaintiffs.

The Sapporo District Court, in a 2015 decision involving the Sapporo Dome, did not adopt the principle of "sense of presence" that had been one of the elements considered in previous decisions. The court held that safety should not be sacrificed in the pursuit of a sense of presence. This same decision limited the spectators' duty to exercise caution and for the first time handed down a victory to a plaintiff, holding teams and stadium owners accountable for implementing safety measures that take into account the presence of spectators who may not be paying attention to the ball. In 2016 the court decided not to adopt the "sense of presence" rule so the plaintiff lost that claim.

3 Comparison of foul ball research

Based on an analysis of 548 foul balls in 25 MLB games, and 448 foul balls in 16 minor league games, the data showed that the most dangerous area in a stadium was down both the first and third base lines (Fried *et al.*, 2012). Professional baseball in Japan does not release the results of foul ball studies. Nevertheless, there is data for Japanese high school baseball for the spring national championship in 2002 and the summer national championship (both held at Koshien Stadium). This research was undertaken to develop safety measures in the wake of an incident at the summer national championship in 2001 in which a member of a brass band who was seated in the infield "Alps" seats was struck and blinded by a foul ball.

As highlighted in table 8.1 and 8.2, the 2002 Spring and Summer National Championships had 289 fouls in 31 games and 531 fouls in 48 games, respectively.

Although this is not necessarily an accurate comparison to professional baseball because these players are high school students using metal bats, it is clear that the areas subject to sharp foul balls are the first and third base sidelines.

4 The extent and height of infield protective netting

MLB issued netting recommendations in December 2015. According to these recommendations, protective nets should be installed along the first and third baselines for a distance of 70 feet (21 meters) from the home plate, and information should be provided when tickets are sold as to whether or not protective netting is provided. The recommendations do not, however, speak to the height of protective nets, saying only ". . .that shields from line-drive foul balls in all field-level seats that are located between the near ends of both dugouts."

Similarly, there are no consistent rules or guidelines for protective netting in NPB. Courts rely on the construction guidelines for baseball stadiums issued by the Exterior Sports Facilities Committee of the Sports Facilities Association. These guidelines suggest that stadium infield protective netting should be approximately 3 meters (9 feet) high. The average height of stadium infield protective netting is approximately 4.59 meters (13.77 feet)(fence and protective net), and judicial precedent until 2013 made use of the question of whether or not the standard was met as a basis for decisions. In the 2015 Sapporo Dome foul ball case, the accident occurred with a net approximately 5.6 meters (16.8 feet) above ground level. The netting was actually lower than it had been in the

TABLE 8.1 2002 Spring National Championship foul balls

	Total number of batters	Right-handed pitcher, right-handed batter	Left-handed pitcher, right-handed batter	Right-handed pitcher, left-handed batter	Left-handed pitcher, left-handed batter	Total number of fly balls
TOTAL	2406	1176	399	642	189	980

Note: Total number of foul balls does not include bunt fouls

Foul balls entering stands		Right-handed pitcher, right-handed batter	Left-handed pitcher, right-handed batter	Right-handed pitcher, left-handed batter	Left-handed pitcher, left-handed batter	Total number of fly balls
Breakdown	1st base Alps	9 (1)	2 (0)	3 (0)	1 (1)	15 (2)
	1st base VIP	110 (5)	30 (2)	10 (0)	1 (0)	151 (7)
	3rd base Alps	12 (1)	5 (1)	10 (2)	0 (0)	27 (4)
	3rd base VIP	11 (1)	4 (3)	74 (10)	7 (1)	96 (15)
TOTAL		142 (8)	41 (6)	97 (12)	9 (2)	289 (28)

Note: Right-handed pitcher, right-handed batter indicates a face-off between two right-handed players.( ) indicates sharp hits.

TABLE 8.2 2002 Summer National Championship foul balls

	Right-handed pitcher, right-handed batter	Left-handed pitcher, right-handed batter	Right-handed pitcher, left-handed batter	Left-handed pitcher, left-handed batter	TOTAL
Total number of batters	1598	348	980	193	
TOTAL					3119

Foul balls entering stands		Right-handed pitcher, right-handed batter	Left-handed pitcher, right-handed batter	Right-handed pitcher, left-handed batter	Left-handed pitcher, left-handed batter	TOTAL
Breakdown	1st base Alps	11(0)	3(0)	9(2)	0(0)	23(2)
	1st base VIP	219(47)	40(8)	16(5)	1(1)	276(61)
	3rd base Alps	17(9)	9(1)	14(0)	1(0)	41(10)
	3rd base VIP	13(1)	1(0)	147(25)	30(7)	191(33)
TOTAL		260(57)	53(9)	186(32)	32(8)	531(106)

Note: ( ) indicates sharp hits.

past. Nevertheless, the court did not attach much importance to this fact, and as indicated earlier, limited the spectator's obligation to exercise due care, which resulted in an initial victory for the plaintiff.

5 Summary

Although the specifications of stadiums in Japan often follow the specifications of MLB stadiums, Japan is actually ahead of the US in terms of protecting more fans with larger protected areas. The key in Japan, given the fact that stadiums have had infield protective netting, is that the netting once up should not be reduced in height. We are also starting to see incidents in Japan in which the responsibility of the teams and stadium owners is called into question for foul ball accidents occurring after netting has been removed.

Finally, the question of how high the netting should be can only be determined on a case-by-case basis examining each individual stadium to determine what is the most dangerous area and then to provide appropriate netting to protect those dangerous areas.

PHOTO 8.2   A foul ball warning sign in Japan

Risk management

The primary means to avoid potential liability associated with negligence claims is risk management. Risk management can range from having contracts that distribute risks (such as insurance policies) to actually examining risks and trying to minimize them (such as putting a warning sign near a recently mopped floor). The key to risk management is understanding risks and taking steps to minimize them. This is where data collection can come in handy. For example, automobile accidents used to be tracked through a two page accident report. How was that information used? Someone would have to go through each one of the accidents to determine if there was a dangerous intersection and to see if there were any other contributing factors that impacted accidents at that intersection. That report has changed after being used for around 20 years. The form was recently replaced with an eight-page form. Researchers examined the new form and determined it would not take longer to complete (compared to the two-page form), but would provide more critical information that can make it easier to track accidents. There was significant pushback from those who did not want any change ("we have always done it this way"), but the change was being mandated by the federal government in an effort to track the most dangerous roads and to hold municipalities accountable for making sure they use federal highway funds to make sure they correct dangerous roads. This is a perfect real-world example of how risk management can be derived from data collected through actual incidents. This same process is used by those who insure sport-related risks. They try to determine the odds of a potential claim, the cost of the claim, and how much they would want to make as a profit to assume the risk. It is a gamble, but based on sound data.

Contract law

Contracts exist throughout the business world. Sport businesses are not immune from these contracts. Contracts cover everything from sponsorship to ticket sales, concession sales, employment contracts, player contracts, coach's contracts, and numerous other contracts that are seen all over the world. These contracts need to be enforced and such enforcement can be significantly difficult. For example, all the counterfeit goods sold at major sporting events have prompted the FBI, Interpol, and other agencies to converge on such events to collect and destroy such goods. Such goods are manufactured outside of a contractual relationship and their production is not authorized. Similarly, many sport broadcasts are pirated and broadcasted to bars, night clubs, and homes that have not paid to receive the broadcast. This represents a violation of a contract for exclusive broadcasting as well as criminal theft. Thus, while a bar owner that steals a broadcast signal could face criminal theft charges, the same owner can be breaching a contract if they had a contract to broadcast other events or if their broadcast contract did not allow them to charge or make money from broadcasting an event. To help protect valuable sport-related rights, contracts are written to provide the broadest potential coverage, but no contract will be completely iron clad, no matter how many attorneys and ideas are covered.

New technologies such as smartphone apps Periscope and Meerkat allow any smartphone user to live-stream video from their phone onto their Twitter feed. Such an approach was not considered when most broadcast contracts were negotiated. This can significantly impact the value of a broadcast contract if fans can start streaming their own videos of an event. If someone is at a sporting event they can possibly broadcast the event live without expensive equipment, technical knowledge, or even permission. If a pay-per-view event is $59 to purchase, how many people would pay that amount if they could get a video feed from a phone for free? These apps will also allow for crowdsourced gamecasts where fans can see video images from many different angles all over a sport facility. This is an example of how technology can outpace the legal system. Thus, while sport events can try to knock out as many illegal broadcasts of their events as possible, there might be numerous other legal broadcasts that are being permitted with new technologies which do not represent a breach of any criminal law or any contract.

Contract terms lend themselves to data analysis. How many units were sold? What is the price point for selling a certain number of items? When will a bonus be paid? And other terms require data to enforce the contract. This might also require parties to work together to ensure accuracy. One approach used when sharing parking revenue at a sport facility is to have a representative from the municipality (if it owns the parking lot) and the team each track cars entering the facility. One party might collect the revenue and the other might deploy a counter (hand counter or a loop in the ground that tracks cars). Data from both are reconciled at the end of the day. If cars are charged $5.00 to park and there are 1,000 cars at the venue then the counter should read 1,000 and there should be $5,000 collected (minus any passes). It is assumed that there might be a small variance, but anything more significant represents a significant concern.

Damages from breaching a contract also require significant data. If a player has an insurance policy on their body and they are injured, what is the value of that injury and how much should be paid? If a player has an endorsement contract with one company, and is seen wearing the clothes of a competitor, that represents a devaluation of a contract and if it breaches the contract, can result in damages. How much should those damages be? If the player was a minor star then the damages would probably be minimal. If the player was a superstar and photographs were prominently displayed then the damages could be significant.

Antitrust law

Antitrust laws are designed to provide a level playing field for businesses. Businesses are not allowed to engage in any anticompetitive activities that maintain a monopoly or to enter into an agreement to limit competition. When examining any antitrust claim, regulators and attorneys will examine the impact on the relevant market. The question then becomes, what is the relevant market? In most cases the court will examine the impact of the activity on those affected by the anticompetitive activity. In dealing between teams in a league, the relevant market and impacted parties are often the athletes, coaches, and referees who often enter into a union to more effectively negotiate with the league and to provide the league with some antitrust protection. In other cases, the relevant market might be customers. For example, if three fitness chains conspire to set prices, then the customers are hurt because they cannot negotiate or search for better terms. All the arguments associated with such cases rely on data to determine if competition is being harmed (through increased pricing or limited product options).

Government regulations

There are numerous government regulations that require data. Taxes rely on financial data. Unemployment compensation insurance and workers' compensation coverage are based on past claims collected from employers and numerous injured employees. Some regulations are very specific. For example, by 2015 14 cities had adopted benchmarking requirements for commercial buildings in an effort to make them more energy efficient. Portland, as an example, passed legislation requiring buildings over 20,000 square feet (6,100 square meters) (in Atlanta the regulations kicks into play at 25,000 square feet and in Kansas City the regulation is applied to facilities over 50,000 square feet) to use ENERGY STAR'S portfolio manager to report energy and water consumption on an annual basis. The data will eventually be made public. The effort is designed to push facility managers to utilize data to more efficiently run their facilities and allow every other facility to compare themselves across a local region to determine how efficient they are ("Three more US Cities add benchmarking requirements," 2015).

Conclusion

There are numerous ways in which sport law and data intersect. While such data might not be as sexy as sport marketing or event management data, it is critical in providing a safe environment and helping to determine possible damages or impact. The key area examined in this chapter for sport executives is the issue of foreseeability and how data can help determine the most likely types of injuries and what strategies might help minimize these injuries.

References

AAP. (2014, August 25). *Stephen Dank loses defamation dismissal appeal.* Retrieved from www.9news. com.au/national/2014/08/28/12/24/dank-s-appeal-dismissed-and-he-has-to-pay

Associated Press. (2013, August 25). *Lance Armstrong settles with* Sunday Times *in Libel Case.* Retrieved from www.csmonitor.com/World/Latest-News-Wires/2013/0825/Lance-Armstrong-settles-with-Sunday-Times-in-libel-case

Coventry v. Lawrence, UKSC 13 (2014). Retrieved from www.bailii.org/uk/cases/UKSC/2014/13. pdf

Fried, G. (2015). *Managing sport facilities* (3rd ed.). Champaign, IL: Human Kinetics.

Fried, G., Pittman, A., Milsten, A., Abell, T., & Mills, J. (2012). Don't sit there. . .or there. . . or there: An analysis of ball park protection and foul ball injury risks. *International Journal of Sport Management, 13*(4), 423–43.

Hickey, N. (2013, May 15). *Stephen Dank's defamation claim for $10 million damages – A good press release, but what about the law.* Retrieved from http://ipwhiteboard.com.au/stephen-danks-defamation-claim-for-10-million-damages-a-good-press-release-but-what-about-the-law/

Pleads guilty to hacking (2016, January 9). *The Hartford Courant,* C6.

Socolow, B. R. (2015). Wearable technology in professional sports: Big money, big data, big problems? *Sport Litigation Alert, 12*(20).

The Wal-Mart litigation project. (2015). Retrieved from www.wal-martlitigation.com/

Three more U.S. cities add benchmarking requirements. (2015, July). *Buildings,* 11.

9

MANUFACTURING/PRODUCTION ANALYTICS

Gil Fried

Introduction

If you were going to launch a marketing effort for a new product where would you start? Most people would say with the product benefits, but the effort actually starts way before that with what it takes to bring the product to market and how to support the effort. Without the back support the most wonderful marketing effort will fail. One recent example I read was very enlightening concerning D-Day. The battle started on June 6th, 1944, but the preparation started two years earlier. The key to winning the battle and the war was the preparation, including the supply chain. By June 1944, 17 million tons of cargo was shipped from the US to Great Britain. This included 800,000 pints of plasma, 17 million maps, and once the invasion began one million gallons of oil, 3,489 tons of soap in the first four months alone, and enough food to give each soldier 2,830 calories a day. The army's "Red Ball Express" on a daily basis transported 900 trucks, 24 hours a day delivering a total of 412,193 tons of materials to the front lines. Without these supplies and the logistics D-Day would not work (Godfrey, 2015).

Not everything was seamless during this effort. Distribution of winter uniforms was delayed because front line units did not provide the right requisitioning numbers. Furthermore, winter uniforms were a priority until October, and by then it was too late for every soldier to receive all the winter gear they needed for the bitterly cold winters. Also, blanket requisitions did not take into consideration the civilian population, prisoners of war, and French free forces. Combined, there was a deficit of almost a million blankets by the winter of 1944.

The Allies were not the first to employ supply chain management to help win a war. The Romans were able to help win distant wars through using their navy, which was a much more effective, economical, and speedier means to supply legions fighting abroad than to rely on locally sourced food and supplies. The key was to generate operational efficiency. Supply chain analytics (SCA) is designed to accomplish the same goal. SCA examines service fill monitoring, loss monitoring, supplier performance, inbound delivery monitoring, supply chain performance management, distribution management, operational performance management, and other similar indicators to help determine if a company is running effectively. SCA is critical because there are so many possible disruptions to the manufacturing and distribution process such as supply distributions, demand volatility, shrinking product life-cycles, and related disruptions. An executive can wait and respond to all changes as they come or they can undertake a predictive process to detect potential problems before they affect the process, lower quality, or increase costs. SCA is only one of a number of tools from manufacturing analytics to enterprise-wide analytics to more effectively bring products from concept to delivery. Numerous sub-systems have been developed over the years to help streamline each step of the product cycle. If there are 50 steps from developing an idea to manufacturing it, distributing it, and then selling it – each step has a cost and if the cost can be reduced at each level then the overall costs can be significantly reduced. That has led to numerous quality improvement programs such as lean manufacturing, Six-Sigma, and Total Quality Management (TQM) which are all designed to lead to continuous process improvement, reliable decision-making, quick response to problems, and reducing overall costs.

The concerns faced by the Romans and the Allies still exist to this day. In a recent example, Chipotle Mexican Grill realized its strength was also its Achilles heel. The restaurant chain prides itself in having locally farmed and natural ingredients. Such a focus helped it increase its sales at 1,900 restaurants in 2014 by 19.8 percent. But a major E. coli outbreak severally impacted sales and stock price in 2015. The drive to have locally farmed and more natural ingredients required a very complex supply chain that included numerous small, independent farmers compared with the large, highly processed, industrial food providers serving restaurants such as McDonalds. Local farmers have a much harder time insuring consistent quality. The local program also primarily ran from June through October, when local farms could harvest the needed produce (Giammona & Patton, 2015). This required Chipotle to have two different supply chains and redundancy systems in case small farmers were unable to deliver produce. Many sport organizations face the same concerns. They need to have the right parts/ingredients the customers desire, at the right price, at the right time, in the right amount, and free of any defects. If the supply chain, manufacturing process, inventory management system, employer scheduling, and related systems are not operating effectively then the sport business will not be able to operate efficiently – thus costing money, lost orders, customer dissatisfaction, and a publicity nightmare. The company's founder and CEO (Steve Ells) apologized on national TV, took out full-page advertisements in national newspapers, and hit the road to convince customers they were taking action. The company aggressively pursued a number of strategies such as aggressive food testing including weekly safety audits, quarterly national audits, and independent lab testing (Chipotle, 2015).

Imagine if a baseball team only had eight players suited to play a game. Imagine if it took Nike 12 months to finally get a shoe to market and by then the design or color was out of fashion. Imagine if a football stadium ran out of beer at the end of the first quarter. These are all disasters that could have been avoided through proper planning. Chipotle could have attempted to minimize the possibility of product disruption through more aggressive testing from the beginning. Some elements, such as an employee getting sick and spreading the norovirus at a restaurant in Boston that ended up sickening members of the Boston College basketball team (along with over 130 others), are impossible to completely predict and prevent. This does not mean that planning cannot help minimize these disruptions and that is why using analytics in the manufacturing and production process can be so helpful.

Value chain firms (those that produce physical assets) will utilize analytics to explore: problems of supply chain fluctuations, costs of assets, flexibility of operations, and interface with others in the supply chain (Davenport, Harris, & Shapiro, 2010). When exploring the supply chain (i.e. the raw goods that go into making the product and how those raw goods make it to the factory), analytics can help explore what happened in the past, what is occurring right now, and how to prepare for the future. When exploring the past, analytics can help examine what happened such as the number of orders, defect rate, and asset utilization as examples. This information can lead to insights such as what process controls have worked and what bottlenecks are impacting the production process. When analytics are used to explore the current situation it can explore bottlenecks, truck rerouting, equipment concerns, and inventory controls. Analyzing the current situation can highlight what should be the next best action – which could entail a recommendation for preventive maintenance of equipment, better routing of supplies, or maybe bundling orders. When examining supply chain analytics for the future, a manager would explore forecasting demand, capacity planning for a factory, and alternate inventory supplies. The information about the future can lead to projections to optimize the plant in the future such as schedule optimization, future products, supply routing changes, and hitting target manufacturing numbers (Davenport *et al.*, 2010). Thus, analytics will help explain what has happened, what is going on now, and what the future will hold for making the supply chain as efficient as possible. Extrapolation from historical data forms the first stage in developing a possible data model.

The supply chain evaluation process starts with problem identification, which is normally an inefficiency that is going to be reduced or determining the optimal inventory rate to save money through minimizing carrying costs. The inefficiency could be that in the manufacturing process a large amount of material is wasted, thus costing money (both in terms of raw goods and the cost to collect and dispose of the waste). Then historical data needs to be reviewed to capture information on products, sources, personnel, equipment, and processing steps. Products can then be segmented on product groups (i.e. all baseball gloves versus bats) based on cost, availability, use, and the impact of any inventory policies. Then a manager can examine the routing of the raw materials, pricing issues, and processing steps. With this information a manager can anticipate future needs so supplies can be automatically reordered through a trigger action (i.e. when supplies dip below ten units, more units are automatically reordered). A manager can then explore how to configure products and maintain efficiency, customizing and modifying the process so that some products can be grouped together if they use the same components or equipment. This can help adjust the process flow (based on quality, cost, demand, etc.) and this helps the organization reach real-time optimization.

The need for forecasting

The key for proper manufacturing and production is forecasting. Forecasting determines the future needs and allows an organization to prepare to meet the demands. A sport team knows how many games they will play in the pre-season and the season, but they do not know if they will make the post-season. If the stadium needs to be used in what would be the post-season time frame they have to determine how likely it is that the team will make the playoffs. Forecasting might be as simple as asking sales personnel how may tickets they anticipate selling. Anticipatory surveys can provide some very useful information. Furthermore, some businesses operate on cycles which can help with forecasting. For example, a sport apparel company can anticipate significant sales volumes in June and July in anticipation of back to school purchases. Similarly, a bat manufacturer would have increased orders and production cycles in anticipation of an upcoming baseball season while demand will taper off after the season ends.

Forecasting customer demand is a central part of supply chain management which leads to a successful lean manufacturing system. This can be especially acute when there is a large manufacturer with thousands of products, but can be just as challenging for a minor league basketball team trying to determine what concessions to stock or how to order promotional items for the next season – such as bobble-head dolls. Managers need to make sure that any forecast is a consensus forecast from across the entire organization. This is often called an ensemble forecast. Using the promotion example, the problem might be identified as how many bobble-heads to order for a given promotion. Past research might show that the team ordered 1,000 bobble-heads of their star player and they needed to place the order six months in advance. Past research might also highlight how many tickets normally are sold for give-away games and what price elasticity existed for these more attractive game days. The modeling and variable analysis might examine what are the projected ticket sales. Data can be obtained from ticket sales personnel and group ticket sales personnel. The ensemble forecast would also use information from concession, finance, marketing, and even legal (in addition to ticket sales). The data can be analyzed and it might be established that more than 4,000 additional tickets could be sold if there were 5,000 bobble-heads given away and that while the bobble-head might cost only $2 to produce, each ticket can be sold for $10 so there is a high upside for holding such a give-away game. These results then need to be disseminated across the organization. It is recommended that there should not be a specific number (i.e. we will have 10,000 fans that game), but rather should represent a range (i.e. from 9,000 to 11,000 fans). For example, what if the coaches are hearing chatter that a player might be traded? Imagine ordering 5,000 bobble-heads six months before the season begins and then the player is traded or retires? That is one reason why manufacturing needs a faster turn-around to prevent such circumstances, which can often occur with fads.

Analytics are often used in the cost–benefit analysis to determine whether to manufacture something in a given country or locale. Even within the United States, as an example, the cost for manufacturing is much less in Alabama compared with Hawaii or Alaska. The same price differential exists across different countries. While manufacturing locally gives a company greater oversight and speed, if there is time, the cost can be significant. Some estimate that the cost of manufacturing in the United States is 8–10 times more expensive than in China – due to domestic labor costs (Finkle, 2015).

Part of the forecasting effort is to respond as quickly as possible to changes. Change in customers' preference requires quick transition from one product line to another without wasting inventory or machinery. In fact, many of the most innovative products that succeed in the US are successful because they use less capital and employees to increase delivery speed to customers. For example, car giant General Motors creates about $1.85 of market value per dollar of physical assets while Tesla creates around $11 (Colvin, 2015). Even though both companies are car manufacturers they are completely different and speed and efficiencies are not the only differences: they operate on different business models. For example, Tesla has tried as much as possible to cut out independent dealers who just add costs to customers without providing significant value. Thus, they try to sell directly to customers. This removes friction from the supply chain similar to how companies such as Uber, the world's largest car service company, succeeds by not owning any cars or Airbnb has become an accommodation juggernaut without owning any real estate. That is an example of removing friction and producing an almost capital-free model. Disruptive processes in other areas such as insurance or travel agencies significantly altered the business landscape when web based options changed how the products were sold.

Forecasting impacts more than just supplies and equipment. For example, scheduling of workers to coordinating delivery drivers requires significant planning so that personnel/vehicles are not underutilized or sitting idle. While some of the forecasting elements might be internal to a business, forecasting is much broader as a company needs to look outside as well. Global and national circumstances such as a recession, striking dock workers, change in currency rates, and numerous other variables can be tracked and acted upon to provide protection. For example, some teams with private chartered airplanes ferrying players around might have pre-purchased airplane fuel in 2015 anticipating possible price increase and they locked in a set price. When oil prices plummeted at the end of 2015, the forecast proved to be wrong and some teams might be caught paying double for fuel costs or risk litigation if they try to back-out of their contracts. Some contracts anticipate (i.e. forecast) potential issues and might have escalator or de-escalator clauses in a contract requiring price adjustments based on possible future conditions. Large buyers have a better chance of negotiating such a clause compared to small companies with little bargaining power. Thus, forecasting is a process requiring constant vigilance both internally and outside the company to identify issues that can impact the company, what might be the impact, and how to take advantage or minimize the impact of future occurrences.

Technology changes

Technology has changed the forecasting process in many ways. One is the ability to collect and process numerous data points from diverse areas under comprehensive models to explore what might happen in the future. In the past, sales people would indicate what they felt the next year's sales volumes might be and then that served as the forecasts. Technology allows numerous entities, such as suppliers, government agencies, wholesalers, customers, employees and others, to weight in and provide information that can be aggregated to explore multiple models as to what might happen in the short as well as long term. That is where the internet of things – where all devices and equipment are connected to one another – can revolutionize the manufacturing process. Imagine in the future a customer might be able to custom order their sports apparel through uploading their measurements and style choices to a specific seller and the order is automatically sent to the manufacturing plant, and the process to have the finished product shipped to the customer is undertaken with one click of the mouse. Each step in the process can then be analyzed to find any inefficiency.

Technology is also increasing the speed at which machines can manufacture products. Similarly, using 3D printers is just one way to speed the time between engineering and manufacturing by reducing the time needed to develop prototypes and cutting the costs on the assembly line. New Balance launched a limited release shoe in 2015 with a 3D printed midsole that allowed for customization and quicker turnaround. Local Motors in Arizona has produced a primarily 3D printed car. While a traditional car has 20,000 parts, the Local Motors car has only 50. Such efficiencies will be seen around the world as 5.6 million 3D printers are expected to be shipped around the world by 2019 and manufacturers who use 3D printers are experiencing a 4 percent saving from deploying 3D printers in their supply chain (Rockwood, 2016). In addition sensors on machines and throughout the assembly process can create a more efficient system and reduce downtime. Robots working the assembly line and moving inventory make less mistakes, take much fewer breaks, and can be reprogrammed more effectively than human workers. Companies are also using augmented reality (AR) where equipment (such as tablets or visors on hardhats in a factory) can examine a piece of equipment at a factory and all the repair information and operating information will automatically be produced to help identify problems. As of 2016, 35 percent of manufacturers use smart sensors to analyze data from factory equipment and an additional 17 percent expect to deploy such technology by 2018 (Rockwood, 2016). While technology can streamline the manufacturing process, there are still numerous customers who want custom or handmade products such as customized golf clubs, tennis rackets, and skis.

Technology cannot solve some problems that are outside the purview of even the most analytic companies. The crumbling infrastructure of many countries makes it almost impossible to plan for supply chain and distribution flow when it is not known whether a travel route would even be usable. For example, using lean manufacturing is focused on reducing the amount of inventory in storage to reduce carrying costs. This is a fine line approach because while money might be saved if inventory stock is low, if the inventory cannot be immediately replaced it can stop production. This happened after a massive blackout affecting the northeast of North America in 2003. While power was out for hours for some, others were without power for almost a week. The traffic problems and inability to ship materials caused many manufacturers to back away from a strict lean system to a lean + system where an amount of inventory in arrears was secured in case of any future disasters or incidents.

One of the most important tools for inventory management in the future is radio frequency identification (RFID) tags. These small devices allow managers to track the item with the tag. While this is often seen in libraries and stores to protect items and merchandise from theft or misplacement, the same technology can apply to inventory. RFID tags can be used to notify not just the manufacturer, but also a supplier when inventory levels reach a certain level. This same data approach is used in stores where new inventory is scanned (by their bar code) when they are placed on shelves. When an item is purchased the item's barcode is scanned and the price is registered. Just as important, the item is removed from the inventory. When a certain number of the item is reached, an order is placed for more of that product. Thus, while barcodes help with the pricing process, they are just as important as an inventory management tool and save stores from having to send employees to the shelves to do inventory tracking every several weeks.

Natural resources also need to be closely monitored to ensure necessary resources are available. For example, what should a natural grass turf field do in California or other draught stricken areas to ensure playability, and not violate laws requiring cutting back on water usage. Natural resources can be measured and analyzed. Israel is a well-known leader in water technology such as drip irrigation for desert land. Israel has been monitoring water usage (the country is on the Mediterranean but used to be swamps and desert land until around the 1930s) since the 1950s, long before they had computers to do the task. All water usage was monitored to track efficiency and overusage. Furthermore, real-world pricing was launched for water which represent what it really costs to deliver water, so all the costs associated with water treatment and delivery were passed on to customers and the higher price encouraged water conservation. Such an analytical approach might be undertaken with other scarce resources in the future.

Technology is not just impacting the production and manufacturing process, but also how products are being used. This can be seen in some high-tech products such as Tesla cars where some were bursting into flames while being driven on highways. Instead of an expensive nationwide recall the high-tech auto company examined data and determined that the Model S lowered its chassis while operating at highway speed to become more aerodynamic. The lower chassis caused some debris to hit the battery pack. Using the internet of things, the company sent updated software to every car that reduced the amount the car was lowered by one inch, thus eliminating the problem and avoiding a costly recall (Colvin, 2015).

Manufacturing/production analytics

So far we have covered various issues associated with manufacturing analytics, but we need to dive deep into what is manufacturing/production analytics. We are combining the two topics because making a sport shoe, producing a baseball game, or producing a sport broadcast require very similar steps to move from idea to execution. Manufacturing is the process of making things. By this definition, manufacturing involves taking some item, transforming it, and creating a new product. Production is the process of making something so manufacturing can fall within that definition. Thus, we need to look at how items are transformed, but also need to look at component parts, how an item moves through the production process, and ends up in the marketplace. This might seem like a straightforward process, but imagine the complexity when there are large numbers of inventory components outsourced from throughout the world, a large number of products, and numerous suppliers – with each one possibly following a different quality standard.

So how can numbers be used to improve the manufacturing process? The first thing to explore is the goal of the organization. From there a manager can examine the currently existing process to really understand what is involved and where there might be concerns or bottlenecks. This could arise, as an example, when items need to be processed in one area, moved to another for further processing, and then returned back to the first location just because machinery is spread out throughout a plant. Through a simple visual inspection a manager could identify such an inefficiency. Managers also need to:

- detect significant events in the manufacturing cycle;
- identify why variations or defects occur;
- drive continuous process improvement;
- support developing best practices throughout an organization;
- change the mindset from reactive to predictive process management;

- increase productivity; and
- decrease costs.

A visual inspection or talking with employees is one approach. All the equipment in a factory can be electronically connected and this can be a great way to analyze their efficiency. From how much electricity they use to whether they need maintenance, the equipment can be monitored for efficiency and optimization.

Managers need to understand that the three areas of bringing in supplies, transforming them, and then transporting the finished product are equally important. The most effective factory floor that sits idle due to supplies not arriving on time, is not efficient. The same goes to loading shipping trucks. If products are added in a haphazard manner they can be damaged and the loading/unloading time can be significantly increased. The same process is used in the facility change-over process where parts of a basketball court need to be stored in such a way that it speeds-up the assembly process when installing such a floor over ice in an arena. The quickest way to ensure the floor can be placed in a quick manner is to store it initially with the parts that need to be removed and placed at the front of the storage area and when the floor is placed back in storage that part should be the last piece placed back in storage.

Analytics can be applied for the entire process of getting a product from concept to delivery. The best way to approach this analysis is to explore all the elements normally found in the process to ensure total quality for a manufacturer. Japanese manufacturers were the ones who really brought life to the total quality process, but it was actually an American, William Deming (1900–93), who pioneered total quality management and launched it in Japan. While his ideas were not initially embraced by US manufacturers, his efforts in post-World War II Japan helped revolutionize their manufacturing process. He focused on several key areas, such as:

- continuous quality improvement as a company's overriding mission;
- implementing a preventive management system, obsessed with quality from the beginning rather than just manufacturing a product and waiting for defects to be detected and reported by customers;
- using good materials, equipment, and processes from the start to ensure quality rather than inspecting finished items just at the end of the manufacturing process;
- establishing long-term relationships with suppliers to provide the best quality rather than just going for the cheapest option;
- train workers so they become a competitive force in improving quality and reducing costs;
- allow workers the freedom to report out of control processes;
- encourage workers and management to work as a team (such as quality circles) rather than everyone competing against each other; and
- instill employee pride by providing workers with the right tools and quality parts to help complete the job.

(Kohler, 1994)

Deming is not alone in his effort to improve quality. The key is developing a process and measuring the outcome at each point. The typical stages of manufacturing are as follows:

- Customer research – identifying customers' desires through analyzing the results of surveys and focus groups.
- Product development – converting customers' wants to design a precisely engineered product and identifying design quality points.
- Purchasing materials – purchasing or refining components and then testing for quality.
- Manufacturing – machines and labor are applied to the purchased material to create the product and the process is monitored for consistency and efficiency such as materials failing to meet specifications, employee issues, or machines wearing out.
- Storing – the finished products need to be warehoused and then shipped to wholesalers or directly to consumers. This process can be monitored for obsolescence, carrying costs, and other inefficiencies.
- Marketing – the product is promoted to customers and then after sale service needs to be provided (such as warranty support). Customer satisfaction can be monitored and manufacturing defects analyzed.

(Kohler, 1994)

One of the most common analytical techniques during the above process is product sampling where several products from the production run (called a lot) are examined to determine if they are acceptable (i.e. quality control). If the sample quality is poor the lot could be rejected and if the quality is acceptable then the lot is accepted. This process can be impacted by how many samples are taken from the lot, if the sampling is undertaken for every lot, what quality standard will be used, and what percentage of defects observed is acceptable. There is always a risk that a good lot will be rejected because some samples are bad or the opposite would be that a sample comes back good and the lot is moved along to consumers and then flaws are found by the consumers. It is also important to know what should disqualify a given product. For example, should cosmetic irregularities disqualify a product?

This process can be seen by examining the cost and process associated with producing a sport-related product. The finance chapter examined some sport finance analytics, but breaking down the cost of a product can also help with the manufacturing analysis and to determine if a product is worth pursuing. For example, what are the cost points in producing a $100 pair of sneakers? It costs Nike around $28.50 to manufacture a $100 sneaker in Asia. This includes $25 to buy the shoe from the factory manufacturing it and an additional $3.50 to cover transportation, shipping insurance, and international duty fees to bring the shoes into the United States (Kish, 2014). Nike will further have expenses of $15 attributable to the shoes (covering marketing, athlete sponsorship, administrative expense, etc.), $2 for taxes, and a profit margin of $4.50 – representing a 9 percent profit. Thus, the shoe would be sold to a wholesaler for $50. This does not take into account the number of shoes that might be defective, waste during the manufacturing process, equipment inefficiencies, even products stolen at a warehouse before they reach the consumers. Many of these inefficiencies or losses are programmed into the bottom line and are often part of the administrative expenses. But, every effort needs to be made to track and reduce costs. Reducing the transportation cost by 50 cents might not seem like a lot, but spread over 60 million pairs sold every year that would result in increased profit of $30 million.

It should be noted that the analytics involved in manufacturing can also be used in the demolition process. Apple's iPhones are repurchased by the company when customers are upgrading and want to turn their phones in for a voucher. If the phone is in good shape it might be resold, while poor conditioned phones are sent to be recycled. To meet Apple's stringent environmental protocols, recycling companies are required to weigh shipments before phones are dismantled and then weigh the end product to make sure the weigh is the same (i.e. nothing is lost in the process that will end up in landfills). Other equipment manufacturers are not as stringent as Apple and they allow recyclers to remove cameras, chips, and other components (Culpan & Kharif, 2016).

CASE STUDY: BUILDING A BETTER PRODUCT

Name: Krishna Vasist
Title: Head – Business Development
Current employer: moonwalkr, Bengaluru, Karnataka, India
Brief work history: I completed my graduate Sport Management degree at the University of New Haven. During my time at UNH I was the chairperson for sponsorships in the sports management department where I was exposed to the US sport industry ecosystem. I moved back to India and became a part of the founding team at moonwalkr. We

PHOTO 9.1   Krishna Vasist

at moonwalkr design and develop high-performance sports gear. I head the Business Development team at moonwalkr. My role as a Business Development Head involves:

- building long-term relationships with professional cricketers;
- designing a proper global sales channel for brand moonwalkr;
- organizing promotional activities to create awareness about the brand; and
- identifying new brands and converting them as our OEM clients (original equipment manufacturers).

How do you think data helps influence your industry segment?

Data helps improve our segment especially in the product ecosystem; cricketers use a host of protection equipment such as helmets, leg guards, chest guard, hand gloves and more.

What example can you share regarding using data to help make a decision?

My case study will examine how we arrived at a breakthrough design insight, due to data gathering and analysis and moving onto setting up the business based on that new product design direction.

The issue

The cricket manufacturing ecosystem works with materials and production techniques that have not moved with the times. In spite of advanced material technologies available, cricket protection gear is still largely made using cotton, cane and Polyethylene foams.

The analysis

Cricket is a sport played in 105 countries and currently the second-most-viewed sport in the world. It is a unique sport that evolved from a traditional Sunday leisure activity to one of the most demanding sports athletically. From tea drinking to balanced diets, from blazers to dry fit kits, from five-day to five-hour games, cricket has not just moved, it has reinvented itself over the years.

Cricket is similar to baseball wherein a batsman and bowler test each other's skills with a wooden bat and a hard leather ball. However, in cricket the batsmen runs a much larger risk of injury from a cricket ball that is bowled at speeds of 80 to 100mph and in 2015 there was an unfortunate fatality due to a player being hit. To protect themselves, batsmen carry around four kilograms (8.8 pounds) of protective equipment when they are batting. This weight can add up with all the running required in an often hot and humid climate.

While the game itself has undergone monumental changes, the same cannot be said for the equipment used. This is especially true for the protective equipment worn by the players.

With these dynamics at place, moonwalkr, a small design start-up based out of Bangalore, India, has made the pursuit of innovation in sport, a sport in itself. The fundamental question remained: Can we redefine protection gear? We believed that by calling it purely protection gear we were limiting the function of the gear. We felt the gear also had a role to play in the speed and agility of the batsman. By prioritizing design and a progressive approach of understanding and using new-age material composites we set out to develop gear that not only protects the player but crucially aids in mobility and enhancing speed and performance during play.

High performance in sports gear is defined largely by the material technology used and design innovation. India with its strong craft ethos and knowledge base of working with natural materials, such as cane and cotton, has contributed heavily to the cricket equipment manufacturing landscape. Our region of the world became the world hub for manufacturing cricket gear. To this day, over 80 percent of the world's cricket brands get their gear manufactured in this region.

Leg guards, chest guards and hand gloves were all traditionally made with a combination of a hard cane outer and cotton inner, all layered and stitched together. The materials were locally sourced and with generations of master tailors available, created an optimized production ecosystem.

More recently, the material used to manufacture the gear has evolved to soft and medium density Polyethylene (PE) foams rather than cotton. We noticed that the adoption of easily available plastic shells, as primary impact alternatives, was surprisingly low.

The leather cricket ball is bowled between 80 and 100 mph. On impact from a cricket ball, there would be localization of impact energy with the cane- or foam-only structured approaches. To compensate for this possible impact, thick and large volumes of foam were added to prevent leg injuries. This bulk, in turn, affects the naturally evolved running stride and thus slows the batsman down a little. The gear also has an effect on the footwork of the batsman during play. Impact energy management was analyzed through a layered foam structure involving both medium- and high-density Polyethylene (PE) and Polyurethane (PU) foams. The high-density foam in the range of 100–140 kilogram impact density took the primary impact of the cricket ball and the medium-density foam (with densities of 30–40 kilogram impact density) formed the secondary foam layer that helped with absorption.

Unfortunately, while the age-old manufacturing techniques produced acceptable products at the right price point, the industry suffered from a malaise of "we will play with what we got" attitude. Customers were not requesting significant customization because they did not think they could find something different. It is similar to how baseball catchers' gear stayed the same for years until some started bravely exploring other gear such as throat protectors and knee rest pads, which initially were revolutionary, but are now commonly used.

The use of new and cutting-edge materials that can be used for superior designs and production were not used because of the sophisticated production systems that those materials required. This is one reason why there has not been significant advancement in cricket gear innovation. Moonwalkr opened conversation with material scientists from the Fraunhofer Institute (Germany) and explored various new-age materials. Special plastics and composites were researched for our specific use. Test simulations, material finite element analysis (FEA), computer modeling, simulation analysis, and multiple prototypes later a ballistics grade composite plastic was identified as the optimal shell material. This composite had a most optimized strength-to-weight ratio required to address our impact challenges.

The goal was to find a combination of materials that would best help with the deceleration of the cricket ball during impact and thus reduce the energy transfer onto the leg on impact. We explored a family of materials that included Ballistic grade plastics, Fiber reinforced materials and new-age fabrics. After considering a host of design parameters, we finally focused our attention on composite plastics and multiple-density foam technologies. The design architecture involved a primary impact layer followed by a medium- and low-density foam combination to aid in the energy absorption as highlighted in Figure 9.1.

Existing leg guards weigh in at around 1 kilogram (2.2 pounds) per guard; we wanted to be in the 600gms (1.3 pounds) region. The design challenge was to not just reduce the weight but also to make the gear as compact as possible. Thus density, volume and strength of the materials were some of the important factors considered during testing and material evaluation.

This approach of a hard composite as a primary shell and a medium-density foam layer yielded much better protection on impact. The property of the composite to dissipate impact energy over the surface area of the shell, as opposed to localization of impact energy that was the feature of pure foam combinations, yielded a better system of

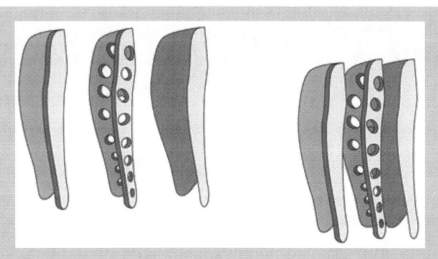

FIGURE 9.1   Leg guard design structure

impact energy management. Our new design (a thin composite shell and foam structure) reduced the gear's bulk by about 50 percent and the weight by 40 percent. This helped the batsman with better footwork and speed between the wickets.

We worked with National Instruments (NI), a company specialized in automated equipment testing, to help us with the impact testing of our product. A prosthetic leg was designed from plaster of Paris. Ten strain gauges were mounted to this leg at various points. Three of them at the knee region, three of them over the shin bone area and four of them over the calf area. These strain gauges were further connected to a data acquisition system where any impact would result in a proportional increase of amperage. NI used a traditional leg guard and moonwalkr's prototype. Uniform test conditions were maintained for both leg guards being tested including:

- test grade cricket ball weighing 158 grams;
- international grade bowling machine;
- distance between bowling machine and test object maintained at 45 feet (15 yards); and
- bowling machine speed maintained at 99 mph (159.32 Kmph).

The peak knee reading was 3.13 micro strain for the old leg guard, 14.37 percent more energy compared to the new leg guard prototype. At the knee area, the peak reading was 1.30 micro strain for the moonwalkr design, which was 58.4 percent less energy compared to existing leg guards. The moonwalkr design had the peak reading of 2.68 micro strain at the chin rather than the old design which caused more strain on the knee from impact – as shown in Figure 9.2.

Though India is a fairly large manufacturing hub, we only found the manufacturing process required for our composite in one other industry, and that was in the automobile industry.

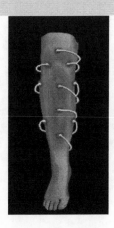
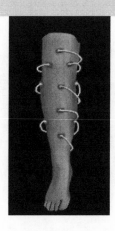

Sensor locations   Area impacted by ball   Area impacted by ball
using old leg guards   using moonwalkr prototype

FIGURE 9.2   Testing location and results

We initially worked with third-party manufacturers to manufacture the trials, mostly the thermoforming of the composite plastic. The biggest challenges were getting machine time from companies (for thermoforming) due to their existing production schedules. In time this led us to invest in our own thermoforming system that helped in quick prototyping and eventually helped us understand and optimize our own production schedules.

We worked with renowned and trusted material manufacturers to ensure material quality used in making our products. We designed and set up a customized production system to yield consistent and quality components. The end-products were batch tested for impact and build quality.

We then proceeded to set up our own manufacturing plant for the composite with a portfolio of cricket protective equipment designed to be made with this new material.

What lesson did you learn from the process?

We learned through this process that product design and research usually absorbs more time and resources than originally planned. You have to prepare yourself for the journey.

New product designers need to be prudent with the research data while employing it in their design process and strategy. Observing and noting data from existing products in the ecosystem is as important. The urge to sidestep this process in the event of a new and exciting product idea is usually high, so it is important to meticulously collect and understand the product's data as this can save iterations, time and resources.

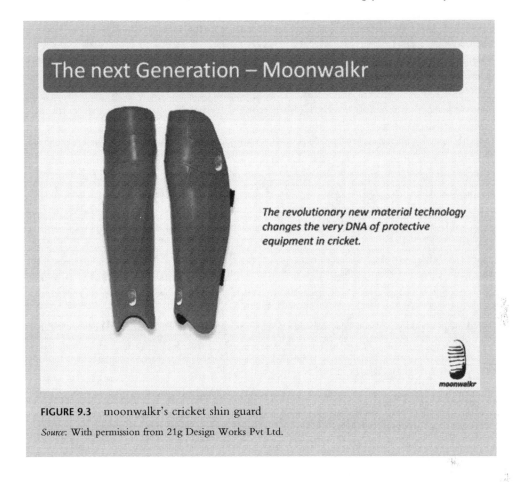

The next Generation – Moonwalkr

The revolutionary new material technology changes the very DNA of protective equipment in cricket.

moonwalkr

FIGURE 9.3   moonwalkr's cricket shin guard

Source: With permission from 21g Design Works Pvt Ltd.

Nike

There is a lot of analytics associated with manufacturing. Take, for example, Nike; they are of course one of the largest sport business in the world. They also are very diverse in their product lines such as: NIKE Brand, Converse, Hurley, Jordan Brand and Nike Golf. Their brands are manufactured in 679 factories in 43 countries, employing over 1 million workers. Just imagine the HR responsibility associated with each factory tracking all these employees. What makes such an effort even more difficult is that in some countries it is not uncommon for children to work in factories, but Nike has an aggressive program in place to prevent child labor at factories producing Nike products and to make sure employees at these plants are earning a reasonable wage.

Nike relies on its analytical approach to help generate revenue and secure major contracts. One such contract is its exclusive contract with the NFL. In 2012, Nike agreed to pay the NFL $220 million a year for five years to make all the league's on-field uniforms and officially licensed apparel such as fan jerseys. Nike won the bid in part by touting its finely tuned supply chain. The ability to tweak the manufacturing process was critical for Nike's push to sell more jerseys to women and children. By 2015, almost 50 percent of the jerseys sold by the company Fanatics were women and children styles. Nike also pushed its factories and partners to shorten lead times and run smaller batches. This allowed Nike to shorten delivery times (to US stores from factories in Asia) for jerseys to several weeks rather than months. This was important for Nike because a number of back-up players might be unpopular jerseys, but a major injury to a starter might thrust the back-up into a starting role and if they do well there might be significant demand that can be taken advantage of now, rather than hoping they still might be popular in several months (Stock, 2015).

At the end of fiscal year 2013, just more than 1 million people – with an average age of 32 – worked in the 785 factories that Nike sourced from directly. It was estimated that another half million people worked in the factories that make the materials used in Nike products, and more than 1 million people worked in raw material production (some factories were vertically integrated, and played more than one of these roles) (Nike, 2015). Nike is more than just people, for example, the overall water footprint across Nike's value chain was 217 billion gallons of which 6 percent (about 13 billion gallons) was directly related to Nike. Similarly, the overall waste footprint across their value chain was 700 million kilograms, of which 14 percent (96.7 million kilograms) was attributed to Nike. Of this amount, 11 percent was incurred in making the Nike gear, 6 percent in moving the goods, and 9 percent in selling the goods (Nike, 2015).

Nike follows the Sourcing & Manufacturing Sustainability Index (SMSI). The SMSI is one component of the company's overall Manufacturing Index, which also assesses contract factory performance on quality, on-time delivery and costing in equal measure. At the end of 2011, 49 percent of Nike contract factories scored bronze on the SMSI. By the end of 2013, 68 percent had reached that score. Factories that did not meet the bronze level were accessed penalties such as having to pay for future audits and continued lack of progress could result in decreased orders or being removed from Nike's list of approved factories (Nike, 2015). In 2013, no factories reached the highest gold level, one reached silver, and 535 reached bronze level (68 percent). That meant that 249 factories (32 percent) did not meet the bronze level requirement.

In 2013, 94 percent of factories went through a full assessment of labor, health, safety and environmental compliance. Nike uses a 10-page labor audit that examined over 250 areas. This audit identified the most common violations of Nike's Code of Conduct as hours (42 percent of all violations) and wages (39 percent of all violations) with overtime and lack of proper documentation being major issues. Nike was hoping that lean manufacturing could help reduce wage and hour related issues in these factories. Educating employees and managers at these international factories was another critical step to help reduce cost and increase efficiency. Nike worked with some factories to improve data quality, and to study and assess absenteeism, worker engagement and well-being, factory management and supervisor skills. Each of these areas helps to contribute to worker well-being and to individual and factory productivity (Nike, 2015). Care had to be taken to make sure that efficiency was not obtained at the expense of worker engagement and well-being. This can be addressed by steps such as supporting external health clinics to making sure the workers and their families were healthy to eliminate absenteeism and ensure factories were operating effectively. The data showed that when such simple steps were taken the factory efficiency and work product increased.

One key area activists wanted Nike to examine was safety in the workplace. Besides underage workers, pictures of unsanitary work environment and hazardous chemicals prove significant fodder for those challenging Nike's practices. Thus, Nike examines contract factories on 35 health and safety factors. These are only some of the measures Nike is accessing.

Other data points their process examines include:

- *Data quality* – 6 measures including validity based on cross-checking, occurrence of errors, team member participation in providing input.
- *Lean* – 21 measures including production efficiency, percentage of rejects and rework, skill levels, absenteeism.
- *Worker engagement and well-being* – 40 measures including employee turnover, problems raised/resolved (production and social), motivation, stress, exhaustion, ability to voice opinions, feeling of well-being inside and outside the factory.
- *Outside the factory* – 10 measures including worker sentiment, participation, impact on turnover or absenteeism.

(Nike, 2015)

As can be seen by this example, Nike is not just saying they are going to do something, they are actively changing their manufacturing process and system and they are relying on numerous data points to determine if they are effective. Additionally, Nike undertakes the data collection and dissemination process in a very open and transparent manner for the entire world to see.

CASE STUDY: PRODUCING A MAJOR SPORT BROADCAST

Name: Mike Boissonneault
Current title: Production Operations, Human Resources and Business Leader and recently retired from ESPN
Brief work history: Mike is a 35-year veteran of ESPN. He spent 29 years in Operations and Production, where he was a team leader in control rooms and studios and award-winning Director of such iconic studio based shows as SportsCenter, The NBA Today, NFL GameDay, Inside Baseball and others. Additionally, as a senior leader, Mike managed the scheduling of technical facilities and operations

PHOTO 9.2 Mike Boissonneault

personnel over a 15-year span. Within those years, the Operations staff grew to more than 500 and the facilities expanded to more than 85 studios, control rooms, edit rooms, etc., in multiple locations. His team connected the studio and remote operations together to support the various programming and production requirements and complement one another. He then spent four years as a Senior Director in Human Resources whereby he hired a recruiting and staffing team to support all company divisions as well as the professional internships at ESPN. His last three years were also spent in senior leadership, overseeing the Business Operations of ESPN Technology, which included resource management, logistics, diversity, workforce planning strategies and management training.

What example can you share regarding using data to help make a decision?

Economics drives decisions. Networks and other providers have realized economies of scale by increasing the innovative technologies to help in covering events. For example, more camera angles could result in a better handle on close or controversial calls in almost any sport; from photo finishes in horse racing to an NBA three-point shot, trying to get all angles covered is tough. It's inefficient to have an operator for every camera position, because some would only be used a few times in a game and, therefore, become cost prohibitive. Automation and remote controls for cameras and lights have made it possible for one operator to handle several camera feeds at once, sometimes from a great distance, saving on human headcount, travel and other expenses. Most of the technical operating roles (audio mixing, technical directing, media and graphics) are all part of a centralization and optimization exercise these days whereby the economics will determine from where and how often they will be on site physically at an event versus at a home base.

This case study will examine some of the various decision-making milestones necessary to stage sports as presented on television, from early planning meetings through post-game ratings interpretation.

Each broadcast game comes with a myriad of issues to solve ahead of time. All stakeholders must bring their expertise to the planning table and help to make the best decisions and mitigate risks that will ensure success. The following breakdown examines some of the key elements in the production decision process including the sport, venue, location, technology, skill requirements, crew, support programming, ratings, and scalability. For each point we will start with the typical questions that must be satisfied to start decision-making and often lead to numbers (facts) to resolve decisions.

Sport

Where does the particular game stack up in the pecking order of its own sport or league? Is it a pre-season, regular or post-season contest? That answer will generally start to determine the quality or quantity of resources necessary to produce a successful show for the host provider. Similar to sports, crews and technology tools also have a ranking, perhaps by skill and talent or perceived value to the same provider. Which game or series gets the top crew is a very important decision to the broadcast provider, as they have vested interests and high priced rights and brand identity at stake. Each event will also require specific technology and equipment. This allocation has to be explored across an entire season schedule that might need different crews and resources at different locations the next night or week. This can be even more complicated when there are simultaneous sport seasons and levels (professional and collegiate as an example) overlapping with one another and stretching a provider's resources. The decision often boils down to economy of scale. For example, to a provider with a limited amount of rights or single sports focus, they can place more emphasis on the sport or games at hand and continually strive to perfect coverage and add innovative measures. In instances where a provider is splitting resources to a number of sports and high-level contests, decisions can include ways to improve coverage through more technology and automation, always making sure the consumer is served well.

In the current state for many of the high-volume providers, the cost of travel and logistics of remote production have forced strategic changes in many of the traditional ways to set up and produce on site. Some of the contemporary solutions include centralizing more of the production control room operations back at a network location and using a studio-based team and resources in lieu of sending a crew to a site for one-off games. The crew at the provider's centralized location can then integrate more feeds similarly throughout a day or night and this clearly saves on travel and expense. Some of the criteria necessary to pull this new operation off successfully include advances in technology and delivery. For example, transmitting a bundled feed together (cameras, microphones, etc.) from a venue has become an economical way to package elements and save travel expenses.

Venue

The physical condition of the venue presents many challenges as well. There are many aging stadiums and arenas across the land where a big production might get staged. The physical condition of these facilities might not afford the same capacity for new tools, systems, cables, or other infrastructure as newer professional venues. Older facilities might not have the strength to handle the weight of cables, people, temporary stages, etc. How does it stack up for everything from power capacity, physical condition of conduits and structures that may support people, equipment and cables? How will it withstand weather and any other emergency situations? These types of decisions are important for proper placement of equipment such as cameras, microphones, cellular bridges and towers, communications, truck and crew parking, etc. Therefore, when possible, site surveys are conducted and realistic expectations are set.

Location

Where is the venue actually located? Is it a professional stadium or arena in an urban setting or on a college campus? Wireless signal strength can be an issue and alternate systems or technology might be necessary to overcome it. All locations should have accessible paths for crews to get to and from and not disrupt the fan experience at the venue. How easy or difficult will it be to get crew and equipment in and out? Traditionally, trucks and staging equipment must maneuver in order to get television and other equipment into position and they need accessible roads or access ways.

Airports and other public transportation stations are also part of the overall travel decision-making as are days, dates and times that the crew needs to travel in or out. Consider the event coverage on holiday weeks when the crew might travel with the rest of the public on high demand days and expected travel delays. There are many more conditions for the complex decisions regarding whom to schedule, when to travel or whether to hire locally instead. Location might also restrict the availability of public transportation, such as taxis and rental cars. Crew mobility is directly related to location.

Technology

Technology is at the heart of a production. Manufacturers create televisions to adapt to the various formats and platforms for exceptional and very personal consumption. Think of the terms 1080p, 1080i, 720p, 4K and 5.1 Surround Sound. These terms became synonymous with better and bigger pictures and sound quality. It also represented a shift in viewing behaviors and drove providers to find ways to deliver the formats home to give consumers a new experience while viewing their favorite teams and leagues. The demand for more personalized consumption and behaviors drove the screen manufacturers to create more dynamic models in so many combinations of capability and performance. This includes size as well as platform. There is no "one size fits all" in the new world of media consumption. Early adopters of high definition pushed the consumer brands to create the new televisions before the broadcasters could even deliver the technology. For example, 1080p capable sets were selling before any 1080p delivery was available. Consumers came to expect true HD and surround sound audio on all news, entertainment and sports programs. The demand was well ahead of the supply. The same issue then moved to widescreen formats; where the media industry had to find a way to meet the consumers' ever growing demand for better quality and picture. The shift in consumer habits also drove providers to figure out how to produce live games in new formats. Producing the game was a major challenge to overcome for providers. The next hurdle would be how to deliver it home or into mobile devices in the new formats, still not available through traditional distribution. The internet helped provide the solution as smart televisions, as well as some computers and mobile devices, could handle the newer formats such as 4K. Subscription services, delivered via the internet, could deliver 4K resolution and, with smart televisions, display on the big screen.

The production crews needed high-definition lenses to shoot the action and all of the operations platforms and formats downstream in the supply chain needed to be HD capable of recording, playing, storing and distributing natively as well. This process took time, research and a lot of innovation to get to the point of normalcy. Similarly, the ability to use specific equipment to air certain games/events often is based on financial constraints. Therefore, decisions on what equipment to use on a regular basis versus special occasion will often drive decisions. These highly sought after tools that create various effects for us on the screens are not just plug-and-play. Often they require some installation within the supply chains and support infrastructure. Some tools are permanently installed and others need to be carried in and out of a particular event, usually when the production trucks are rented for the game or multitasked in a season. Deciding on what technology solutions to use involves many stakeholders such as experts in design, engineering, operations, sales, production, finance, logistics, etc. Each has a vested interest in getting the most bang for the buck, making decisions based on economy of scale principles, ensuring that the tools will be properly used and at what cost, that will bring the greatest returns over a game, a season or an annual time frame. This is often a cost–benefit analysis based on analytical underpinnings.

One example of the decision-making of event production, in recent years, was how to produce high definition (HD) and standard definition (SD) signals simultaneously. The aspect dimensions for this example are 4:3 for SD and 16:9 for HD. One is taller and the other wider. These would require two distinctly different pictures. Using two production cameras at every position would be too expensive, and there wouldn't be enough room for both cameras at most facilities. The solution was derived using common sense and digital converters. Since the future was HD, it made sense that the productions would originate as HD and convert to SD for that audience. Any new cameras would have HD lenses and that would be the native signal flow. The focal point of any camera shot was still in the center of the lens. The camera operator still shot focal point through the center of the lens and the 16:9 aspect would be the natural overflow of the shot, basically filling the side bars or "wings" of the picture for HD viewers. One lens could produce the shot and the signal would go through a converter that took HD 16:9 aspect in and after a down conversion, sent SD 4:3 out to the older format TVs and distribution services.

Crew

Scheduling people at the remote events is simply known as crewing. This is a science with a lot of analytics. For the sake of this case study, let's use the A/B/C method, where "A" level events are tops in value, prestige, consumer engagement and the "C" level events are at the lower end. Similarly, the "A" level crew is the most experienced and successful, not just be by tenure or years; instead they are proven through skills, ratings and rankings. This is a challenge for providers as many of the experienced and most talented teams are not full time and salaried employees. Many are contracted by sport, by season and/or by event and available to multiple providers based upon their individual business plans. In the end, decisions on whom to hire and where to send them are not just built on cost, experience and skill, but also the qualitative pieces need to be examined such as the chemistry of a crew, adaptation to change, and team oriented goals.

Skill requirements

There are many roles that may be used in events which typically require facilities, such as a production unit or truck, a transmission unit, on-site management and an announcer stage or set, in addition to the game coverage. Many members of a remote crew may be independent contractors who lend their services to multiple providers. The production personnel alone could include: producers, directors, associate producers and production assistants. Technical personnel could include: a technical director, audio mixer and assistants, tape or media specialists, studio (booth) lighting, camera operators, and perhaps graphics producers/operators, editors, utility roles, runners, etc. The logistics of getting all these individuals to the right location at the right time is where the science and balancing act takes place. Add to this any number of conditions, such as holiday travel difficulties, weather delays, games running into several overtimes, crew coming in from many locations, etc., and the logistical nightmare of crewing is never over. Also, there can be any number of union regulations, given certain cities and venues that have contracted themselves with union crews locally. Some venues may require that union workers fill critical roles on a crew. This also presents some challenges in how to blend the team together and succeed. One key is to use analytics to help resolve challenges and maximize resources while minimizing costs due to skills, travel, transportation, etc.

Support programming

The addition of shows and supplemental coverage often enhance the value of a major event. For example, to maximize the overall value to The World Series rights holder, the provider could add ancillary programming to support the event. Whichever events are added to the primary event, there will be significant demand for resources and logistics to effectively deliver the support programs. It's one thing to cover a game from a proven stadium or arena. It's another thing to bring a studio-based show out to the same venue and add that to the coverage. While it translates into cross-pollinated ratings increases and often shares some revenue and even some crew or technology, at times it is a logistics nightmare. News and information type shows often need a different set of foundational pieces, are used to a news gathering format of operations and not game production. This presents a lot of challenges to pull off smoothly and many industry providers have honed their execution of the shared stage, especially at major events.

Ratings

Television networks have traditionally relied upon research and ratings to determine their audience size, demographic and, at times, behavioral patterns. Ratings services used to make phone calls, collect "diaries" from consumers, use scientific factors from small samples and predict the overall audience numbers as a result. These findings were important for sales and programming decisions alike. Ratings directly drive revenue and are incorporated into game coverage as well as storytelling. Multimedia providers have forced a shift in ratings interpretation as they serve simultaneous audiences. Recently, ratings have undergone an overhaul that now includes behavioral traits, spending habits, searching trends and time spent online. The advent of the second and third screen consumption to accompany television has forced providers to split their energy into several directions and platforms to serve many other audiences with the same contest, covered specifically and discreetly differently for each screen.

Scalability

Today, providers are looking for even more cost savings solutions that won't disrupt or downgrade a production. Centralizing key production components can create efficiencies. Providers will now plan to centralize the resources at site, making each of the dozens of signals (camera feeds, microphones, etc.) available to be paired up in whatever combination works for the intended audience. For example, in a big college football or basketball game, the provider might send a secondary feed out, featuring the team announcers, and share the network's sounds and pictures from the game "pool" of resources. The schools may have online streaming of their games available to parents and alumni, which allows customized commentary as well.

Breakthrough technological solutions are helping this effort. At the game end, multiple signals can be bundled and fed together as one source to a central location through video compression. At the provider's home base, the feed is unbundled and treated there as if they were on site. The studio control room can cut cameras and mix in the announcers and game sounds, add graphics and even roll in replays. It's quite economical and done with no apparent loss of quality or integrity to the consumer. Centralizing the production control room back at a home base or HQ, gives the provider the technical solution to re-create the onsite experience for the consumer, albeit with less travel and other location based expenses. This is a very rudimentary example of cost reduction without sacrificing quality.

The producer and director, technical director, audio mixer, graphics and media specialists can all work in the centralized home base control rooms and potentially work on multiple games from different locations in the same day, further stretching the cost savings.

Each one of these elements has changed over the years, based on finances, technology, programming, and even customer changes. To produce a high-quality broadcast event has changed over the years, and through using numbers at every stage the production quality has improved and provided the viewing audience with a better product and the teams, leagues, events, producers, distributers, and all other parties with a better product to generate revenue.

What lesson did you learn from the process?

Personally, this report scratched the surface and there is so much more that goes into the world of remote or event production. Inside the network (provider) planning sessions is a very intense and often rapid pace of decision-making. Vested stakeholders from Production, Engineering and Operations are always present. In the more valued games and events, you'll find representatives from Programming, Distribution, Digital Media, Sales, Marketing, Travel, International, Studio Production, Creative Services and more. It's a high priority event anytime the provider takes it on the road; the brand and the reputation for the company is always at stake as well. Finance is always in the forefront as so many decisions are held accountable to a budget or a bottom line.

What suggestions do you have for students about data in your discipline?

Learn that decisions are generally made due to financial criteria and there are technological solutions to most challenges. At times it takes many people to prototype what will become a smaller or automated operation in the future. Don't be scared to place physical resources to play the role of a future technology solution. Research your audience and listen to the feedback. They will factor in ratings and that will drive future decisions.

ESPN

Significant resources are needed to produce a game, event, or a broadcast. For a major broadcaster such as ESPN, there needs to be significant resources to help deliver the content to the end viewers and each element needs to be effectively managed through analytics. For example, there are numerous trucks that are crossing the country traveling from venue to venue to broadcast games and each truck requires maintenance, fuel, drivers, loaders and unloaders, power supplies, and numerous other elements. Using the truck example, how much does each driver rack-up each year in terms of toll costs? Can those costs be reduced to help decrease the overall event production costs? Similar questions can be asked about each element of the organization and with such a large organization the numbers can be mind-blowing. Let's examine some of ESPN's numbers from 2015:

- They have 26 satellite dishes (located in the Connecticut (CT) teleport, including the Torus which handles 35 feeds, functionality meaning they have the equivalence of 60 dishes) and in 2012, they facilitated 49,000 inbound signals.
- They are not one stand-alone company, but rather a portfolio of over 50 different business entities (each with budgets, expenses, deliverables, etc.).
- There are approximately 4,000 employees in CT and another 4,000 throughout the world.
- The ESPN Plaza in CT has 1.2 million square feet (with an extra 500,000 nearby) including 17 buildings spread over 123 acres.
- They produced 51,000 hours of live event/studio programming in 2015. ESPN Radio provides more than 9,000 hours of talk and event content annually over 500 affiliated stations.
- Besides US operations (eight domestic cable networks), they have 26 international networks reaching all seven continents. Their additional businesses allow the company to reach sport fans in 61 countries.
- Besides CT, they have production facilities in Bangalore, Buenos Aires, Hong Kong, London, Mexico City, Miami, Melbourne, Mumbai, New York City, Rio de Janeiro, São Paulo, Singapore, Sydney, and Toronto.
- Their website averages 62.6 million unique visitors a month. SportsCenter is viewed on average by 115 million viewers a month. ESPN Radio reaches 20 million listeners every week. WatchESPN is available to 93 million homes through major multichannel programing distributors across platforms such as tablets, laptops, and smartphones.

(ESPN, Inc. fact sheet, n.d.)

All these numbers reflect the size and scope of the company, but also countless areas to explore analytics as a way to save money. Imagine how much money the company pays yearly for electricity. Should they change light bulbs to save money? Should they do a cost–benefit analysis of installing a fuel cell tower or some other energy alternative? These are just some of the utility related questions that can be analyzed by tracking current usage and exploring ways to reduce them or become more efficient.

Besides using analytics to be more efficient and produce more, better, less expensive content – the company collects significant data from their subscribers and viewers. Such information can be a treasure trove that ESPN can sell to others who are interested in marketing towards very engaged sport fans. Thus, while manufacturing and production often explores trying to develop a product or event, the process can also produce data that can become its own valuable product.

Conclusion

This chapter has tried to cover some basic issues associated with how analytics are impacting the production and manufacturing process. The key is normally focused on finding inefficiencies and then finding ways to quantify them so they can be assessed and hopefully reduced. There is no one correct way to reduce costs or speed up the process, but numbers will help find a better path as long as the right data is available, analyzed, and acted upon.

References

Chipotle (2015). *A focus on food safety*. Retrieved from http://chipotle.com/food-safety?_ga=1.258 944522.122844595.1450293201

Colvin, G. (2015, November 1). 21st century corporation. *Fortune, 172*(6), 103–12.

Culpan, T., & Kharif, O. (2016). Where iPhones go to die (and be reborn). *Bloomberg BusinessWeek*, 35–6.

Davenport, T.H., Harris, J., & Shapiro, J. (2010, October). Competing on talent analytics. *Harvard Business Review*, 1–6.

ESPN, Inc. fact sheet. (n.d.). Retrieved from http://espnmediazone.com/us/espn-inc-fact-sheet/

Finkle, V. (2015, November). Choose your own manufacturing adventure. *Inc.*, 44–5.

Giammona, C., & Patton, L. (2015, December 14–20). Small suppliers, big problems. *Bloomberg BusinessWeek*, 21–2.

Godfrey, Major F. (n.d.). *The logistics of invasion*. Retrieved from www.almc.army.mil/alog/issues/ NovDec03/Logistics_of_Invasion.htm

Kish, M. (2014, December 16). The cost breakdown of a $100 pair of sneakers. *Portland Business Journal*. Retrieved from www.bizjournals.com/portland/blog/threads_and_laces/2014/12/the-cost-breakdown-of-a-100-pair-of-sneakers.html

Kohler, H. (1994). *Statistics for Business and Economics* (3rd ed.). New York, NY: Harper Collins College Publisher.

Nike (2015). Labor. Retrieved from www.nikeresponsibility.com/report/content/chapter/ labor#sthash.EXyFB2Hm.dpuf

Rockwood, K. (2016). Manufacturing's next act. *Inc.*, 82–4.

Stock, K. (2015, December 21–27). No matter the score, Nike always wins. *Bloomberg BusinessWeek*, 18–19.

10

EVENT MANAGEMENT BY THE NUMBERS

Juline E. Mills

Introduction

More than 10 million meetings and events are held worldwide annually, costing over $565 billion (Frost & Sullivan, 2013). The execution of these events consists of the completion of numerous tasks and the application of a wide variety of skill sets including a solid understanding of general business principles, hospitality operations, and the management of related data. Both quantitative (numeric) and qualitative (descriptive) data are particularly important in event management from planning to design to overall management. Events are defined as "temporary and purposive gatherings of people," (Bladen *et al.*, 2012, p.3). Many definitions exist on the term event management and the differences between event management and event planning. The two terms are often used interchangeably and overlap in meaning. Event management "is the organization and coordination of activities to achieve the objects of events," (Bladen, Kennell, Abson, & Wilde, 2012, p.3). Officially, the Bureau of Labor Statistics (2016) defines event planning as, "meeting, convention, and event planners co-ordinate all aspects of events and professional meetings. They arrange meeting locations, transportation, and other details." More precisely, the Institute of Event Management (2015) describes event planning as "the process of managing a project such as a meeting, convention, tradeshow, ceremony, team building activity, party, or convention." Some authors distinguish event planning as more small-scale and event management as large-scale events such as major sport, festivals, concerts, and conferences (Ramsborg, Miller, Breiter, Reed, & Rushing, 2008). Whether small (e.g. Board Meetings/Weddings), large (Conferences/Conventions), minor (Major League Baseball), major (Super Bowl), or mega (Summer Olympic Games, World Cup Football); event management is carried out using the five project management processes – initiating, planning, executing, monitoring and controlling, closing/debriefing – and involves the consideration of a wide variety of data driven factors (Project Management Institute, 2016). These factors include time management, risk management, financial costs, quality management, scope, security, attendee/customer services, supervision, human resource audit, venue management, communications, project integration, procurement, and stakeholder management (Masterman, 2014; Project Management Institute, 2016).

Is event planning a lucrative career? The data speaks for itself. The US event planning industry currently employs approximately 78,000 event planners with an average annual salary of $51,000; sports event planners make an average of $42,000. The employment of event planners is expected to grow 44 percent from 2014 to 2024, 10 percent faster than the average for all occupations (Bureau of Labor Statistics, 2016). In the United States the top four industries that employ event planners are Business, Labor, and Political Organization; Hotels and Motels; College Universities and Professional Schools; and Grant and Giving Services. The top five states for event planning jobs are California, New York, Texas, Florida, and Virginia. Washington DC, Massachusetts, and New Jersey are the top three highest paying states for event planners (Gaille, 2013).

The old adage "if we build it they will come," does not work with events and careful planning and management is critical to achieving event outcomes. Neither can the "one approach fits all mantra," be used. Event management decision-making is embedded in the type of event of which there exists a sizeable range. Getz (2012) identified events either by function (the reason why the event is being held) or form (the overall design). There are 11 functions (e.g. cause related, spectator, participant, or premier/launch parties) and 23 forms (e.g. sporting events, festivals, exhibitions) (Getz, 2012).

From planning to design to management

Event management is about the delivery of *exceptional guest experiences*, a high priority for consumers. On average 86 percent of US adult consumers will pay 25 percent more for a better experience (Customer Experience Impact Report, 2011). Fan Experience Expert Ruby Newell-Legner, of 7starservice.com, advises clients to engage event attendees by turning transactions into experiences, always seek to discover what truly motivates fans and attendees, and continually reward customer loyalty as it costs six times more to attract a new customer. Event service management should equal service that sells and must be integrated into each stage of the event planning process. Often the service experience is added at the end of the event development process. Service should be integrated in the theme, the sense of place and ambiance, and the designed "wow" factors. Event managers as they go through the planning, design, and management of an event must continually ask or remind themselves:

- What is the event environment that I am seeking to design?
- What is the experience I am seeking to provide to attendees?
- What problem does this event solve? or Why is there a need for this event?
- What is the role and behavior of attendees at this event?
- What techniques will be used to heighten guest participation?
- Is the developed experience worth patrons' time, money, and emotional engagement.?

(Berridge, 2014)

One of the first decisions in event management is determining whether this is a single/ one-time only event or an effort to develop an *event portfolio*. An event portfolio is the creation of a series of interrelated small and/or large-scale events; with unique programmatic elements that appeal to a wide cross section of consumers, and which take place at different times of the year (Ziakas & Costa, 2011). Event portfolios can greatly increase visitor arrivals to a destination, define the culture, and build community cohesion. Event portfolios often develop a fan base that makes it easier to increase participation with each event staging.

The pre-calculation of potential *economic impact* of a single event, event portfolio, or a mega-event to determine value optimization is also critical. Economic impact is a measure of the effect of visitor spending (direct impact); changes in sales, income, and employment due to the supplying of goods and services to an event (indirect impact); the effect of employee spending of their income at other local businesses (induced impact). For both major and mega-events the realization of true economic value is often controversial as to whether or not there is much gain from such endeavors. Following the 1996 Olympic Games in Atlanta, Georgia counties with an Olympic venue saw a 17 percent increase in employment (Hotchkiss, Moore, & Zobay, 2003). In addition to contributing to infra-structure development, enhancing a destination's image, and increasing local pride, the National Football League (NFL) and the NFL Players Association estimate that the league supports 110,000 jobs in NFL cities and adds approximately $5 billion to local economies (Almond, 2014). Cities that build stadiums for the National Football League (NFL) often do so based on expected increased revenues and economic benefits. Various academic research studies, on the other hand, have found that this economic impact is over esti-mated. NFL stadiums and arenas produce an extremely small, and in some studies, a nega-tive economic impact for cities hosting the Super Bowl (Almond, 2014; Baade & Matheson, 2004; Coates & Humphreys, 2003; Stephenson, 2014). The primary reasoning for the lack of increased economic impact is often referred to as the substitution effect, being that consumer entertainment spending is typically consistent. Consumers therefore rather than spend more when a new football or major league sport stadium comes to the community, shift their entertainment budget to football (Almond, 2014). At the Super Bowl consumers may spend very little at the destination beyond tickets, transportation, accommodation, and food (Taks, Green, Chalip, & Kesenne, 2013).

The development of a *formal strategic plan* for the event including the management, design, and execution process follows. The average event planning lead-time is 6.7 months. A classic perspective to strategic planning in event management is recommended in which time and focus is spent formulating a specific written plan for the event including a clear description of the goals and mission of the event, the implementation and monitoring process, and a thorough evaluation. Once the strategy is reviewed with input from all major parties, and consensus achieved, then action is taken to execute the defined steps to achieve event objectives. This is not to say that changes cannot be made or that an event cannot evolve as it is developed but changes are made using the goals and mission of the event as a guide. A key part of strategic planning is to clearly define a knowledge management approach to efficiently handle the resources and often times massive amounts of event related information. *Knowledge management* includes defining the information, skills, experience, specific actions, specific targets, and judgment needed to effectively execute the event. Knowledge management also includes understanding employees' strengths and abilities, and using these to effectively manage the event. Event planning and management are critical for event success but also to avoid a myriad of risks and pitfalls and the resulting negative publicity and lawsuits.

Perhaps one of the most crucial factors in event success, planning, and design is *location analysis*. In sport, an estimated 50 million adults will travel 50 miles or more to attend organized sport events (Travel Industry Association of America, 2003). A unique stadium and/or sport facility designed with appropriate "wow artistic features" and a unique ambiance or "sense of place" may also influence consumers to attend events at that location more frequently. Choosing a venue for a sports event where the weather becomes questionable at certain times of the year, may result in cancellations, loss of income, and loss of life. The 1998 Sydney to Hobart 628 nautical miles yacht race in Australia saw six sailors dead, 55 rescued, and only 44 finishing from a starting line-up of 115 due to severe weather problems. Event organizers were blamed for failing to listen to weather reports and implementing proper safety procedures (Mundle, 2000). Choosing a venue for a conference, where the closest hotel is 10–15 minutes away by car, the venue is without on-site food service, or with alcohol restrictions can cause reduction in attendance as well as event participation and enjoyment. If alcohol is available, determining transportation needs so that guests do not drink and drive or calculating sufficient security needs to defuse potential situations is important. Data is critical throughout this process as driving time and distance can significantly impact whether participants and spectators will actually attend an event. The devil is in the details and failing to identify potential weak points for an event can cost money and even possibly lead to tragedy. In 2015, a wrongful death lawsuit was filed against Zombicon, the annual Halloween-themed event held in Fort Meyers, Florida, at which one person was killed and five others injured when a gunman opened fire on the crowd. Event organizers are accused of negligence caused by improper procedures and inadequate security staff who did not check the weapons of attendees to ascertain whether the guns used by patrons as part of their costumes were real and loaded or fake. The non-profit event aimed at fund-raising for the arts and the local community sees attendance of approximately 20,000 participants annually (Helsel, 2015). Venue location selection becomes even more serious with major and mega-events given both the short and long-term impacts. The 2008 Beijing Olympics, for example, displaced an estimated 14 percent or 1.5 million residents (Shin & Li, 2013) resulting in continued discussions on the true value of mega-events to host destinations. Is obtaining worldwide broadcast coverage worth the cost to build facilities, disrupt a city for years, and displace millions? That is a question on which data can provide input, but ultimately that is a policy question which can only be answered by the host country.

Typical factors such as suitability for the type of event, target audience and their income level, venue cost and fees in relation to budget, maximum attendee capacity, layout, parking, insurance, accessibility, vendor restrictions, and acoustics are often among the first decisions made and checked off the event to-do list. However, small oversights in capacity misjudgment can result in significant problems for attendees and at times lead to critical incidents. Forty-seven people were crushed to death and 250 injured during a crowd stampede to get seats at a soccer match in Johannesburg, South Africa, in 2001. The incident caused by improper ticketing procedures resulted in stadium overcrowding (Mason, 2001).

Budgeting oversights can also lead to significant problems. Super Bowl 50's public events cost the City of San Francisco, California, approximately $4.8 million. However, despite the NFL announcing the Bay Area as host in 2013, City departments, such as Fire and Emergency Management, only included expenditures in the 2015–16 budget for services for the Super Bowl at $307,843. The significant shortfall was covered by the City's General Fund followed by an appropriate solution for reimbursement determined after the event (City and County of San Francisco Board of Supervisors budget and legislative analyst report, 2016).

According to Howard and Crompton (2004), sports events experiences face the continued challenge of the resistance from customers refusing to pay increased pricing while at the same time expecting increased event quality. Guaranteeing event quality begins with understanding the event customer and planning the event experience accordingly. Participant motivation should influence event design, services provided, overall event programming, and ultimately the advertised brand personality for the event. High-quality services enhance customer satisfaction, increase customer retention and loyalty, increase willingness to pay, and ultimately enhance event profitability. In spectator sports, consumers' overall impression is based on game performance, amenities, service delivery systems, event staffing, and over-the-top services. The overall image of the event leads to the development of *brand value*. Among sporting events the top ten event brands worldwide (2016), calculated based on revenue-per-event-day, are:

1. The Super Bowl ($518 million);
2. The Summer Olympic Games ($384 million);
3. The Winter Olympic Games ($285 million);
4. International Federation of Association Football (FIFA) World Cup ($229 million);
5. WrestleMania ($170million);
6. The National Collegiate Athletic Association (NCAA) College Basketball Men's Final Four ($150 million);
7. Daytona 500 ($136 million);
8. Union of European Football Associations (UEFA) Champions League ($127 million);
9. College Football playoff ($106 million);
10. Major League Baseball (MLB) World Series ($101 million).

Music, marching bands, mascots, cheerleaders, dance teams, and special theme nights are considered standard entertainment fare at both professional and collegiate sporting events (Apostolopoulou, Clark, & Gladden, 2006). The social experience of attendees now plays a significant role in event enjoyment (Xing & Green, 2014). While "avid sports fans" focus on the core game elements, casual fans need other motivators to maintain game interest. The Super Bowl halftime show is important to attracting casual (low to moderate) sport fans increasing overall attendance and viewership (Apostolopoulou *et al.*, 2006). *Event experience* includes creative theme development (pre, actual, and post), event design, props and staging design, and related entertainment experiences. The staging of event experiences includes attention to detail in ensuring technical performance (execution) and creative/artistic performance (appearance) (Ellis & Rossman, 2008). One primary tool often overlooked in the develop-ment of both the technical and creative aspects is the development of an event experience based on qualitative and historic research. Many themed events are planned from memory versus using historic information to increase event authenticity. From this process, an event design agenda that embraces all aspects of the event including integrated services emerges. It is important to check for intellectual property rights and copyright infringement in event theme design. In 2011, The Academy of Motion Picture Arts and Sciences (The Oscars) sued an event planner in Atlanta, Georgia, for copyright infringement in using seven-foot gold "Oscar" statuettes at an event. The event planner quickly complied and settled the lawsuit out of court (Hurley, 2011).

In recent years, event design and management have faced criticism for the toll events take on the environment. Much focus has shifted to designing furniture, fixtures, and equipment (FFEs) for event execution that is sustainable and/or reusable and in maximizing waste reduction at events. *Merriam-Webster Dictionary* (2016) defines sustainable as being "able to be used without being completely used up or destroyed; a method of harvesting or using a resource so that resource is not depleted or permanently damaged." The International Organization for Standardization (ISO) defines *sustainable event management* (also known as event greening) as "the process used to produce an event with particular concern for environmental, economic, and social issues." ISO notes in its 20121 standard, developed by event industry professionals for managing local celebrations to mega-events, for sustainable event management that:

> The "great time we had today" can leave an aftermath of problems for tomorrow. When people get together, particularly in large numbers, they can put a strain on local resources such as water and energy, and create significant waste, or tensions related to culture or sheer proximity with neighboring communities.
>
> (Frost, 2012)

Waste Management (WM) in its report on Sustainable Stadiums and Arenas (2013), estimates that the four major professional leagues (NFL, MLB, NBA, NHL) generate approximately 35,000 metric tons of carbon dioxide (CO_2) each year from their fans' waste activities alone. Recognizing the need for change, mega-events over the past 25 years have made steady progressive steps to increasing sustainability. Super Bowl 49 in Phoenix, Arizona, was able to divert 80 percent of the waste from trash (Karidis, 2016). The London 2012 Olympic Games was the first with a zero waste vision, measuring the carbon footprint over the entire project term, saving 400,000 tons of carbon dioxide, achieving 62 percent of reused, recycled or composted waste, and reusing and recycling 99 percent of installed items at game venues (London 2012's sustainability legacy lives on, 2013). Sustainable event management involves developing sustainable sport event policies, health protection, community-wide participation, as well as clear identification of primary areas of conservation, biodiversity, water, waste, transportation, and energy.

Arguably the number one most common mistake in event planning is inappropriate *staffing management*. Failing to allocate the right human resources with the right skill set to the right task. Prior to the event, metrics need to be established for the number and type of event staff, the selection process, developing application and interview procedures and questions, testing and vetting, and finally training the selected applicants. During the event, much attention needs to be paid to supervising staff, assessing progress in meeting event goals, communicating effectively with employees their fixed posts and event tasks as well as emergency evacuation and emergency medical operations. Attention must also be paid to monitoring staff traffic controls and bottlenecks (for example, waiters and waitresses or staff congregating in the service area of an event instead of checking guest tables and surveying the room for guest needs). In mega-events *volunteers* are crucial to event success. The recruiting, training, and management of volunteers can impact overall guest experience. Volunteers for events are notorious for being unreliable. Good volunteer systems, that psychologically invest the volunteer in the process, can lead to increased participation from residents. Vikersund, Norway, is home to the world's largest ski-flying venue and hosts an annual ski-flying competition. The town has approximately 3,000 residents; a third of whom volunteer and are the primary labor force for the event (Kristiansen, Skirstad, Parent, & Waddington, 2015). Just imagine how much it would cost to employ such a workforce, and the amount of time and energy that would be required to annually prepare for such an event. Only through a built-in volunteer base of this size and with such commitment can such an event take place. After the event it is important to de-brief staff highlighting what the key highlights of the event were and what areas need improvement. Given that events are temporary, taking time to evaluate employee performance and developing a database of future potential employees will help to alleviate recruitment problems at future events. Furthermore, the debriefing process can generate data upon which future events can be run more effectively. Think of it like a recipe. If you baked a great cake, do you remember the ingredients you used and in what quantities? If not, you might not be able to replicate the cake again. If you document the entire process you have the data to bake the cake again or decide what changes might be needed to get the right results.

Perhaps the greatest gain in the field of event data management is the rapid development of *technologies and systems* geared at improving event execution of the myriad of duties necessary to ensure a successful event. These systems integrate both front of the house functions (attendee interfacing), such as ticketing, registration, travel and accommodations, and back-of-the-house features including staffing, floor planning, catering management, itinerary scheduler, task management, sales management, and communications log. According to Frost and Sullivan (2013) in a study of over 14,000 industry participants planners using event management software saw a 20 percent increased event attendance, a 27 percent productivity increase, a 22 percent increase in response time to requests for proposals (RFPs) and a 15 percent decrease in booking costs. Event planners using mobile technology saw a 33 percent increase in attendance engagement, a 13 percent increase in sponsorship sales, and a 7 percent decrease in printing costs. The web and social media also play a significant role in event promotion and management. The average event uses at least five methods to promote and increase event attendance. Eighty-eight percent of US marketers use social media to increase awareness about their events before they occur; in addition RSVPs rates are higher online than with paper invitations (FreemanXP & Event Marketing Institute, 2015). Technology readily extends the life of an event and increases community engagement from year to year by the ability to post online videos and other information. Technology in event planning is not without its problems and event planners need to ensure they are effectively managing online presence pre-, actual, and post-event. The 2008 Beijing Olympics is perhaps a good example of the importance of managing online presence for an event. The official Beijing Olympics website received more than 1 million visitors daily and often crashed. Scammers created a mirrored site selling fake tickets to more than 10,000 fans (Fairbairn, 2011).

CASE STUDY: PERSONNEL DEPLOYMENT

Name: Russell Mucklow
Title: CEO and Co-founder of AwareManager
Current employer: AwareManager
Brief work history: When I graduated from business school in 1984 in Massachusetts, the personal computer industry (as it was referred to then) was just taking off. I began my career as an entrepreneur, creating accounting and financial systems for clients overseas.

In 1988, I returned to the United States, and after post-graduate studies, co-founded AwareManager in 1988. Our focus by that time had expanded into developing property management and operational

PHOTO 10.1   Russell Mucklow

solutions. Over time, the type of facilities and venues we worked with became more complex. Our first foray into the sport industry was with the New York Mets in 2003. At the time of writing, 12 of the top 25 most valuable franchises in the world (according to *Forbes Magazine*) actively use AwareManager. We have achieved this through organic growth without external financing or long-term debt.

How do you think data helps influence your industry segment?

Our clients' ultimate goals are to provide world-class experiences for all their stakeholders, not just their fans, tenants or guests. This doesn't happen by accident. High-profile events can often take years of preparation, and comprehensive management systems are critical to ensuring a consistently excellent experience.

As technology has become increasingly more sophisticated, so have the facilities and events themselves. This poses a real challenge. In the past, one could get by with informal communication and management techniques, such as MBWA (Management by Walking Around). Facility and event management is much more complex today, and data has become critical to the managing and operating of high-profile venues. Data helps in two fundamental ways.

The first is as a measure of success. Often, it's not apparent what constitutes success or worse, this becomes subjective. Therefore, it is important to create objective metrics and KPIs to measure performance.

Secondly, data has transformed communication. With the invention and widespread usage of mobile devices and the internet, we now have much greater transparency. By taking a holistic approach to information, stadium and event managers can now "see" what is happening in real-time and also have the ability to start anticipating or predicting problems before they occur.

What example can you share regarding using data to help make a decision?

The issue

With any event, there are important decisions to make. One of which is determining if you are ready to open the gates to the public. To know that you are ready, all staff and contractors must be in place, and all necessary checks must have been performed.

This is not only important from a safety perspective, but also for the stakeholder experience (fans, sponsors, media, etc.). You want to be sure that everyone is at their post, and you are open for business.

A delay in opening your gates not only poses logistical and safety problems, including having too many people trying to access the stadium at once, but you also reduce the amount of time that fans are in the venue. This has a significant, negative impact on discretionary spending by fans.

It is not sufficient to know that you have the correct number of people scheduled for the event, you also need to know when they arrive, where they are at any point in time (and have then been through access control) and that they are sufficiently qualified for the roles you are expecting them to perform.

This is most evident when working with Premiership Football (soccer) in the United Kingdom. They rival US sports teams in size of venue, complexity of event management and actually exceed them in terms of overall stock market valuations.

Two factors make Premiership Football even more challenging. The first is the nature of the fans (more fights, ejections and arrests) and that they need to be segregated into home and away sections of the stadium. The other is that, due to the horrendous accidents that have resulted in hundreds of deaths, the sport is highly regulated. To operate a sporting event you legally need a safety certificate. The Green Guide (which was first published as a result of the Ibrox disaster in 1971 when 66 people tragically died) is the official standard, which outlines all safety measures that need to be taken to host sporting events.

The analysis

The Green Guide provides guidance on the number of stewards required for an event. While this can get somewhat complicated, there is a minimal requirement of one steward for every 100 to 250 fans, given the logistics and layout of a venue.

In reality, experienced staff are able to gauge this to some extent as staff begin arriving at the venue. However, given the complexities and scale of today's events, this analysis is best shown through stadium dashboards ideally using a RAG (Red/Amber/Green) analysis. Where Red indicates that the designated staff member has not entered the stadium or been through access control; Amber (or Orange) indicates that he/she is not ready at the post; and Green indicates that the staffer is in place and ready for the commencement of the event.

Rule-based analysis can be used to determine the status of sections as well. For example, it may be acceptable to open the gates if 80 percent of designated staff/

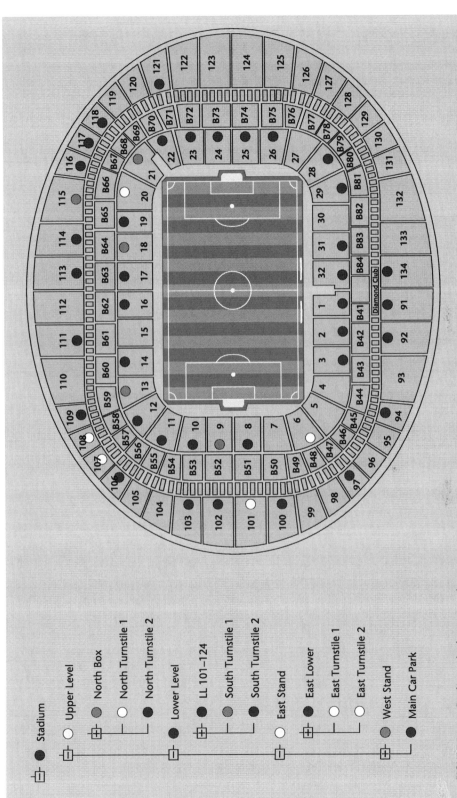

FIGURE 10.1 Stadium deployment chart

Source: Courtesy and with permission AwareManager

contractors are in position in their specified sections (see Figure 10.1). Depending on regulatory requirements, the percentage of staff (security/stewarding) may be mandated by a governing body.

This type of analysis can also be used for pre-event checks and tracking incidents throughout the event.

The end results

Stadium and event managers can now open their gates when they know that the right people are in the right place and that all of the necessary checks have been done.

By creating an event plan that is updated in real-time, there are fewer surprises. The last minute reallocation of staff and resources decreases, allowing staff to focus on more pressing, unexpected issues.

Having this degree of transparency also means that each person is tracked individually through the system. Thus improving security and making the event safer for all stakeholders.

What lesson did you learn from the process?

What we subsequently found once we began implementing these types of solutions was that by creating greater transparency, this not only improved the efficiency of running an event but it also helped all stakeholders communicate better.

Implementing AwareManager introduced a greater level of proactive management. This allowed staff to anticipate issues before they became significant problems. Also by providing mobile devices, it enabled them to record information at the source and in real-time.

The heart and often the most memorable part of an event, good or bad, is the *food and beverage*. The US commercial foodservice industry saw a 3.1 percent increase in sales to $440.1 billion in 2015 (The NPD Group, Inc., 2015), of which $40 billion was contributed by the catering industry. The US commercial foodservice industry employs 12 million people of whom approximately 600,000 were food service contractors or caterers. In 2013, independent caterers in the US made revenues of approximately $8.1 billion. These revenues rose to $12 billion in 2015 (United States Census Bureau, 2015) with the average catered event feeding 100–250 people. Event catering is considered particularly profitable as no single company has a dominant market share; and only 0.07 cent of capital is spent for $1.00 of labor (Gaille, 2014). Event guests are valuing the quality of food as being critical to the success of the event from weddings to conventions to mega sports events. Event food and beverage has changed considerably with the "standard event fare" being replaced by food experiences that tap into the psychological need of guests and serve as an added event attraction. Most stadiums offer a level of upscale fine dining that serves to increase revenues. Ballpark food, however, has become a unique feature of sport events, with specialties such as the Houston Astros' Chicken and Waffle Cone; an ice-cream cone stuffed with mash potatoes, honey mustard, and topped with fried chicken. Another gastronomical wonder is the Wilmington Blue Rocks' Sweenie Donut Dog; a hot dog with a donut bun, topped with bacon and sides (Berg, 2015).

At the same time that creative foods are being designed for consumers, food allergies are increasingly becoming a major concern at events. According to Food Allergy Research and Education (FARE, 2013) approximately 4 percent of, or 9 million, American adults have food allergies with eight foods – milk, eggs, peanuts, tree nuts (e.g. walnuts, almonds, cashews, pistachios, pecans), wheat, soy, fish, and shellfish – responsible for 90 percent of all allergies. Fish and shellfish (2.8 percent) followed by peanuts are the most prevalent allergens. The push to buy local is also increasing, but can create complications in production and service as highlighted by Chipotle E. coli incidents mentioned earlier in the text. Data can be used to help identify the most effective ways to protect fans with allergies and monitor food production to avoid any cross-contamination. But data is needed even before any food gets to a customer. It is estimated that more than 80 percent of the emissions associated with food are in the production phase. Large farms are much more efficient than small farms. In contrast, only 11 percent of the cost is associated with transportation. Thus, when someone wants to buy local they are helping to reduce the transportation costs, but the production costs might be significantly higher, thus alleviating the potential green savings hoped for by the end purchaser (Levitt & Dubner, 2009). Concession related equipment is getting more high tech and can help make food faster and at the right temperature to avoid food-based illnesses. Various manufacturers are now making food timers (based on ideal cooking times), temperature controllers (which operate based on product load size, ideal temperature, and food moisture level), and equipment that monitors market conditions in real-time to advise how much to produce, when to start/stop cooking, and when to throw away food that would no longer be considered fresh/safe. Such systems produce less waste, lower overhead costs, result in greater efficiency, and increase annual sales. Concerns are also increasing regarding food safety at events. In 2009, ESPN in an examination of health department inspection reports for the food and beverage outlets at the 107 US professional sports arenas and stadiums found that 28 percent of the venues had at least one "critical" or "major" health violation that could potentially affect patron health (Lavigne, 2009). Event managers must ensure that food is sourced correctly, and their staffs are appropriately trained to serve food at correct temperatures and within the recommended safe zones.

Conclusion

In closing, event planners and managers, once the door is closed to patrons, and the clean-up complete, must take the time to examine *attendee satisfaction* and *return on investment* (ROI). Seventy-five percent of companies with event budgets between $50 million and $100 million expect a return on investment of more than 5:1 for live event and experiential programs. However, 48 percent of brands only realize a ROI of between 3:1 and 5:1 with their events and experiences (Event Marketing Institute, 2016). While 95 percent of events collect feedback from attendees, only 35 percent actually use the feedback to improve and/or make event improvements (Gaille, 2013). Further, 90 percent of dissatisfied customers often do not return to a follow-up event, with 48 percent of "wronged customers" telling ten or more people about a bad event experience. Only 23 percent of customers who have a positive experience tell 10 or more people about it (Dixon, Freeman,

& Toman, 2010). Customer Service Manager (2016) notes from a Lee Resources Inc. study that, most importantly, 91 percent of unhappy customers will not willingly do business with you again.

References

Almond, S. (2014). *Against football: One fan's reluctant manifesto*. Brooklyn, NY: Melville House.

Apostolopoulou, A., Clark, J., & Gladden, J. (2006). From H-Town to Mo-Town: The importance of Super Bowl entertainment. *Sport Marketing Quarterly, 15*, 223–31.

Baade, R., & Matheson, V. (2004). Super Bowl or Super (Hyper) Bole? Assessing the economic impact of America's premier sporting event. College of the Holy Cross, Department of Economics Faculty Research Series, Working Paper No. 04–03, 2004.

Berg, T. (2015, April 6). *The 17 best new MLB ballpark foods for 2015*. Retrieved from http://ftw.usatoday.com/2015/04/best-ballpark-foods-2015-opening-day-bacon-sriracha-waffle-churro.

Berridge, G. (2014). Designing event experiences. In S. Page and J. Connell (Eds.) (2014). *The Routledge handbook of events* (pp. 273–288). London: Routledge.

Bladen, C., Kennell, J., Abson, E., & Wilde, N. (2012). *Events management: An introduction*. London: Routledge.

Bureau of Labor Statistics, U.S. Department of Labor. (2016). *Occupational outlook handbook, 2016–17 edition, meeting, convention, and event planners*. Retrieved from www.bls.gov/ooh/business-and-financial/meeting-convention-and-event-planners.htm

City and County of San Francisco Board of Supervisors budget and legislative analyst report (2016) *Super Bowl 50 city budget analysis*. Retrieved from www.sfbos.org/Modules/ShowDocument.aspx?documentid=54799

Coates, D., & Humphreys, B. R. (2003). The effect of professional sports on earnings and employment in the services and retail sectors in US cities. *Regional Science and Urban Economics, 33*(2), 175–98.

Customer Experience Impact Report – Consumer and Brand Relationship. (2011). Oracle. Retrieved from: http://www.oracle.com/us/products/applications/cust-exp-impact-report-epss1560493.pdf

Customer Service Manager. (2016). http://www.customerservicemanager.com/customer-service-facts/

Dixon, M., Freeman, K., & Toman, N. (2010, July–August). Stop trying to delight your customers. *Harvard Business Review*. Retrieved from https://hbr.org/2010/07/stop-trying-to-delight-your-customers.

Ellis, G., & Rossman, R. (2008). Creating value for participants through experience staging: Parks, recreation, and tourism in the experience industry. *Journal of Park & Recreation Administration, 26*(4), 1–20.

Event Marketing Institute (2016). Trend tracker 2016: Largest annual report of top event marketing trends. Retrieved from www.eventmarketer.com/institute/

Fairbairn, E. (2011, July 12). *Gang jailed for £5m Beijing 2008 Olympics ticketing scam*. Retrieved from www.telegraph.co.uk/sport/olympics/8632321/Gang-jailed-for-5m-Beijing-2008-Olympics-ticketing-scam.html

Food Allergy Research and Education (FARE) (2013). *Facts and statistics*. Retrieved from www.foodallergy.org/file/facts-stats.pdf

Freeman XP & Event Marketing Institute (2015, February 17). *The viral impact of events: Extending & amplifying event reach via social media*. Retrieved from http://freemanxp.com/insights/insights-papers/the-viral-impact-of-events-best-practices-to-amplify-event-content/

Frost, R. (2012, June 20). New ISO 20121 standard for sustainable events management. Retrieved from http://www.iso.org/iso/home/news_index/news_archive/news.htm?Refid=Ref1598

Frost & Sullivan (2013). *Beyond the horizon: A look at how technology is changing the events industry*. Retrieved from www.prnewswire.com/news-releases/frost–sullivan-technology-key-in-transforming-meetings-and-events-232840181.html

Gaille, B. (2013, November 14). *14 Event planning industry statistics and trends.* Retrieved from http://brandongaille.com/14-event-planning-industry-statistics-and-trends/

Gaille, B. (2014). *Delightful catering industry statistics.* Retrieved from http://brandongaille.com/catering-industry-statistics/

Getz, D. (2012). *Event studies: Theory, research and policy for planned events.* London: Routledge.

Helsel, P. (2015, November 3). *Family of man killed at ZombiCon event files $5 Million Lawsuit.* Retrieved from www.nbcnews.com/news/us-news/family-man-killed-zombicon-event-files-5-million-lawsuit-n456826.

Hotchkiss, J. L., Moore, R.E., & Zobay, S. M. (2003). Impact of the 1996 Summer Olympic Games on employment and wages in Georgia. *Southern Economic Journal, 69*(3), 691–704.

Howard, D. R., & Crompton, J. L. (2004). *Financing sport* (2nd ed.). Morgantown, WV: Fitness Information Technology.

Hurley, L. (2011, February 9). Planner threatened with lawsuit over "Oscar-style" décor. Special Events. Retrieved from http://specialevents.com/news/planner-threatened-with-lawsuit-over-oscar-style-decor

Karidis, A. (2016, February 5). *3 Super Bowl waste stats TV Announcers may have missed 90% diversion rate, 155 tons of trash, $200k grant.* Retrieved from www.wastedive.com/news/3-super-bowl-waste-stats-tv-announcers-may-have-missed/413188/

Kristiansen, E., Skirstad, B., Parent, M., & Waddington, I. (2015). "We can do it": Community, resistance, social solidarity, and long-term volunteering at a sport event. *Sport Management Review, 18,* 256–67.

Lavigne, P. (2009). *What's lurking in your stadium food?* Retrieved from http://espn.go.com/espn/eticket/story?page=100725/stadiumconcessions

Levitt, S., & Dubner, S. (2009). *Super Freakonomics: Global cooling, patriotic prostitutes, and why suicide bombers should buy life insurance.* New York, NY: Harper Collins.

London 2012's sustainability legacy lives on. (2013). Retrieved from www.olympic.org/news/london-2012-s-sustainability-legacy-lives-on/205777

Mason, B. (2001, April 14). *South African football stampede kills 43.* Retrieved from www.wsws.org/en/articles/2001/04/afr-a14.html

Masterman, G. (2014). *Strategic sports event management* (3rd ed.). London: Routledge.

Merriam-Webster Dictionary. (2016). Sustainable [Definition]. Retrieved from www.merriam-webster.com

Mundle, R. (2000). Fatal storm: The inside story of the tragic Sydney–Hobart Race. *International Marine/Ragged Mountain Press*; 1 edition (May 17, 2000).

Project Management Institute (2016). *A Guide to the Project Management Body of Knowledge (PMBOK® Guide).* Newtown Square, PA: PMI, Inc.

Ramsborg, G. C., Miller, B., Breiter, D., Reed, B. J., & Rushing, A. (Eds.) (2008). *Professional meeting management: Comprehensive strategies for meetings, conventions and events* (5th ed.). Dubuque, Iowa: Kendall/Hunt Publishing.

Shin, H. B., & and Li, B. (2013). Whose games? The costs of being "Olympic citizens" in Beijing. *Environment and Urbanization, 25*(2), 549–66.

Stephenson, J. (2014). Letting teams walk: Exploring the economic impact of professional sports franchises leaving cities. MPA/MPP Capstone Projects. Paper 25. Retrieved from http://uknowledge.uky.edu/mpampp_etds/25

Sustainable stadiums & arenas. (2013). Waste Management. Retrieved from http://www.wm.com/sustainabilityservices/documents/insights/Stadiums%20and%20Arenas%20Insight.pdf

Taks, M., Green, C., Chalip, L., & Kesenne, S. (2013). Visitor composition and event-related spending. *International Journal of Culture, Tourism and Hospitality Research, 7*(2), 132–47. Retrieved from http://scholar.uwindsor.ca/humankineticspub/28

The Institute of Event Management (2015). What is event planning? Four unique perspectives from event planning experts. Retrieved from https://institute-of-event-management.com/what-is-event-planning

The NPD Group, Inc. (2015). U.S. Commercial foodservice industry trends. Retrieved from www. npd.com/wps/portal/npd/us/news/data-watch/commercial-foodservice-industry-scorecard/.

The top ten event brands worldwide [Statistics Report]. (2016). Statista. Retrieved from http://www. statista.com/statistics/253353/brand-value-of-sport-events-worldwide/

Travel Industry Association of America (2003). *Travel statistics and trends.* Retrieved from www.tia. org/travel/TravelTrends.asp#s

United States Census Bureau (2015, December). *Caterers market research report | NAICS 72232.* Retrieved from www.census.gov/econ/isp/sampler.php?naicscode=722320&naicslevel=6#

Xing, X., & Green, C. (2014). Marketing a social experience: How celebration of subculture leads to social spending during a sport event. *Sport Marketing Quarterly, 23*(3), 138–47.

Ziakas, V., & Costa, A. (2011). Event portfolio and multi-purpose development: Establishing the conceptual grounds. *Sport Management Review, 14,* 409–23.

11

FACILITY MANAGEMENT ANALYTICS

Kimberly L. Mahoney

Introduction

In sports venues today, we have more data and information available to us than ever before, relating to everything from utility usage, concessions inventory, effectiveness of marketing campaigns, parking lot ingress/egress, security incidents, and more. The challenge is figuring out how to manage it and how to use it. Analytics, and the corresponding platforms, provides a means for facility managers to use data to increase efficiencies and improve the overall guest experience. "Analytics acts as funnels to increase the granularity of the data – as the data becomes more granular, it may become more relevant to different roles within the facility management organization" (Building Automation, 2013). For example, facility management executives may be most interested in high level metrics related to ticket sales and revenues, while engineers may be more interested in the energy consumption of a specific system or sub-system (Building Automation, 2013).

The emerging field of data analysis and knowledge discovery can be used for such applications as managing traffic, planning tourism infrastructures, or analyzing professional sport matches (Fort, Sellares, & Valladares 2014). Facility databases contain valuable information that can be extracted using geometry analysis, data mining techniques, and visual analytic methods to answer numerous questions. There has been specific interest in finding trajectory patterns exhi-bited by many entities, also known as group movement patterns. Such an approach can be used in facility management to help determine the best location for a new facility, aid in identifying best locations for event advertisements or sponsor advertisements, traffic management strategies, and numerous other possible facility solutions (Fort *et al.*, 2014). In this chapter we will focus on the use of analytics within venue marketing, operational systems, food and beverage, parking and transportation, safety and overall event management, ticketing, and the overall guest experience.

Venue marketing

Traditionally, professional teams have been most effective at utilizing data in their marketing and sales efforts with advanced analytics. Venues face a unique challenge because the customer base may change with each event. The fans attending the basketball game today are not the same as the fans attending a concert, professional wrestling event, or circus which may be taking place the following day. Not only is the customer base different for each event, but how you market to them varies as well. All this makes it difficult to figure out how to make the data actionable in venue marketing. As a result, venue marketing departments may utilize analytics differently in some areas than the marketing department with a professional team or a college athletic department.

Venue marketing staff are able to track the return on investment (ROI) for marketing campaigns and track website traffic and methods of access. However, they must focus on long-term trends as spikes in website traffic may result from specific event announcements (Mahoney, Esckilsen, Jeralds, & Camp, 2015). The marketing department also works closely with the ticket office and their ticketing provider (i.e., TicketMaster, etc.) for customized marketing efforts and re-targeting, where online advertising is targeted to consumers based on their previous online activities, particularly in situations where these actions did not result in a sale. Though some industry professionals have expressed concern about readers tuning out online advertisements. Once a customer makes a purchase at the ticket office, the venue marketing personnel can then track that user online and direct customized marketing to him/her. Through the ticketing system, customers are also linked to previous purchases by matching their data which helps build a history of their interests.

According to David Redelberger, Director of Interactive Marketing with Columbus Arena Sports and Entertainment (CASE), they can also track what cities buyers are from and can use that information to target future advertising to those geographic areas for similar events. The venue can track ticket pre-sale activity for each partner (i.e. fan clubs, suite holders, insider clubs, etc.) by utilizing different pre-sale passwords for each. The venue marketing staff is also able to track marketing campaigns for specific events and can target particular groups through social media by their interests, income, geographic location, and more.

Most venues today have their own customer database, or "insiders" club, they use to communicate regularly about upcoming events, pre-sales, on-sales, and promotions. They are able to track click-throughs and sales to identify exactly how many tickets were sold and how much revenue was generated from a particular email. This is significant when the marketing department is working to determine the format, design, and frequency of correspondence through their database.

Some venues are able to use their ticketing system to communicate with event attendees before and after the event. These communications can also be used to learn a great deal. Pre-event they may warn customers of possible construction traffic, make them aware of a special promotion at the concession stands, or invite them to a pre-event party at the venue. They may also use that email to promote other events. As in other areas, they can then track the click-throughs and the number that convert to sales. Post-event, venues may send an email thanking guests, marketing other events, and asking guests to complete a post-event survey. In such a survey, beyond learning about guests' event experience, venue marketing personnel may ask how they heard about the event. Responses to that question allow them to make changes for similar, future shows. Such surveys can also be used to determine top operational areas of concern from the guests that can be used by other departments to identify means for improvement.

While venue marketing departments are still working to catch up with their counterparts in other segments of the sport industry, they have made great strides. Historically, venues have relied on more traditional media outlets such as television, radio, and print to promote their events and drive ticket sales. Unfortunately, with traditional media there is no definitive calculation on the return they may see in ticket sales. Today, available data from online activities has enabled them to better track the impact of their efforts and increase overall marketing efficiency.

Operational systems

The operations department in any venue is responsible for the complete physical environment (including maintenance, housekeeping, engineering, etc.) and providing a safe, pleasant atmosphere for clients and customers, all while managing the conversions and production as required by the event schedule. In addition, they are continually working to decrease reaction times, manage expenses, and project expenditures. In this regard, the use of analytics in managing the operational systems within a venue may be particularly impactful.

The amount of data available to the facility manager continues to increase, but it is important for facility operations personnel to know how to use the tools effectively. According to Sean Delehanty, sustainability manager for BAE systems, "the largest benefit of utilizing energy analytics is to benchmark and monitor utility consumption and quantify cost savings that result from understanding how utilities are used" (Building Automation, 2013). Some products that support analytics, benchmarking, and dashboards in existing buildings include electrical outlets and switches (replacement or plug into existing) that allow data collection down to the receptacle level (as opposed to the breaker level) and send data across the electrical wire or wirelessly (Building Automation, 2013).

According to SkyFoundry (2013), "Analytics works by identifying patterns that represent faults, deviations, and opportunities for savings." Such basic systems may include alarms, fault detection and diagnostics, and analysis tools. Every system has both strengths and weaknesses. Table 11.1 outlines some of the key operational aspects of such systems, as well as potential limitations.

Analytics, on the other hand, automatically crunches the data to identify and report any issues. One of the most important characteristics of analytics is the ability to expose things that venue management personnel are not expecting or looking for. Analytics can be applied to real-time data and offers the ability to define more sophisticated alarm conditions and FDD rules. With the use of modern analytic solutions, human interaction and reaction is not generally needed beyond contributing to the selection or definition of the initial parameters (SkyFoundry, 2013).

Modern analytic systems can be implemented and adjusted at any time without reaching back to make changes to the alarm levels or logic. There is flexibility to define rules, and analytic rules crunch through large volumes of data to find patterns that may be difficult or impossible to see when looking only at real-time data. For example, an alarm may tell us that the venue is above a specific kilowatt (kW) limit at a given point in time, while analytics tells us things like how many hours in the last six months we exceeded the electric demand target, how long each of those periods lasted, what time of the day they occurred, and how those events were related to the operation of specific equipment, the weather, or building usage patterns (SkyFoundry, 2013).

True analytics for venue operational systems allows the use of multiple data sources, within different formats and different time sampling frequencies. This allows for analytic

TABLE 11.1 System operations and limitations

Systems	Operational aspects and limitations
Alarms	• Typically evaluates a sensor value vs. a pre-assigned limit and may include a time delay (condition must be true for a designated amount of time before the alarm sounds). • Must be able to define the condition required to sound an alarm when programming the system. • External data is not used, therefore providing a limited scope of data. • Alarms are typically evaluated at that given moment and require different techniques to identify patterns and correlations over time. • Alarms do not typically allow for logic that interrelates multiple data items from multiple sources. • Adding new alarms generally requires modification of control logic or alarm parameters in controllers, which may be particularly difficult when you are trying to analyze data from a system installed and managed by others.
Fault detection and diagnostics (FDD)	• Serve to identify equipment performance issues. • These tools are typically equipment-specific and characterized by pre-defined rules based on an engineering model for a particular piece of equipment. • Programmable analytic tools provide more flexibility enabling engineers to implement rules based on their knowledge equipment systems specific to their venue. • Results may include timelines showing the occurrence and duration of faults along with their correlation to other conditions or issues, thereby potentially providing insight into the cause of the issue.
Analysis tools	• Analysis tools is the term most often used to describe software used to analyze time-based data, such as energy meter data. • These tools provide the user with the ability to examine data graphically and manipulate it to identify peaks, anomalies, and perform normalization against weather, building size, baseline data, and other factors. • A human is still an essential part of the analysis process and requires someone to interpret the charts and graphs.

Source: SkyFoundry (2013).

rules that look for correlations between age of equipment, manufacturer, service history, and weather conditions, amongst others. Perhaps most importantly, analytic tools can often be applied on top of existing systems as long as the data is available. They typically do not require changes to the equipment or automation system and can be hosted in the cloud or installed on-site.

According to Colin Thompson, Director of Operations at the Jerome Schottenstein Center (20,000+ seat multi-purpose arena in Columbus, Ohio), "we live by exceptions, rather than rules." Often, these are not venues with a consistent schedule like an office building. Their usage and operational needs depend on the venue type, ownership, mission, geographic location, and event schedule.

Traditional venues may elect to use re-commissioning or retro-commissioning. Re-commissioning refers to the process of reviewing building systems to ensure they are functioning based on the original design criteria. Retro-commissioning is the comprehensive review and testing of venue systems to identify deficiencies and correct them (Roper & Payant, 2014). Neither of those approaches allows for the dynamic environment which exists in sport and entertainment facilities. Facilities like an office building only need a couple of operating scenarios (fully occupied or unoccupied), while the environment at event-oriented facilities fluctuates with the event schedule. Because of this complexity, standard re-commissioning or retro-commissioning have limited potential for meaningful savings and efficiencies over time. Sport and entertainment facilities require systems and platforms that can adapt to their respective needs.

One such example is SHIFT Energy's EOS system which was the world's first implementer of Intelligent Live Re-commissioning (ILR) based on cloud computing, big data analysis, and real-time machine to machine control (SHIFT Energy, 2014). Essentially, the EOS system provides software which overlays existing venue systems thereby allowing venue personnel to learn from their usage and make automatic adjustments. SHIFT partnered with the NHL Vancouver Canucks to implement the EOS system at Rogers Arena, a 475,000 square foot, 18,000+ seat, multi-purpose facility that opened in 1995.

The Rogers Arena venue systems include four separate control systems for HVAC, chillers, lighting, and the ice plant. The EOS platform was enabled by the integration of the various control systems and the solution collects 5 million data points per day, which is then used to derive an optimal plan for the building. EOS started running unsupervised in April, 2014 and by June the system was trimming 20 percent of energy costs in the building. According to the SHIFT Energy case study (2014), examples of EOS implementation include the following:

- infiltrates spaces with cool outdoor fresh air at night when it is advantageous;
- connects to the local weather forecast and uses it along with the facility schedule to determine which equipment should run at night to achieve energy savings; and
- EOS automates the shutdown of lighting when not needed. It even balances daylight and electric lighting in spaces with access to outdoor lighting.

Today, other cloud-based systems are available including Schneider Electric's Building Analytics, which also enables venues to pinpoint which systems and equipment have irregularities, with prioritization based on energy cost, severity, and comfort. Their cloud-based automated diagnostics use artificial intelligence to identify problem conditions and guide resolution through suggested actions and then periodic engineering reviews ensure the system is continuously driving action and tracking performance over time. Such systems can:

- enable venues to take advantage of existing building data;
- find hidden costs and inefficiencies;
- optimize operational performance;
- reduce energy expenditures;
- create more environmentally friendly, high-performance buildings.

(Schneider Electric, 2015)

Such systems can reduce the cost of facility operations primarily in utility cost savings, maintenance efficiency, and operational improvements. They may also produce ranked recommendations on the most impactful fault remedies and energy savings available for a particular facility, as well as evaluate system performance to identify items that directly impact ongoing energy consumption and equipment operation (Schneider Electric, 2015).

While some venues may not have the resources available for a comprehensive analytic solution, venue personnel can pull data that is available within specific venue systems. For example, a lighting control system, such as Musco Lighting's Control-Link® platform, enables facility managers to control lighting systems and other electronically related systems, and provide real-time data regarding system usage and utility savings (Musco Lighting, 2016). Therefore, venue operations personnel can track utility usage relative to the event calendar and area weather to assist in system programming efforts. Musco can also use existing venue data to analyze the return on investment (ROI) timeline for those venues considering a switch to LED lighting.

According to Colin Thompson, the primary focus is generally on HVAC (heating, ventilation, and air conditioning) because it is the largest energy driver. Analytics can be used in other operational areas as well, including inventory control (monitoring levels and predicting lead times) and sustainability (waste hauling/trash management, smart trash cans, and recycling). As with all systems, it is important to evaluate the return on investment (ROI) before proceeding.

Food and beverage

Another area within public assembly facilities demonstrating rapid growth in the use of analytics is within food and beverage operations. As always, venues are working to identify ways to maximize revenue streams, not only by providing added services to meet customer expectations, but also to capitalize on existing opportunities. For many venues, food and beverage service represents one of the most important revenue producing ancillary services (Mahoney et al., 2015). Many guests attend events planning to spend money on food and beverage as part of their event experience. In order to maximize the revenue potential and enhance the guest experience, the venue must be strategic in their efforts. Many of the large food and beverage contractors are working to provide additional services to their clients in this area including those identified in Table 11.2.

According to Don Muret (2015), "Big data is being used to study what fans eat, drink, or buy to wear." Evolving technology enables new approaches to food service and provides data on customer habits. Today, more teams and venues are turning to their outsourced concessionaires to help make sense of all the information and determine how to use it.

Levy Restaurants' E15, launched in 2014, are working to drive new revenue through the information gleaned from customer transactions in arenas and stadiums. They utilize four applications, including:

- *Dynamic, digital menu boards* – includes the ability to apply dynamic pricing late in the game to cut down on food waste.
- *Video cameras with heat mapping technology* – placed above concession stands to analyze operations and make adjustments as needed to reduce wait times and streamline the overall food delivery process.

TABLE 11.2 Several of the large food/beverage providers and their branded analytic efforts

Food and beverage provider	Analytics initiative
aramark	INSIGHT TO IMPACT
Delaware North. Sportservice	TOTAL LISTENING
Levy Restaurants	E15

- *Programmed tablets in suites* – enables fans to control their experience by ordering food and drink on their own and paging attendants as needed.
- *Mobile strategy* – uses data to help teams and venues develop a mobile strategy for in-seat delivery, adding self-serve kiosks to order food and merchandise, and install mobile payment systems.

(Muret, 2015)

E15 have extended their successful use of analytics to improve food and beverage performance to now assist teams in filling seats, optimizing pricing, profiling fan bases, identifying new potential corporate partnerships, and improving the overall fan experience (Levy Restaurants, 2014).

While historically protective of their information, teams, venues, and concessionaires are now working together to consolidate data from all sources in efforts to develop a complete 360-degree view of their customers. For example, after working with E15, the Portland Trailblazers revamped the club level at the Moda Center and advanced into the NBA's top eight teams in arena per caps (average spent per person in attendance at the event) during the 2014–15 season (Muret, 2015).

As the industry evolves, concessionaires are continually conducting research and testing both data collection methods/sources and means to make the best use of the available data. According to Jaime Faulkner, CEO at E15, one of their most interesting studies examined the impact of the team's winning or losing on fans' per cap spending at the venue. While winning was a significant per cap driver for some teams, for others they found it was not as important as factors like the number of television timeouts per game, percentage of ticket sales sold on the secondary market, and the game-score differential. In another example, according to Dan Marmion, technology director with Delaware North Sportservice, their findings helped them improve the optimized range of beverage sizes in certain types of stadiums. According to Bob Pascal, chief marketing officer for Centerplate, they are using analytics to understand the differences in fan experience expectations by country, region, sport, and audience segment (Muret, 2015).

When asked what data is requested most often, Amy Cross, Chief Information Officer at Aramark, indicated that the data they are asked for most often relates to spending activity in relation to location in the ballpark and in relation to time of game. While according to Jaime Faulkner, CEO at E15, the data they are asked for most often relates to the impact of corporate sponsorships on food and beverage revenue (Muret, 2015).

Venue managers and team executives are still learning what to ask and there is significant potential for growth in this area. The successful use of analytics related to ancillary services has the potential to positively impact the bottom line for both the tenant and the venue, while helping to meet guest expectations and enhancing their overall event experience.

Parking and transportation

Managing parking and transportation logistics for maximum efficiency is a continual challenge for venues. Their efforts are impacted by a number of factors, some of which are generally consistent and others which may vary. Venues vary based on whether or not they manage/operate surrounding parking lots and the number of spaces available. Within the parking and transportation operations of a single venue, their efforts are impacted by event variables including day of the week, time of day, expected attendance, and customer demographics. In addition, parking and transportation operations may be impacted by external factors such as weather, construction, and existing infrastructure, as well as other events in the area.

In an effort to improve the parking experience within the Pittsburgh Cultural District, the Pittsburgh Cultural Trust (PCT) initiated a smart-parking technology-based program (Park PGH) within downtown Pittsburgh (Fabusuyi, Hampshire, Hill, & Sasanuma, 2014). The primary goal was to reduce search-time variability and make the district a more desirable destination for patrons by reducing parking related anxiety and uncertainties. They also hoped to attract patrons who were previously deterred by the uncertainty of parking availability. At the time of the study, they were monitoring eight parking garages with 5,000 parking spaces in downtown Pittsburgh (Fabusuyi *et al.*, 2014).

The Park PGH application was the first real-time, predictive parking analytics system based on input from multiple stakeholders. While the prediction approach was not new, the environment in which it was deployed was unique and they included stakeholders in the design with an evaluation platform, which allowed modifications as necessary. Park PGH falls into the category of smart-parking solutions and provides data and outcomes that may be of value to public assembly venues (Fabusuyi *et al.*, 2014).

These smart-parking solutions typically fall into two broad categories: parking guidance systems (PGS) and real-time prediction information systems. Parking guidance systems use variable message signs (VMSs) to inform drivers about available parking spaces and are concerned with transit and park–and–ride lots. Park PGH is not coupled with transit and does not employ VMSs. In addition, parking information is updated each minute and is only available through mobile devices, interactive voice response (IVR) units, or the internet (Fabusuyi *et al.*, 2014).

The Park PGH prediction model is an event-based model for use before the trip begins and uses historical parking and event data to predict future parking availability. For example, if an individual was going downtown for a concert on an evening when there was an

NHL Pittsburgh Penguins game, he/she could establish with some degree of certainty the probability of finding a parking spot (Fabusuyi *et al.*, 2014).

In working to predict parking availability, the focus is on predicting the number of parking spaces at a given time, based on a set of events and weather data using neural network-based predictors. A key assumption in this approach is that the time-varying arrival rate is a function of events occurring in the vicinity. Real-time information is useful for short-term predictions and prediction algorithms are more useful for long-term predictions (Fabusuyi *et al.*, 2014).

According to Fabusuyi *et al.*'s (2014) findings, the application was effective in reducing search time for finding a parking space and led to less trial and error parking situations. They also found that perceptions changed regarding the downtown Pittsburgh parking situation. Their approach combined systems development and integration with a parking-prediction algorithm that uses two systems to make predictions with a high degree of accuracy (Fabusuyi *et al.*, 2014).

While each venue, in conjunction with local law enforcement and transportation, is constantly working to improve efficiency, they may be able to benefit from such an approach. Depending on the circumstances and estimated ROI, such an application may not make sense for some venues. Regardless, any venue can certainly track simple data such as:

- total number of vehicles parked per event;
- if and when parking lots reach capacity;
- ingress/egress times on each route; and
- license plates (states represented).

Such data can be entered into a simple spreadsheet to allow venue managers to track data for all events and examine it to identify trends related to days of the week, time of the year, or event type. All of which could be useful in preparations for future events.

Safety and overall event management

The primary directive for any public assembly facility manager is safety, which applies to employees, participants, guests, and spectators (Fried, 2015). Historically, venue personnel (often the part-time event staff) would complete incident reports to address any safety or security issues at the end of the night, which were then filed in the corresponding event file. Once resolved, those reports may never have been viewed again (unless necessitated by litigation) and their contents forgotten about. Modern-day safety and security issues have become more important and more complicated since the events of September 11, 2001, which unfortunately has been reinforced by events in Boston, Paris, and Brussels (Mahoney *et al.*, 2015). As a result, the industry has responded with an enhanced focus on safety and security.

The International Association of Venue Managers (IAVM) created the Academy for Venue Safety and Security (AVSS), which is a training program for venue and event managers, security professionals, and others; designed to equip them with the best practices, resources, and tools needed to face the evolving challenge of providing a safe venue for everyone (IAVM, 2016). Likewise, the National Center for Spectator Sports Safety and

Security (NCS4) collaborates with professional leagues, intercollegiate and interscholastic athletics, private sector firms, and government agencies to support the advancement of sport safety and security through training, professional development, academic programs, and research (NCS4, 2016).

Truly effective venue safety and security programs are best supported by analytic tools, which enable tracking of related data to be used in decision-making and event preparation. Commonly used tools in the industry include AwareManager and ISS 24/7. As with other solutions, AwareManager offers an incident tracking and resource planning system to improve transparency, better mitigate risk, and run events as efficiently as possible. Their system enables clients to create event templates to track personnel (including roles and qualifications), dynamically redeploy resources during an event as needed, and better manage risk with a real-time venue map displaying staff and incidents (AwareManager, 2016).

ISS 24/7 enables clients to reduce risk and maximize the guest experience by developing solutions to enhance awareness, communication, documentation, and analysis of incidents that occur in public assembly facilities. ISS 24/7 allows clients to digitally document and track incidents, requests, tasks, work orders, preventative maintenance, inspections, security guard tours, and lost-and-found items (ISS 24/7, 2016).

According to Scott Dickson, Director of Event Services and Guest Experience at the Jerome Schottenstein Center and former AVSS faculty member, data from such tools allows venue management personnel to track incidents per event and provide periodic reports to identify trends related to types of events, types of venues, etc. Venues can also establish their own databases, which may require manual data-entry with information from incident reports, post-event surveys, and other sources depending on the venue.

Regardless of how it is collected and tracked, this data can be useful in determining door times, staffing types, staffing levels, and alcohol sales. This data can also be considered in conjunction with the data provided by the ticketing company regarding expected demographics for each event and tracking the arrival/movement of guests. This data can also be used when responding to customer inquiries and complaints, all of which may help to identify needed change (whether for safety or improving the guest experience) that may not be as readily distinguishable when viewed as a singular incident.

Many facilities are able to distribute online post-event surveys to ticket buyers after the event. These brief surveys can provide in-depth information on the guests' experience that can be used as educational tools in training and to assist with future event preparations. Venues are also able to learn a great deal based upon the data from ticket scanners at the entrance gates, including the flow of ingress, the number of people in the venue at any given time, and which entry points require higher staffing levels and security presence.

According to Scott Dickson, the next big trend in venue safety and security is behavioral identification. Event personnel can be trained to recognize behavioral indicators leading to a second level of investigation. The behavioral identification approach is built on the knowledge that individuals planning to commit violent acts display recognizable behavioral indicators that expose them to possible detection (Rozin Security Consulting, 2016).

CASE STUDY: CMMS PROVING THE RESULTS

Name: Matthew Kastel
Title: Stadium Manager for Oriole Park at Camden Yards
Current employer: Maryland Stadium Authority
Brief work history: My name is Matthew Kastel, and I have worked in professional baseball in one capacity or another since 1985. For the last seven years I have been the Stadium Manager for Oriole Park at Camden Yards, the home of the Baltimore Orioles. My employer is the Maryland Stadium Authority, and my primary responsibility is managing maintenance and housekeeping as well as making sure events that take place in Oriole Park and the surrounding campus go smoothly.

PHOTO 11.1 Matthew Kastel

I haven't always been in facility (stadium) management, and my career has allowed me to do just about every job possible in professional baseball. My first job out of college was working on the grounds crew making $5 a game for a minor league team, and once the game started I would head into the stands and hawk beer where I earned a 15 percent commission on everything I sold. Along the way, I have been a General Manager for a minor league baseball team, worked for the Houston Astros for several years, including handling their pre-game activities and helping with promotions. At a certain point in my career I got into managing the logistics of events and facilities in professional sport and thoroughly enjoyed it.

The Maryland Stadium Authority is a State agency which was formed in 1986 and not only owns and operates Oriole Park but also operates M&T Bank Stadium, home of the Baltimore Ravens. Both stadiums share the same parking lot, including the same 92-acre parcel of land. Needless to say it is a very active complex. Keeping the stadiums in world class shape is of extreme importance to not only our organization but also the Baltimore Orioles and Ravens and all the millions of fans that visit each season.

What example can you share regarding using data to help make a decision?

The issue

Both stadiums are multimillion dollar assets for the State, and keeping them in the highest working order is paramount. A little over a decade ago our maintenance records were kept by hand at Oriole Park, and we had dozens of checklists to make sure we had our maintenance and other work taken care of. It eventually dawned on us that we were behind the times and realized this was no way to operate a stadium in the twenty-first century. After doing research on how other large non-sport facilities operated, it didn't take us long to conclude that we would never modernize or move forward as an organization without having a computerized maintenance management system (CMMS).

Due to having just paper records, we were embarrassed to discover how little we knew about our own facility. Answers to basic questions could stump us, such as, how much does it cost to operate Oriole Park? How much did projects and events really cost us? Was all our equipment getting proper maintenance in a timely manner? How do our personnel spend the work day? In short, we concluded that unless we implemented a CMMS and used it extensively we would never truly grasp the working knowledge we needed to manage Oriole Park in the best possible manner.

Under the leadership of our Vice President, Jeff Provenzano, we set a goal that eventually became a mandate. That goal was to purchase then use a CMMS to manage every possible aspect of our operation. This included, at the minimum, tracking the following: maintenance, housekeeping, energy management, scheduling of employees and contractors, managing leases and tenants, work requests, events, work orders, billing, etc. Our ambition is to use our CMMS at a level unheard of in the sporting industry.

Situation

When I stepped into my current position we had two basic but substantial maintenance problems to deal with. As Oriole Park was aging, equipment was failing at an alarming rate, and the cost to repair or replace this equipment was staggering. Additionally, it seemed no matter how hard we worked our maintenance staff we were never able to keep up with our preventative maintenance. Often basic maintenance on key pieces of equipment lagged well behind manufacturer recommendations. Given this we turned to our CMMS to sort through the data on why this was happening and how to best manage this problem.

Before detailing how our CMMS helped us through this crisis, it is important to note that a CMMS is only as good as the information you put in it. The (GIGO) garbage in garbage out rule is applicable to any CMMS, and because of this we invested a lot of time and manpower upfront to make sure we had the correct data in our system. If you don't invest the proper amount of resources doing this you set yourself up for failure. From a preventive maintenance perspective, the key data we needed to put into our system included the following elements:

- every single piece of mechanical equipment had to be in the system;
- each piece of equipment had to include the manufacturer recommendations for maintenance;
- each piece of equipment had to have a frequency on how often it needed preventative maintenance, including an estimate on how long it should take for this work; and
- notes and past work history also had to be linked to each piece of equipment.

Once we had our CMMS set up we could tackle why our equipment was failing at an alarming rate. The first thing we did was analyze the data our CMMS provided us. Our CMMS records showed that in the past 365 days our maintenance team needed to do over 14,000 man hours of preventative maintenance work to satisfy all our preventative maintenance needs. Assuming an average full-time worker works 1,800 hours annually, this would mean we would need the equivalent of approximately eight full-time employees to handle our preventative maintenance load each year. At first glance it appeared we shouldn't have had a problem completing our preventative maintenance, as we had more than eight full-time maintenance workers. This puzzled us, as to why we couldn't accomplish our preventative maintenance on time. Next, we analyzed what we called break/fix work. Break/fix work is exactly what it sounds like. It isn't preventative but reactive maintenance. For example, changing a light bulb that has burned out is break/fix work. To our surprise the CMMS data showed that we were also doing 14,000 hours of break/fix work annually. We had no idea it was that high, and without the accuracy of our CMMS we never could have figured this out. Our numbers told us that between our break/fix work and preventative maintenance demands we needed at least 16 full-time employees to accomplish what we were doing. That number didn't include the man hours needed for game coverage. During Oriole games and other large events we have maintenance workers on hand to respond to trouble calls. Once we reviewed all this data from our CMMS it became obvious we didn't have enough workers to fulfill all our requirements: preventative maintenance, break/fix and event coverage. What was happening, unwittingly because we didn't have a CMMS to help track progress, was our maintenance supervisors would handle first what they considered to be the most pressing needs, which in their minds was break/fix and event coverage. With this our preventative maintenance often got deferred, which meant we were always behind in fulfilling our planned preventative maintenance. The irony of this, of course, is the less preventative maintenance we did the more things would break which caused more break/fix work which gave us less time to do preventative maintenance. It was a vicious cycle we had to break.

We didn't want to be reactive and just hire maintenance people willy-nilly to try to solve this problem. We decided to use the data from our CMMS to tell us specifics on our situation and come up with a plan best suited to match our needs. We also tried an experiment regarding our break/fix work. Going forward our maintenance people had to have permission to do break/fix work. No more, for example, allowing any maintenance personnel to be flagged down by our stadium partners with a maintenance issue. From now on all maintenance requests had to be logged into our CMMS, and the maintenance supervisor would dispatch the work orders as he saw fit. By doing this we controlled the schedule and made preventative maintenance the priority. After this process was implemented, we saw less break/fix work, as things were breaking down less often since we were now doing more upfront maintenance.

Even with this improvement our CMMS still showed we needed more maintenance personnel to get all our preventative maintenance done. We used our CMMS to make good business decisions on how to best do this. Thanks to our CMMS, which tracked all our labor and material costs real-time to the penny, we had a great working knowledge on not only what each trade cost us, but what each task and project cost us as well. After crunching the numbers from our CMMS we soon realized for some trades it would be cheaper to hire contractors, and for others it would be more economical to hire full-time personnel. In the end we made the business decision to supplement our workers with contractors from the following trades: electricians, painters and HVAC workers. In the case of plumbing we found it would be a better business decision if we hired two new plumbers.

Results

In short we used our CMMS to spot and diagnose two real problems and then also used it to come up with the most cost effective and productive solution possible. Today we complete all of our preventative maintenance work on time and have reduced costs, as we now have less break/fix work, not to mention better peace of mind that we will have less breakdowns and unexpected costs.

Moving forward

As we move forward as an organization we are totally vested in CMMS and use it in the following ways:

- Maintenance employees get their daily work assignments via a phone app from our CMMS. They then use their phone to record how much time they spent working on the work order, what they did, and can even use their cell phone to attach any relevant photos to the work order.
- We use our CMMS to schedule our preventative maintenance a month out. This way we know it will be done and we know how much the work will cost us in advance.
- To track manufacturer warranties.
- For accounting to track PO balance, and give us up to date numbers on how much we spent on labor and materials for things like work orders, games, projects, trades, etc.
- To track game day incidents.
- To track contracts and leases.
- To monitor housekeeping's daily reports and game day calls.
- To record all meter readings, such as gas, electric, steam, etc.
- To highlight patterns and trends.
- For forecasting.

   In short, our CMMS has now become, by far and away, the most important management tool we have.

Ticketing

The technology and capabilities of modern ticketing systems are evolving at record pace. Those venues contracted with ticketing providers have a distinct advantage regarding the accessibility and usability of data. In 2012, John Forese, SVP and General Manager with LiveAnalytics (Ticketmaster), reported that they averaged 26 million unique visitors per month. That year they were involved with the sale of over 150 million sports tickets and boasted over 200 million records in their global database. With such data available, they are able to provide in-depth information regarding customers that is useful in a variety of ways. Today's advanced ticketing system capabilities may include the following:

- fan segmentation and profiling;
- prospect and retention modeling;
- dynamic and variable pricing;
- secondary markets;
- social sentiment; and
- mobile.

(Forese, 2012)

This data can be helpful when calculating RFM (recency, frequency, and monetary value) scores to analyze customer value. RFM analysis is a marketing technique used to quantify which customers are best by examining how recently a customer has purchased, how often they purchase, and how much the customer spends. RFM analysis is based on the marketing adage that "80% of your business comes from 20% of your customers" (Tech Target, 2016).

On the ground, clients are able to track click-throughs and follow-up with customers who abandoned ticket purchases (Mahoney *et al.*, 2015). According to Cait Schumman, Director of Ticketing for Columbus Arena Sports & Entertainment (CASE), they can track sales trends as they relate to marketing efforts and for recurring events they can review previous price levels and results to assist with recommendations for promoters regarding pricing for upcoming events in the market. They utilize the system to generate reports for various stakeholders, use the available data to help determine staffing levels for on-sales, and track how tickets are selling and whether or not to put certain seats on hold to dress the house.

Overall guest experience

With the ongoing competition for the customer's discretionary income, venues and event organizers are continually working to improve the overall guest experience. "In order to improve the customer experience, you must first know who the customer is" (Wallace, 2014). Announced attendance is generally based on ticket sales rather than actual attendance and when corporations buy tickets in bulk or tickets are exchanged on the ever-expanding secondary market, it can be impossible to know who is actually in the venue. One solution is WiFi, which provides an avenue to learn more about customers on-site while also building the venue or team's database (Wallace, 2014).

In addition to the competition for customers' discretionary income and time, venues and events have to face the challenge of overcoming the increasing cost to attend events and elevated fan expectations for the perfect event experience (Schlesinger & Bazzell, 2013). Facility executives can now employ analytic solutions that connect customer sentiment data and facility-experience data with what they already know about their customer base, though that tends to be easier for teams with a more consistent fan base. Nevertheless, facility managers need to learn as much as possible about their customers and work to understand their specific desires so the venue can provide targeted products and services (Schlesinger & Bazzell, 2013).

Venues and the events they host provide a number of sources of easily measurable data, such as tickets sold, sales of specific food and beverage items, parking operations, mobile application usage, and ticket scan data (Splunk, 2016a). According to Schlesinger and Bazzell (2013), "Advanced, social analytics against these known, measurable variables creates advanced insights by analyzing data from the customer experience." Examples of predictive analytics using both operational and social conversation data may include the following:

- Aggregate and correlate popcorn sales to locations in the venue that may inform analysts why that location demonstrated such high sales activity, if it is likely to repeat, or if it is a desirable location to make it consistently repeatable.
- The correlation of sales to tweets may tell analysts that someone spotted a celebrity buying a pizza at the game and that fans near that section rushed to the location (not likely repeatable).
- The correlation of Facebook check-ins to sales may also indicate that pizza purchases were made just prior to and during the first inning as fans are arriving at the venue.

(Schlesinger & Bazzell, 2013)

It may be helpful for venue managers to categorize their data and analytical approach into three areas: pre-event, in-venue, and post-event. Venues can leverage data to engage fans with pre-event alerts (traffic, construction, pre-event parties, etc.), parking offers and logistics (discount options, availability, accessibility, etc.), VIP hospitality access, and/or merchandise availability and promotions. Once in a venue, most guests are planning to spend money and venue managers need to determine where they want customers to spend. Analysts can draw data from past purchases, loyalty programs, and other sources to aggregate in order to drive group-level engagement or personalize to drive individual engagement (Schlesinger & Bazzell, 2013). Today's technology includes Bluetooth activated beacons that can be placed throughout the facility and enable the venue or team to push specialized messages to customers providing information regarding purchasing upgraded seats or notifications regarding food and beverage specials. Ongoing engagement post-event may include follow-up emails to thank customers, engage them in online surveys, and ongoing interaction through the venue's customer database.

Deeper insight can be gleaned when venue managers track social data to look for sentiment patterns and other correlations. "Social listening can turn seemingly random interactions into meaningful insights for venue marketers that will extend the experience of the fan beyond their seats" (Schlesinger & Bazzell, 2013). Schlesinger and Bazzell (2013) also suggest that properly leveraging analytics allows venue managers and team owners to understand the fans they want to target and differentiate those with a higher acquisition and retention cost who, therefore, should be allowed to remain in the comfort of their living room.

In a specific example, performing arts venues are beginning to use digitized program books, not only to reduce expenses and their carbon footprint, but also to enable data collection from key audience members and ongoing engagement. The venue asks patrons to use the virtual program, but in order to do so they must complete an online survey, which provides an opportunity to measure what they are doing (Riley, 2016). Additional benefits include the ability to offer the information in other languages (without significant expense) and it allows the venue to connect the audience with the talent in a way that was never possible through printed programs. They can add Twitter handles for the artists and facilitate the connection and engagement between the fans and the artists, which is certainly a value-added for both the customer and the client (Riley, 2016). There are other applications designed as a digital companion to the playbill. Once the customer downloads the app all they have to do is scan the cover of the playbill, which then provides them access to the plot, photos, videos, backstage insight, and information regarding nearby restaurants.

VenueNext, on the other hand, provides a more comprehensive platform that ties together typically isolated venue systems, including location services, ticketing, points of sale, and concession services (Splunk, 2016b). The VenueNext mobile app is used at Levi's Stadium, home to the NFL San Francisco 49ers, where they leverage mobile technology that enables any customer with a smartphone to experience VIP services on-site (Splunk, 2016b). With this app customers can:

- download their tickets and scan them at the gate;
- order food in advance from an express order menu and pick it up on their way in;
- place food orders on-site and have them delivered to their seat while tracking the delivery process (the app remembers their orders from previous visits); and
- watch video replays through their phones.

(Splunk, 2016b)

The same system also provides real-time data for venues to assist in directing resources based on demand in order to optimize the fan experience. For example, concessions operators can track which concession stands are overcrowded, identify blocks in the delivery system, and assess ongoing inventory levels. They can reallocate inventory to meet higher demand at certain locations, thereby reducing cost and waste, while maximizing revenue opportunities and meeting customer needs. Tracking such trends over time assists in managing inventory and enhancing efficiencies (Splunk, 2016b).

As the competition for fans increases, public assembly venues must be proactive in order to stay competitive. One way to gain that competitive advantage is to use readily available data to better understand their customers, the event experience, and what can be done to positively impact that experience while increasing revenues for both the venue and the tenant(s). While not all venues have the resources to purchase an advanced analytic solution, they can make better use of what data is currently available.

Conclusion

Venues are competing to attract both events and ticket buyers. To remain competitive, venue managers must ask the right questions and work closely with their partners to make the best use of the collective data. As we have discussed, the use of analytics impacts nearly all venue operations including venue marketing, operational systems, food and beverage, parking and transportation, safety and event management, ticketing, and the overall guest experience. We also have more data and information available to us than ever before. While it may not be necessary or realistic to implement some of the sophisticated systems referenced in this chapter, today's venue manager must look for ways to gather, manage, and use data to increase efficiencies, reduce expenses, generate revenue, and enhance the overall guest experience.

References

AwareManager. (2016). *Facility management systems.* Retrieved from www.awaremanager.com/our-facility-management-solutions

Building Automation (2013). *Facility analytics can help facility managers make data-based decisions.* Retrieved from www.facilitiesnet.com/buildingautomation/tip/Facility-Analytics-Can-Help-Facility-Managers-Make-Data-Based-Decisions--28146

Fabusuyi, T., Hampshire, R. C., Hill, V. A., & Sasanuma, K. (2014). Decision analytics for parking availability in downtown Pittsburgh. *Interfaces, 44*(3), 286–99.

Forese, J. (2012). *Ticketmaster LiveAnalytics: Big data and sports ticketing.* Paper presented at the 6th MIT Sloan Sports Analytics Conference. Boston, MA, USA. Retrieved from www.sloansportsconference.com/?p=7351

Fort, M., Sellares, J. A., & Valladares, N. (2014). Computing and visualizing popular places. *Knowledge and Information Systems, 40*(2), 411–37.

Fried, G. (2015). *Managing Sport Facilities* (3rd ed.). Champaign, IL: Human Kinetics.

IAVM. (2016). *Academy for venue safety and security.* Retrieved from http://www.iavm.org/avss/avss-home

ISS 24/7 (2016). *About us.* Retrieved from www.iss247.com/about-us/

Levy Restaurants (2014, August 19). *Levy restaurants launches e15, bringing next-generation analytics to sports, entertainment, hospitality and retail industries.* Retrieved from www.prnewswire.com/news-releases/levy-restaurants-launches-e15-bringing-next-generation-analytics-to-sports-entertainment-hospitality-and-retail-industries-271879571.html

Mahoney, K., Esckilsen, L., Jeralds, A., & Camp, S. (2015). *Public assembly venue management: Sports, entertainment, meeting, and convention venues.* Coppell, TX: International Association of Venue Managers.

Muret, D. (2015, February 23). Concessionaires go deep with analytics. *Sports Business Journal.* Retrieved from www.sportsbusinessdaily.com/Journal/Issues/2015/02/23/In-Depth/Analytics.aspx

Musco Lighting (2016). *Control-link.* Retrieved from www.musco.com/clink/controlsystems.html

NCS4. (2016). *About NCS4.* Retrieved from www.ncs4.com/about/overview

Riley, N. L. (2016, February 3). Venues digitize program books. *Venues today.* Retrieved from www.venuestoday.com/news/detail/venues-digitize-program-books-2216

Roper, K. O., & Payant, R. P. (2014). *The Facility Management Handbook* (4th ed.). New York, NY: American Management Association.

Rozin Security Consulting (2016). *SIRA training (behavior detection training).* Retrieved from http://rozinconsulting.com/264-2/behavior-detection-training/

Schlesinger, S. H., & Bazzell, D. (2013). *For sports venues, analytics improve fan experiences, and revenues.* Retrieved from http://data-informed.com/for-sports-venues-analytics-improve-fan-experiences-and-revenues/

Schneider Electric (2015). *Building analytics: Improve the efficiency, occupant comfort, and financial well-being of your building.* Retrieved from www.schneider-electric.us/documents/buildings/Building-Analytics-Brochure.pdf

SHIFT Energy (2014). *Case study: Rogers Arena kicks off the season with EOS.* Retrieved from http://shiftenergy.com/wp-content/uploads/doc/case_study_rogers_arena.pdf

SkyFoundry (2013, October). *Making sense of the data-oriented tools available to facility managers.* Retrieved from www.skyfoundry.com/file/82/Understanding-the-Data-Oriented-Tools-Available-to-Facility-Managers.pdf

Splunk. (2016a). *Case study: VenueNext helps venue operators grow business while bringing fans a superior experience*. Retrieved from www.splunk.com/content/dam/splunk2/pdfs/customer-success-stories/splunk-at-venuenext.pdf

Splunk. (2016b). *Levi's Stadium visitors score with VenueNext and Splunk* (press release). Retrieved from www.splunk.com/view/levis-stadium-visitors-score-with-venuenext-and-splunk SP-CAAAPHA

Tech Target. (2016). *RFM analysis (recency, frequency, monetary)*. Retrieved from http://searchdatamanagement.techtarget.com/definition/RFM-analysis

Wallace, T. (2014, June 24). *Big data's athletic moment: turning sporting arenas into preferred business venues* [Web blog post]. Retrieved from www.umbel.com/blog/sports/sporting-arenas-business-venues/

12

PUTTING IT ALL TOGETHER

Gil Fried

Why analytics?

So far throughout this book we have provided significant examples of how analytics are affecting all facets of a sport organization. The reader should know at this point that the numbers can answer numerous questions and hopefully solve numerous problems. The numbers do not just magically arrive on an executive's desk in a beautiful package. While some managers can ask data-oriented employees to crunch some numbers, that is the weak way to apply analytics. The proper way is to engage these data-oriented employees and work together to identify problems, review prior conclusions, select the appropriate variable, examine data collection opportunities, analyze the data, and then present the findings. This chapter will explore this process and how to apply everything covered in this book to be an effective data user.

Analytics is pursued by managers seeking an edge to understand past occurrences, current conditions, or future possibilities. When examining the past, analytics examine what happened and why it happened. When examining current conditions analytics can help identify what is happening now and what might be the next best action. Using predictive analytics, a manager can try to figure out what will happen in the future. In statistical parlances estimation samples an existing population. In contrast forecasting makes estimates related to future populations. Either approach requires an analytical approach. Not everything is open to analytics, such as when there are variables that cannot be measured (can anyone quantify love?), or when there is no past history (such as a brand new technology). Nevertheless, we want to apply analytics to past instances so we can help determine why events might have occurred – and then we want to use analytics to hopefully project what will happen in the future. There are no guarantees, but using appropriate, accurate and sufficient information can help increase the odds for the accuracy of the results and the certainty of the outcome taking place in reality. Analytics is the answer, even if it will not always provide the right answer.

So how do we become analytical?

Before we walk through the process of applying analytics, it is important to understand what makes a manager an analytical manager. The key is an openness to data and numbers. Even if a manager is scared of numbers, that should not limit their ability to implement a numbers culture. Part of this effort is a desire to have evidence for any decision. Instead of relying on intuition or "we have always done it this way" a manager needs to demand from employees that they prove their point with hard facts. The mantra around an analytic business should be – is there any data to support that opinion? This does not require being a math genius. It requires being a good quantitative thinker, and that does not require that much math beyond what everyone has learned through sixth grade (Davenport & Kim, 2013). Asking for data allows others to appreciate how a person is thinking. Was the person able to leverage the numbers to prove a point or did they find data to justify a previously reached opinion? It is not the math that really should be the focus, rather it should be a curiosity about numbers and to learn what they really mean. This includes appreciating the laws of probability and randomness.

Analytical managers should focus on projects that might produce the best results such as:

- complex decisions with numerous variables and steps;
- simple decisions which for legal or other reasons (industry standards) need to be consistent;
- places where the company needs to optimize a process or activity;
- decisions in which the manager needs to understand correlations/connections and their significance;
- places where the company needs better forecasting; and
- areas where there has been little success so any improvement would be celebrated.

(Davenport, Harris, & Morison, 2010)

Even the most ideal issue for analysis might not produce the desired analytical results. It should be noted that while some sport executives are called geniuses because of their on the field record through putting together a winning team, their success might be considered a typical period of randomness. The team might have done well regardless of the executive. That is why all too often one of the top executives in a league will all of a sudden start losing and then they do well again, in an often never-ending pattern of random winning and losing seasons. Is this because they lose their touch, or is it that they have very little control over how well the team does? What if a baseball team's general manager won 100 plus games three years in a row, then won 90 games, and then won 70 games? The team's fans would be screaming for a new GM, new coach, new owner, etc. Some might say it is a rebuilding year. Others might feel the world is coming to an end. The team's owner might fire the general manager and hire a supposed superstar to quickly fix the team. The next year the team has 110 wins and makes it to the playoffs. Was the team's success based on the new hotshot GM or the team created by the prior GM that took time to really jell?

Part of the answer depends on probability – the likelihood that a given event might or might not occur ("Probability," n.d.). Probability can be boiled down to a number.

Most insurance policies are priced based on probability. Over the long run insurance normally does not save someone money, but it does protect them from the unacceptable high loss concerns (such as open heart surgery or a house that burns down). Insurance companies will ask "what is the likelihood that someone will get into an accident?" One of the easiest ways to measure this probability are past accidents and statistics that show younger male drivers, as an example, have more accidents. Insurers will also examine other numbers that might not seem to be as relevant, but help determine the probability of a driver getting into an accident. Some of these external variables, which have proven to have relevance to pricing, include educational level of the driver, credit scores, and home ownership as examples. These variables tend to show that people who have more stable lifestyles (i.e. not big spenders who owe lots of money) are more reliable drivers. That is why insurance companies undertake significant research on each insured driver and ask about past driving records, along with employment and residential related questions. The data is designed to determine how likely someone will get into an accident, keep paying their premium, take care of their car, etc.

Probability can examine how dangerous various items are. For example, are swimming pools or guns more dangerous? Most people would say guns, but as Levitt and Dubner (2009) calculated, it is actually more likely a child would die in a pool than from a gun. Roughly 550 children die every year from drownings while 175 die from gun accidents. This would tend to mean for many that overall pools are more dangerous. There is one drowning for every 11,000 residential pools while there is one adolescent gun death for every million guns. One way to express this is that a child is 100 times more likely to die from drowning in a pool than being shot by a gun. Probability is being used for numerous applications; from what web searches someone really wants, or spellchecking to suggest intended words, to predictive policing where data can help identify when and where a crime might occur. This is why understanding the probability around numbers is so important – that is where analytics comes into play. It should be noted that perception can be proven and destroyed by data. But, the data has to be correct.

Are the numbers telling the truth?

Statistical analysis rarely provides the truth, but rather provides a circumstantial case for review based on the normally imperfect data we have. Statistical analysis provides accurate results based on the significance level chosen by the researcher. With any analysis of numbers it is important to figure out what is being analyzed. If one was asked to identify the "best" baseball player of all time, it would be impossible to make such an analysis. There are so many variables, positions, eras, etc. that such an analysis would never produce one number that would encapsulate the best player. Furthermore, the term "best" is very subjective and many people would have a different idea of what is "best." Some of the key variables examined when trying to compare baseball players include the on base percentage (the proportion of times a player reaches base successfully), slugging percentage (calculates the total bases reached per at bat), and at bats (to examine consistency over several years). Using these variables to examine "greatness" one can argue that at least using one criteria, Babe Ruth was the "best" because his career slugging percentage is still the record at .690 (Wheelan, 2013). Others could argue that dominant pitchers such as Nolan Ryan or Sandy Koufax were in fact better players, but they should not be judged by the same criteria as sluggers. We always want to make sure we are using the right numbers and examining the correct issue.

When it comes to randomness and probability, a good story is often more believed than a less plausible story. Thus, when an employee provides significant detail in a story they are more often believed than someone who gave a short, curt answer. The same with data – when more data is present, it is perceived to be more accurate by some people. People often misinterpret a significant amount of data rather than a single data point. Even if the large data set is accurate, that doesn't make the data practically significant. This could be said in a different way – the more data does not necessarily mean the better data.

When making decisions we often are thrown for a loss by simple, but often critical, issues such as:

- Lying with statistics such as selecting a biased sample, publishing only positive results and hiding negative results, recall bias (our memory can be biased and influenced), survivorship bias (where poor performers fall by the wayside making results appear better when in fact only the better athletes are still around), and healthy user bias (are people who take vitamins healthier or do healthier people take vitamins?) (Wheelan, 2013).

- Availability bias – when we reconstruct the past (look into our memories) we give unwarranted importance to memories that are the most memorable and easiest to retrieve. For example, a star player hitting a home run is not as memorable as a poor player who hits several home runs unexpectedly.

- Errors in the data – where even the best data can be confounded by flawed data already in computers or data entry mistakes that can skew the results. Furthermore, if decisions are based on old data or a model that no longer applies that can cause an error. One example is when the housing bubble burst in 2007–08 the lenders had assumed a zero probability of a large housing market decline and were caught off guard when it occurred.

- Normal accident theory – which refers to the fact that due to our complex world accidents or results can occur without a clear cause and may just be the result of an accident rather than a straight forward cause and effect.

- Instances, and how they can occur. The likelihood of something occurring is often based on the number of ways in which the event could occur. If there are multiple ways a team can win then there are more chances that a team can win compared to if there is only one or two ways to win.

- Expectations and the fact that we often fall victim to expectations. If you think you will not close a sale, you probably won't.

- Clusters sometimes occur with every large series of random events. While flipping a coin might result in a 50/50 chance of getting a heads or tails, that does not prevent a run where there might be four or five heads in a row.

- Assuming events are independent when they are not, and not understanding when events are independent.

- Regression to the mean occurs over time. Similar to the *Sports Illustrated* jinx, many people feel that once someone appears on the magazine's cover they fall back down to Earth. The truth is that they got on the cover by being great for a short period of time and then return to their normal performance. That is an outlier outcome (far from the mean), which will normally be followed by outcomes that are more consistent with the long-term average.

- The law of small numbers is a term that refers to the fact that sometimes people try to apply the statistical findings from small data sets to a large number of data points. Another way to explain this is that a researcher can try to make inferences about a large population by relying on a small sample.

- The gambler's fallacy occurs when a person feels that since an event has not occurred in a while it is due to happen soon (i.e. such as a slot machine that while it is supposed to be random, might attract more gamblers hoping the machine is due to make a large payout).

- The Bayes' theory refers to the thought that the probability of an event occurring is contingent on another event occurring. Under this theory a team would probably win the Super Bowl if ten players on the team make the all-pro squad.

- There can be a problem with number scores due to problems with the measurement tool. While a scoring matrix might help assign a grade for an assignment, most grades involve an element of randomness – such as why did a student get an 89 rather than a 91 on an assignment? If the instrument is not precise, the grading would not be as precise.

- Black swan events can skew the means. While there might be an average number of home runs hit during a given season, every once in a while someone might deviate from the mean and hit a very large number of home runs. This outlier will throw off the statistical numbers and should not be considered the norm. Certain central tendency measures are influenced by outliers, and they should be evaluated carefully.

- Significance testing allows researchers to identify false patterns through statistical analysis. For example, false assumptions are sometimes based on shared illusions or heuristics (rules of thumbs and short cuts people apply that might be based on mistakes or randomness). Such misinterpretations can be based on our desire to be in control and when people are not in control we might misinterpret random acts (Mlodinow, 2008). This can lead to confirmation bias where we try to find evidence to support our opinions rather than potential evidence that our opinions are invalid. This concern is often undertaken by managers searching for evidence to validate their actions or opinions rather than looking for evidence that their actions or opinions are incorrect.

- If the sample is not representative of the whole or is a flawed sample, good statistics cannot save a bad sample. The best samples will be the largest (which will be based on context and having a large enough representative sample) so the small number issue can be avoided. Randomness (which allows a representative sample) and longitudinal studies are the gold standard for any sample related analysis.

- Does the data provide some base of comparison? If a team has ten wins that might be impressive, but if the team won 15 games the prior year then the comparison shows the team did very poorly.

While randomness occurs, numbers can dispel numerous superstitions, theories, and even hoaxes. But numbers can also lie. The numbers aren't really lying – it is people using statistics in a manner that is incorrect or outright deceitful. This is not to say that a manager should not trust the numbers, but they should never take any numbers at face value. This means that whenever any numbers are presented, a manager should ask what bias might the presenter have and what is at stake. If the presenter can prove the numbers – great.

However, if numbers are just thrown out then they should have very little value. As the joke goes, 73.6 percent of all statistics are made up on the spot (but you can substitute any number you want in the joke).

Statistics can also hide really important data. If a company gives everyone a 10 percent raise that sounds impressive. However, if an average employee would receive a $3,000 raise while the CEO receives a $1 million raise, then while the 10 percent raise is accurate, it skews the data which would appear a lot less benevolent if the real dollar amount was disclosed. If the company had ten employees then the total average raise including the CEO's raise would be $93,636. Of course, the average employee did not get anywhere close to that amount, but using an average without any additional clarification can be misleading. Similarly, when we examine school-based testing, those numbers are skewed by new students entering the school, students dropping out of the school, and the ability and background of students entering and finishing the school. The true measure most people would want to see is how much a student learned from when they came in to the school until they exited the school. This can be called the value added. Pre-tests and post-tests are often relied upon to assess whether value was added. The problem with such an approach is that students learn at different rates and some of the best schools with the best test scores are self-selected because they have rigorous admission processes that select out the poor learners and test takers. The same approach can be used for a coach and whether they were able to really improve the athletes in their charge or if the athletes would have done well regardless of their coach. This analytic approach has been examined by several recent management authors who have expressed little faith in leadership and that most leaders are just lucky they became leader at an apropos time and that if they had come a couple years earlier or later they might have been a failure rather than a great success.

Precision can mask inaccuracies. When one hears statistics they might assume there is research supporting the numbers and that the numbers are accurate, even if they are not – whether intentionally or unintentionally. Those using numbers need to make sure the numbers are right, useful, and can help the organization move forward.

Some key things to remember include:

- While focusing on the numbers, don't forget the human element that there are people behind the numbers and these people have feelings and emotions that numbers might not grasp completely.
- With numbers it is important to fail on a regular basis. Failing allows a researcher to test assumptions and keep refining any potential model and data analysis to find the best fitting model. Failure also can be attributed to not having data on all the relevant factors. If a researcher gets it right from the beginning they actually might miss some major potential areas for growth and success.
- People need to know basic statistics. Managers should understand some basic stats components such as measuring central tendency (mode, mean, and median), probability, randomness, sampling, visual analytics, basic modeling, and correlation.
- Managers need to minimize logic errors (such as making inappropriate assumptions or using analytics to justify a position, as highlighted previously) and process errors (such as failing to properly consider alternative actions or processing data incorrectly).
- Fact-based decisions should be rewarded whenever possible, even if the fact-based conclusion is not followed.

- The best analysts do not need to espouse numerous formulas, but should be able to explain what the data means in plain English – and without insulting those who might not be as well versed in numbers.
- Look beyond what is going on in one industry to help differentiate the organization and find new/different approaches to solve a problem or find new data. For example, publications in magazines such as *Popular Mechanics* or *Scientific American* can shed light on future issues impacting the sport industry.
- Quantitative reasoning should never replace sound reasoning.
- Start with small steps, projects, and victories to gain acceptance and support.
- Find allies across an organization that can help share or process data and provide insight.
- Approach analytics from an enterprise perspective reflecting the entire organization rather than just individual organizational silos.
- Try to find unique data that others do not have or the manager will just be a follower rather than a data leader (also remember that even if new data is used, the competition will try to take away that competitive advantage – this was seen after the release of *Moneyball* and how everyone wanted to adopt analytics). For example, no one else knows what Team A's customers have purchased so that is unique and protected data – especially in relation to their completion. The situation might be different in a league where teams might share information to benefit each other. Unique data can also include how data from the team can be integrated with other data from outside the industry or within a league.
- While data needs to be protected, sometimes there is a benefit to sharing data with suppliers or others to produce a more seamless operation such as to create the best supply chain system where the inventory is monitored by a third party and such logistics help reduce inventory carrying costs.
- Try to collect data in a way that moves it from transactional (what was purchased at the concession stand) to a more analytical format for ease in future analysis (i.e. so the data does not need to be reformatted or otherwise manipulated – thus saving time and money).
- Managers need to protect the privacy of customers and not improperly disclose confidential data. This information stewardship should extend for the information's entire lifecycle.
- Researchers should not hesitate to use non-numerical data such as videos, texts, pictures, voices, scents, colors, and other information that might be more difficult to quantify.
- Don't spread analytical efforts across too many projects so that no one project has enough resources to reach a conclusion.
- Hunches are fine – just make sure they are tested. Analytics should also not discount hunches or intuition.
- While analytics is known for helping to make better strategic decisions, it is equally useful for making tactical and operational decisions.
- The best analytical companies try to embed appropriate analytics in all major processes, reinforce a culture of analytical decision-making, and are fluid to adapt to ever-changing conditions.
- Analytics requires developing a connection between patterns and business activities – and then making decisions that are carried out.
- Use analytics to search for the truth. By seeking data, a manager will find more than just stories or anecdotes.

- Temper the search for data with making a decision. It might be that all the data is not available, but waiting to get all the data will normally result in no decision ever being reached.
- Analytics is designed to produce better decisions, not perfect decisions.
- A manager should encourage transparency and should never shy away from sharing data with necessary collaborators.
- A great model today might not be worth anything tomorrow if conditions change.
- Data should help identify patterns and help managers find the root cause of a given result.
- Always ask questions such as what data are being used, what assumptions are made, and can the results be explained in plain English and in one paragraph? The opposite of this is failing to ask the right questions.
- Other key questions to ask include:

  o How can a manager best leverage data now and for the future to address real business issues?
  o How does the current data differ from past data and what are the ramifications of the new data?

So far this chapter has examined what are the best analytic projects, what problems can impact the appropriateness of the data, and how can a manager make analytics an effective tool. Such information is critical to make sure the data is appropriate and for the right project. Now we have to examine the analytical process in some real examples to put it into the right framework. The process is as follows:

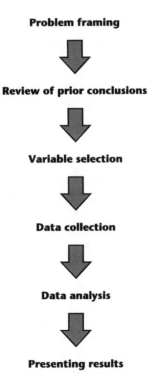

Problem framing

Review of prior conclusions

Variable selection

Data collection

Data analysis

Presenting results

FIGURE 12.1   Analytics problem solving approach

Problem framing

How effective are we in selling tickets? Why did the team win? How can we make sure the right employees are getting promoted or receiving the appropriate merit bonuses? These are just some examples of a problem and the question that can be asked to help answer the problem. This is when a manager or researcher can be very creative. There are numerous problems and numerous questions that can be asked. The key is narrowing down the problems and questions to maximize the potential for finding the data and solving a problem. A good example that many readers can relate to is deciding to go to a college. The first question is, should I go to college? That is followed by can I afford college? can I get into college? what other options do I have? and numerous other questions. The one that most people focus on is what college or university should I attend? There are numerous options normally available so why is one chosen over another? The problem to be framed is, which college should I attend? This is followed by numerous sub-questions such as do I want to live on campus or commute? can I receive a scholarship for athletics? do they offer the major I want? do they have an active Greek or social life? and numerous other similar questions. There is no one correct answer to any of these questions, but they provide the framework to obtaining the right data to help make a college decision.

When examining the problem the following questions should be asked:

- Is the problem clearly defined?
- How can the problem be solved?
- Who are the stakeholders and how involved are they in the problem?
- Who will make and implement the final decision?
- Have you examined the broader issues and narrowed the key issue(s) you will examine through analytics?
- Can you explain the problem in a simple story that anyone can understand?
- Have previous findings associated with similar decisions been examined?
- Is there a creative way to present the problem?

Another consideration is identifying what the key questions are for the organization to move forward. There are several approaches that can be taken to examine what actions might be appropriate for a sport organization. These program evaluation approaches could include: needs assessment, implementation evaluation, outcome/impact assessment, cost–benefit analysis, utilization focused evaluation, logic model, and data-driven decision-making.

Needs assessment

The needs assessment is often undertaken by a sport organization to determine a potential problem or opportunity. For example, the problem could be to identify factors that are affecting the number of youth participating in sport. This can help answer the question of what sports might grow in the future and a manufacturer or sport retailer can leverage this information to help determine what products to manufacture and sell.

Implementation evaluation

An implementation evaluation examines existing programs (rather than future programs) to determine how it is actually working compared with what was supposed to happen. This approach examines theory with actual practice.

Outcome/impact assessment

This might be one of the most difficult, but most important, forms of analysis. This approach examines whether the program actually works. This is where a researcher might try to show causality or to rule out any other alternative explanations.

Cost–benefit analysis

The often used cost–benefit analysis assumes that an impact assessment has already been undertaken to prove the value of the program. Both costs and benefits need to be expressed in monetary terms so if the analysis results in a 1/3.5 ratio that would mean that for every $1 in cost the program produced $3.50 in benefits.

Utilization focused evaluation

Using the utilization focused assessment a researcher examines how the program is used and who uses it. This approach starts at the end result and determines if the project was successful.

Logic model

Using the logic model can help explore why a program should work. Based on what was intended, this approach moves away from making decisions based on faith and uses logic to support the decision. This approach helps identify what data to collect to make sure results can be reached.

Data-driven decision-making

There are two approaches that the data can help resolve – data-driven and data-informed decisions. The data-driven approach uses good data to help make a decision – and this is a weaker strategy. The data-informed approach is stronger because data is just one piece of the puzzle and other issues and side effects need to be explored before making a final decision.

Some of these approaches can overlap when helping to make a decision. The key is to have an approach and the data helps move the decision-making process based on the intended goal.

Review of prior conclusions (research phase)

Internet search engines and business archives can be a great source of initial research results. The issue is how comprehensive was the research? Did the researcher spend 20 minutes or 20 days doing the research? This is actually a false comparison because a well-trained researcher who knows the right questions and can access the critical information might only take 20 minutes. In contrast, someone can spend 20 days undertaking research, but if they are looking at the wrong search terms or cannot accurately process the information then those 20 days might have been completely wasted.

If we take the college choice example from above, prior research might come from:

- siblings who might have undertaken a college search;
- guidance counselors in high schools;
- college recruiting fairs;
- former classmates who researched colleges;
- online sources;
- independent ranking entities;
- accreditation bodies;
- college view books, videos, and webpages;
- attending college open houses and other recruiting visits.

There is no one correct source and someone can learn from each one of these sources. The same holds true for most problems. Yes, there are some very unusual problems and questions that might arise, but most problems and questions have some basic information or background material that can provide some relevance and direction. It should be remembered that past research can help provide information, but should not serve to replace actual customized research. Some folks might find something online and apply that data or solution to their problem. However, every problem and situation is different and just finding a similar problem and using that approach for a different problem is often asking for trouble.

Variable selection – developing the right model

As highlighted by Davenport and Kim (2013), a model can be likened to a cartoon-based caricature. The best caricatures normally have an outstanding feature such as a big nose or large eyes. This becomes the focus and the rest of the face is not as critical. Similarly, a data model will focus on some key variables and ignore rest. This allows the researchers to focus on the key problem and ignore other areas. Often researchers will get bogged down when they uncover so many different issues that the primary problem being researched gets lost in the shuffle.

That is why data uncovered in the research phase needs to be examined and any irrelevant findings (that will not help solve the problem) need to be eliminated to avoid distractions.

The primary variables will be the dependent variable – the one the researcher is trying to predict or explain – and the independent variable which will affect the dependent variable. It should be noted that cause and effect are often very difficult to prove unless there are very few variables at play. For a sport example, the dependent variable might be the total number of wins in a season. The independent variables will be the schedule, total number of games played at home, the quality of competition, the cohesiveness of the team, and numerous other variables that can impact whether a team will win a game.

What a researcher is trying to find is any potential pattern among the variables in the data. This pattern could denote a relationship that needs to be explored. This pattern might be, as an example, that fans who unsubscribe to a team's e-newsletter are more likely to stop buying ticket packages. Such patterns can be found through using various data mining software.

Some questions to consider include:

- Why are you using a certain model?
- Who developed the model and how can they prove its accuracy/ability?
- What assumptions would make the model invalid?
- How will the data need to be tweaked to work with the model?
- What other possible approaches could be used to help solve the problem?
- Are the independent variables actually causing the change in the dependent variable or are there other reasons?

Going back to the college example, once various data is collected, the prospective student can develop the proper model. The model might include colleges/universities within 100 miles of home, with certain athletic programs, with certain degree options, and other variables. From the initial option of maybe a large number of choices, the model might limit the potential colleges to a handful.

Data collection

The problem that has been modeled above produces information which becomes data after it is measured. Data can be collected from numerous sources such as webpages, interviews, surveys, purchasing data, and even equipment with sensors. Data can also be purchased from third parties. Data can be obtained from almost everything and everywhere. Even if the data is not numeric, data can still be observed and there are ways to make some often obscure data more numeric. For example, a person can be asked about the smell of food, and the answer can be evaluated on a five point Likert Scale where the number 1 represents a bad smell, 3 a neutral smell, and 5 a great smell.

Some questions to ask about the data include:

- Can you find all available data (such as all internet searches or all sales from a cash register), and if so you might not need to undertake random sampling because you have all available data?
- Is the sample analyzed representative of the general population?
- Is there any data that support or dispels the hypothesis raised by the problem?
- Are there any outliers in the data (black swans) and how do they impact the data?

Once again, with the college example, our hypothetical student might develop a spreadsheet with the pluses and minuses (similar to a cost–benefit analysis) with all the key variables. That spreadsheet might have a column for every issue the student might have (maybe they have a column associated with living conditions, food options, religious opportunities, etc.). Anything important and of value can be added to the list and data can be collected for analysis. The data need to be updated whenever there are changes. For example, if one school's tuition is reduced through a scholarship offer then the new number needs to be added to the spreadsheet.

Data analysis

To analyze the data you might need a good quant. A quant is someone who is proficient with numbers and feels comfortable analyzing the numbers to spot issues or trends. Many organizations have quant types available, but if not, a smaller team or entity can always hire a consultant or even work with professors or graduate students who understand numbers. But not every decision requires a quant person. They might just need a quant perspective. If someone went to the supermarket and compared the price of several drinks based on the price per fluid ounce, they have just undertaken this process. They have a problem, they might have some information about prior brands they liked, they develop a model to examine the cost per fluid ounce rather than the final price, they collect data, and now they analyze the data to make a decision.

One of the important points is that more data is not always better. This is not to say that if you have a lot of great data you shouldn't use it. However, if you have lots of bad data then just having a lot of data will not help make better decisions. It is important to get the best possible data. Better data is often different or new data that can shed a new light based on changed conditions. Organizations can leverage both primary and secondary data. Most organizations generate significant amounts of data. Imagine the concession counter at a stadium. Every time a sale is completed, data is developed such as what was purchased, what time, how often a credit card was used, and other data. This data can be structured or unstructured. If the data collection system puts the concession data in the right format it could be easy to analyze. Otherwise the information will probably be saved in files that would need to be converted. Lots of data is unstructured and technology has allowed even written text by famous authors to be inserted into a structured format for analysis.

For example, fingerprints are unstructured images. What is analyzed on TV shows is not the fingerprint, but some key points on the fingerprint. The structured information in databases can be applied to analyze the structured part of the unstructured image. The data doesn't tell anything – it is how the data is analyzed that represents the story. The story can take the form of a report or statistics can be used to understand the relationship between variables and to make inferences from the sample to the larger population.

The data should be analyzed to examine if there are any correlations. Correlation analysis examines at least two variables and determines if they vary together. For example, do schooling and future income level correlate? When schooling increases, future income normally increases so a positive correlation exists. When there are more than two variables, statisticians can use regression analysis to explain how multiple variables together predict a dependent variable.

In the college example, the data on the spreadsheet needs to be analyzed. Just because the information is on a spreadsheet does not mean all the information is equally influential. Maybe our hypothetical student will give more weight to the college that has a great sport program compared to high academics. However, if the decision also requires parental involvement then maybe another party will value the cost and academic quality more than other elements. That is why the same data might have different value for different parties. Based on all the available data and people involved, our student then makes a decision.

Presenting the results

The most successful analytics folks can tell a story with the data. The story needs to be told in a way that everyone can understand, appreciate, and act upon. A long, drawn-out story that takes forever to tell and doesn't quickly get to the point will lose interest and supporters. A great story from the data presented in one paragraph will resonate more with the intended audience. An even better story uses limited text and includes graphical or visual analytics to help make the story easier to understand.

The best story will explain the problem that was examined, how the problem was approached, what data was available, what solutions were examined, what final solution was chosen (and why), and then the story proves the business case for implementing the solution.

To conclude our prospective college student example, our prospect picks a college and then approaches his or her parents and says I want to go the XYZ College and here are the reasons I choose that school. Some parents might ask follow-up questions while others will examine the data and if the reasoning was sound, hopefully agree with the decision. Then the action process continues with actually sending in the deposit check. The same basic process goes into deciding on whether and what car to buy, if one should buy a house or rent, and any other major decisions for which data can help provide a perspective and address a problem/question.

Putting the pieces together in an example

The following is a very simplified example that can walk the reader through how to use analytics to answer a common problem faced by a professional soccer team every year. It is simple because transfers can be explored from numerous perspectives such as cost–benefit, media attention, broadcast opportunities, licensing potential, and numerous other issues that are both quantifiable and qualitative.

Problem framing

Imagine a soccer team deciding whether to acquire a given player from another team. Should the team pay 10 million euros a year for the player and an acquisition fee of 50 million euros to his current club?

Review of prior findings

There are numerous sources of information on professional soccer players. This information can look at the number of minutes they play, their general fitness/health, how much wear and tear their body has endured, how well they play in certain playing schemes, what their dominate foot is, and numerous other pieces of data readily available.

Variable selection

The variable will be the cost associated with acquiring the player and the yearly cost over the term of the contract. Other variables could include how well they played in the past in similar schemes utilized by the acquiring team and what could be the expected impact of having the player on the team. The cost also has to assume the opportunity cost of not signing other players.

Data collection

There is significant data available on the player, but also the player's stats can be run through a computer simulation to help determine the number of potential wins with the player in the line-up compared to existing or other potential players that could be acquired. Running the data through the simulation connects the data collection with data analysis in the next section.

Data analysis

The team could use a plus/minus analysis where they can put into a computer the player's data and play out scenarios to determine how likely it is the team would perform better (a plus) with him in the line-up versus the likelihood of them performing worse without him in the line-up (a minus). While this seems like a straight forward analysis, some players might bring team leadership (to mentor younger players) or playoff experience that might be hard to quantify.

Presenting the results

If the final decision is that the data shows the player is worth the investment then the researchers can present a detailed finding – based on the data – to the team owner recommending whether to acquire the player or not.

Conclusion

This chapter has examined some of the key points in determining what should be examined, issues that impact data, and how to develop a process upon which to make decisions. There is no one set way to solve a problem, but using a framework, the right data, and the right model can give the best approach under the circumstances to hopefully make the best decision (notice all the caveats – and that is important because it is very rare to always make the "best" decisions).

References

Davenport, T., Harris, J., & Morison, R. (2010). *Analytics at work: Smarter decisions, better results*. Boston, MA: Harvard Business Review Press.

Davenport, T., & Kim, J. (2013). *Keep up with your quants*. Boston, MA: Harvard Business Review Press.

Levitt, S., & Dubner, S. (2009). *Freakenomics*. New York, NY: Harper Collins.

Mlodinow, L. (2008). *The drunkard's walk: How randomness rules our lives*. New York, NY: Vintage Books.

Probability [Definition]. (n.d.). Math dictionary. Retrieved from http://www.webquest.hawaii.edu/kahihi/mathdictionary/P/probability.php

Wheelan, C. (2013). *Naked statistics*. New York, NY: W. W. Norton & Company, Inc.

INDEX